The Bedside
Guardian 2019

The Bedside Guardian 2019

EDITED BY
ADITYA CHAKRABORTTY

guardianbooks

Published by Guardian Books 2019

2 4 6 8 10 9 7 5 3 1

Copyright © Guardian News and Media Ltd 2019

Aditya Chakrabortty has asserted his right under the Copyright, Designs
and Patents Act 1988 to be identified as the editor of this work.

First published in Great Britain in 2019 by
Guardian Books
Kings Place, 90 York Way
London N1 9GU

www.guardianbooks.co.uk

A CIP catalogue record for this book is available from the British Library

ISBN 978-1-9162047-0-6

Cover design by Guardian News & Media Ltd
Typeset by seagulls.net

Printed and bound in Great Britain by
CPI Group (UK) Ltd, Croydon CR0 4YY

Contents

Foreword

YANIS VAROUFAKIS

'The government has failed – it's time to go back to the people.'
The rousing title of the *Guardian*'s editorial at the beginning of the
year was aimed, of course, at Theresa May's dog's Brexit. Alas, its
wording carried a universal truth, suiting, as it does, the current
situation not only in Britain but also the United States and the
European Union, not to mention Brazil, Argentina, India etc. etc.

If one conclusion emerges from revisiting the past 12 months,
it is that governments have failed almost everywhere. As a result,
there is an urgent need to go back to the people if we're to stand
any chance of finding answers to our existentialist crises – be they
climate catastrophe, social misery, geopolitical threats to peace,
involuntary migration, or other assorted forms of depravity.

The past 12 months were not the worst of times. And they
certainly were not the best of times. Rather, the past year has
proved depressingly predictable to anyone who has observed,
since 2008, our steady global slide into a postmodern 1930s. The
failure of our governments, as highlighted by the *Guardian*'s editorial, felt almost inevitable. With its roots in France's National
Front, Italy's Lega and Hungary's and Poland's governments, a
paradoxical 'Nationalist International' emerged on the strength
of Brexit and Trump. The rise of Vox, Spain's neofascists, proved

that recalcitrant nativism is not confined to Europe's north-east. Bolsonaro's triumph in Brazil and Modi's domination in India show that the North Atlantic is part of a larger disaster, rather than a special case.

STIFFEN YOUR UPPER LIP, YOU ARE NOT ALONE – A MESSAGE TO BRITISH FRIENDS

When I speak to my despairing British friends, I feel a need to lift their spirits. Not out of solidarity, but because they have no reason, I believe, to feel more downhearted than the rest of us. While their anguish is understandable, I tell them they have good cause to stiffen their upper lip and, despite Boris, Nigel, Labour's divisions and the overall sorry state of the House of Commons, to remain relatively upbeat about British democracy. I remind them that one of nationalism's hidden symptoms is a creeping feeling of inverse exceptionalism – a false sense that our country, our democracy, our parliament is in a worse state than our neighbours'.

Inverse exceptionalism is a great gift to xenophobic populists as they can weaponise it with the promise to make our democracy great again, to make us proud again. Thus, my unexpected message to British friends: you are not in greater trouble than we are. We all live downstream. The toxic algae engulfing you in Brexit's wake is a general condition that we all suffer from. If anything, having immersed yourselves in it since June 2016, your democracy is perhaps better suited now to be tough not just on Brexit but also on the causes of Brexit, which can be pinpointed both within and without the British Isles. In short, stop feeling sorry for yourselves, desist from self-absorption, and let's join forces to help the people take back control. In Britain. In Europe. Everywhere.

I know that, during the past 12 months, it was hard to resist the spectre of national humiliation. Theresa May's strategic error of agreeing to Brussels' two-phase negotiation (first, London gives the EU everything and only then will the EU discuss London's demands), coupled with red lines that boxed her into an impossibility, guaranteed the former prime minister's abject defeat. However, the UK media did you a disservice by setting the British prime minister's foolishness, and the House of Commons' divisions, against a fictional EU that is rules-based, democratic, united and, above all else, competent – a European Union, in other words, that could not be further from reality.

Back in 2015, three days into my tenure as Greece's finance minister, the president of the Eurogroup, comprising the finance ministers of EU countries sharing the euro, threatened me with Grexit if I dared insist on challenging the self-defeating, inhuman austerity programme our people had just rejected in a democratic election. Shortly afterwards, at my first Eurogroup meeting, Wolfgang Schäuble, my German counterpart, declared that elections cannot be allowed to change previously agreed economic policies, to which I responded that his words were music to the ears of Chinese Communist party apparatchiks who think along similar lines.

In short, the enemies of democracy and common decency are in power on both sides of the English Channel. So, my message to British friends is: stop wallowing in self-pity and, instead, join us in a common, transnational movement to build a democratic Europe.

A UNIVERSAL CONDITION

Our condition, we must realise, is truly universal. Yes, as Patrick Kielty says in his article on page 103, an EU official said the UK needed to be taken care of 'like a patient'. But so too should almost every country I know of, including those firmly within the EU. With the possible exception of China, the planet's major economic zones seem to be governed either by regimes trying their best to resemble the Weimar Republic's last days or by politicians, Donald Trump and Matteo Salvini for instance, who seem worryingly inspired by the organised misanthropy that followed Weimar's collapse.

The aftermath of the European parliament election of May 2019 was quite telling about this state of affairs. The day after the election, the European Union's 'liberal' establishment were breathing a sigh of relief that the extreme right did not fully dominate the European parliament. Readers of Europe's mainstream press would be forgiven for missing what would have, a few years before, been declared a shameful result and, indeed, a global emergency: the extreme right had actually *won* the elections in France, in Italy and in the UK. Only sorrow should flow from our establishment's readiness to celebrate the smallest of pickings, namely that the fascists did not win everywhere.

Meanwhile, as described in Ed Pilkington's piece, every day on the other side of the Atlantic, Presidents Trump and Bolsonaro deploy a lethal blend of machismo, fear and loathing with a dexterity not seen since the early days of Mussolini. Worse still, their Nationalist International has a clear plan for the world, in sharp contrast to progressives who are more disorganised than ever: a transactional world comprising reactionary countries divided by lethal borders – as described in Patrick Timmons' vivid article – but connected by bilateral deals that bypass all democratic mechanisms for limiting the power of multinationals with gigantic investments in fossil fuels, in wrecking national health systems, and with a transparent agenda to level all forms of worker solidarity in their path.

HOW DID WE END UP LIKE THIS?

Capitalism changed in the 1970s. The United States turned from a creditor nation to the largest consumer of other people's net exports. Germany, Japan and, later, China grew on the back of America's trade and budget deficits. In turn, German, Japanese and Chinese profits flowed back to Wall Street, in search of higher returns. This recycling system broke down because Wall Street and its UK side-kick, the City of London, took advantage of its central position to build colossal pyramids of *private money* on the back of the net profits flowing from the rest of the world into the United States.

This process of private money-minting by Wall Street and the City of London banks, also known as *financialisation*, added much energy to this global recycling scheme. Under the cover of its very own ideology, neoliberalism, and with political support provided first by Maggie Thatcher and soon after by Ronald Reagan, finan-cialised capitalism generated huge, ever-accelerating levels of demand within the United States, in Europe (whose banks soon jumped on to the private money-minting bandwagon) and Asia. Alas, once the bubbles burst, it also brought about its demise in the Fall of 2008 – our generation's 1929.

The only significant difference between 1929 and 2008 was the speed and determination with which central banks came to the aid of the financiers. While the majority, in the UK, in the US, in Greece, in Germany too, were treated to the cruelty of austerity and associated ignominies such as universal credit and means-testing (as Frances Ryan describes on page 166), the central banks printed mountain ranges of public money to refloat the failed banks, especially in the UK and in the US. Expansionary mone-tary policy succeeded in creating a semblance of recovery while, underneath the surface, austerity was destroying our communi-ties – Patrick Butler discusses this on page 28, as well as Helen Pidd and Jessica Murray on page 200.

The European troika, Greece's Golden Dawn, Brexit, Trump, Salvini, Germany's AfD, the shrill demands for electrified border fences and so much more were the fruits of this topsy-turvy policy of socialism for bankers and austerity for the many.

GOING BACK TO THE PEOPLE – EVERYWHERE!

The *Guardian* editorial was right: It *is* time to 'go back to the people'. But *Guardian* readers who interpreted this as a simple call for a second referendum were wrong. Our democracies are too damaged for a quick fix. In Britain's case, in particular, the demos cannot be put back into a broken democracy simply via a second vote. Something more is needed.

In the run-up to the June 2016 referendum, I addressed several anti-Brexit meetings. The one that sticks in my mind took place in Leeds, where I shared a platform with John McDonnell to campaign for the DiEM25 (Democracy in Europe Movement 2025) line of 'In the EU. Against *this* EU!' Afterwards, a lovely old lady approached me to tell me why she could not agree: 'My dear boy,' she said tenderly, 'if I vote to remain, it won't be you or Jeremy in 10 Downing Street to fight to transform this EU. It will be Cameron, who will treat the result as a vote of confidence in himself and a licence to hobnob with the Brussels people who crushed you and your democracy.'

Every time I encounter demands for a second referendum by people keen simply to annul the first, I think of that lady. However much I wish Brexit had lost, telling her to vote again, until she gets it right, is not something I would ever do. It would confirm in her mind that a vote is allowed to count only when it does not change anything. It will remind her of the power that she, her children, her neighbours and her community have been denied ever since trade unions and local authorities were neutered. So, if we are going to go 'back to the people', let's do it properly.

Bankers and neoliberals never let a good crisis go to waste. Nor should we. The Brexit crisis is our opportunity to rethink democracy in the UK and to do whatever it takes to 'go back to the people'. Similarly, across the EU, in the United States, in Africa, in Asia. Of course, this is easier said than done. 'None of us are free' if 'one of us is chained', as the old rhythm-and-blues song proclaimed. The British people will never be given full power to decide their future if the Germans, the Greeks, the Brazilians or the Nigerians are denied it. Antisemitism will never die if Islamophobia is not snuffed out too. As Edward Said once said, the Palestinians will never be liberated if the Americans and the Israelis are not emancipated also.

In the past 12 months, in the midst of all the soul-searching and despair caused by the Nationalist International's triumphs, the idea of democracy proved its resilience. We saw the idea of citizens' assemblies gaining ground, especially after its successful deployment in Ireland. We noticed that Aristotle's definition of democracy (as a system in which the poor, being in the majority, govern) is making a comeback. We admired children across Europe who decided that it was time to act like adults because the 'adults in the room' were behaving like spoilt brats (see Jonathan Watts' remarkable profile of Greta Thunberg on page 117). We saw young women win office in Trump's America, ready to confront patriarchy, exploitation and climate change.

On a personal note, the past year has been a rough diamond. In the May European elections, DiEM25, our Democracy in Europe Movement, did something crazy: we ran in seven countries simultaneously. We wanted to demonstrate that transnational progressive politics is possible. I stood as a candidate in Germany, while a German comrade stood in Greece. For our manifesto, the *Green New Deal for Europe*, we consulted thousands of Europeans over the course of three years. And our list of candidates in each country, from Portugal to Denmark to France to Greece, was selected by an all-member vote, where the Germans also had a say on the candidates in Greece and vice versa. In the end, we attracted one and a half million votes but won no seats in parliament. On election night, however, the Greek prime minister called a snap general election for six weeks later and MeRA25, our DiEM25 party in Greece, won nine seats.

Campaigning across Europe nearly broke me. But it also convinced me of the deep well of progressive energy waiting to be tapped in a Europe that to the naked eye looks beholden to the fake clash between an austerian establishment and the xenophobic ultra-right. Discovering some of the most progressive people I have ever known in the midst of conservative Bavaria, meeting poor brave pensioners putting up a fight against fracking in north-western Greece, supporting Sicilian comrades in their struggle to shield migrants from Salvini's attacks – those were the precious moments that over the past 12 months helped me counter Bertrand Russell's tendency to despair at 'the unwillingness of the human race to acquiesce in its own survival'.

Introduction

ADITYA CHAKRABORTTY

The historic turmoil chronicled in this book unfolded while the country was waiting for something else to happen. We saw a prime minister destroyed by colleagues, 10 of whom promptly lined up to succeed her. We saw yet another overconfident and underqualified Etonian march through the entrance to Number 10, while remembering how not so long ago he'd been gurning his way through TV comedy shows. We went on marches; we moaned to our friends; we got angrier and angrier.

All these were ripples churned forth by one big event that didn't even show up. The UK was meant to leave the European Union on 29 March, but it missed that long-held appointment as well as the one after that – and as the following weeks and months slipped by, people began to wonder/dread/hope that it might never happen at all. Until Boris Johnson became prime minister promising that, 'do or die', Britain would be out by Halloween.

So by all means consider the ructions covered in this anthology as the last gasp of the chaotic interim between the 2016 referendum and the whatever-comes-next; but that doesn't make them mere displacement activity, the anxious fidgeting of a political class awaiting its *18 Brumaire*. Rather, the events captured here shaped the future we are about to enter. Over these pages, you go from Theresa May trying every trick to get her backbenchers to back the deal she'd struck with the EU, as documented by

Jennifer Rankin and Daniel Boffey, to Johnson breezily claiming Britain could 'easily cope' with the chaos of a no-deal Brexit. You see the jeering backbenchers of 2018, subjected to splendid gavel-bashing by Martin Kettle, become the cabinet ministers of 2019 and flounder as badly as the last lot. You can read Sam Wollaston's profile in January of the band of preppers stockpiling everything from prescription drugs to dried falafel mix, knowing that by September cabinet ministers were promising Britons would get 'the food they need', although not presumably the food they want. That desiccated cliche about journalists writing the first draft of history comes to life over this volume.

Covered here in real time is the most profound political change of all. Over the 90s and 00s, the common complaint about our politicians was 'they're all the same', that all parties offered broadly the same Davos politics – credulous of 'investors', critical of labour, claiming to be interested only in 'what works'. Then the banking crash showed that 'what works' really didn't, and by 2019 the two main parties were poles apart. As Jonathan Freedland observes, the Conservatives have gone from being the 'natural party of government' to a self-destructive sect, even while Labour has tried to harness the political energy of Greta Thunberg and the school strikers, probed here by Jonathan Watts and Rebecca Solnit. As the 21st century enters its third decade, the choice our first-past-the-post system offers is utterly stark: between 'Britain Trump' [sic], as the US president terms Johnson, and European-style social democracy from a party that wants to be more radical but doesn't know quite how. The big question on which the future of this country depends is which way those politicians, civil institutions and voters who feel themselves to be somewhere in between will jump.

Versions of this question are now being asked across the world: in India, Turkey, Brazil and most of all in the US. The striking thing about our reportage from the Amazon, the Texas-Mexico border, Kashmir is how far they chime with each other.

These themes dominated this year and this book, and I make no apology for that. But other lives were lived, full of the usual glorious human idiosyncrasy. In this volume, the first man to swim around Great Britain describes how it feels when your tongue disintegrates, while a 15-year-old schoolboy recounts how he came to rap with a musical hero in front of a giant crowd at Glastonbury. Elsewhere, Hannah Jane Parkinson hymns night buses, Andy Bull stalks the gents' toilets at Lord's during one of the greatest one-dayers ever, and the demise of Joe Grundy prompts a tribute from another radio great, Nancy Banks-Smith.

Regrets? This editor has a few and here is the place for them to be mentioned. A solitary hardback can't do more than hint at the variety of work that appears in our newspaper and online every minute of every day. I read as much as I could as diligently as I could for this book and would regularly feel as if I were drinking from a fire hose. Even vital reporting loses its impact over time and pieces that run long mean denying places to others. I'd have liked to feature more reporting from Europe and across the world, more on the economics that, while not always top of the news, is often driving it, as well as obituaries. Put simply, in an ideal world I'd have given you even more.

One obit I hated losing was of WL Webb, who for decades curated *The Bedside Guardian*. His life was remembered in our paper by another *Guardian* colleague, David McKie, who noted how Webb would assemble the books pages: 'For years his devotion to the supremacy of the word over mere presentation was such that when a strong book review exceeded the space available, he would simply reduce the closing paragraphs to a smaller type.' Many times during the editing of this book did I want to follow suit.

Today's *Guardian* newsroom is very different from the one I joined in 2007, with more women in senior positions and an increased range of writers and editors from ethnic minorities. Much work remains to make our newsroom more representative of the society of which it is part, but this book showcases the diversity of voices and perspectives that makes the *Guardian* so different from the rest of what used to be called Fleet Street.

Just before I joined the paper, a friend gave me a copy of the latest *Bedside*, which happened to be edited by one Katharine Viner, so there was a particular pleasure in being asked by her to carry the torch this year. Later editions, I noticed, featured acknowledgements of Lindsay Davies, who I can confirm is as wise and encouraging as predecessors say. Former *Bedside* editors Gary Younge and Claire Armitstead gave helpful advice. My thanks to various section editors who racked their brains or their colleagues' memories to nominate especially good pieces. And Amit Chaudhuri kindly agreed to the inclusion of one of his poems, originally published in our Review section.

This book has an editor and a guest foreword and a collection of choice pieces by great journalists, but the names listed are not the only ones responsible. There are section editors who commission and encourage ideas, subs and graphic designers and production staff who launder prose and make the pieces look inviting enough to read, moderators who get the best out of the ensuing conversation below the line, others responsible for our digital operations, films and podcasts, live events. Then there are the cleaners, security, mailroom and canteen staff. All make up the *Guardian*, of which some of the best is collected here. This is an age impatient with institutions, sometimes rightly so. Yet the *Guardian*, at 198 years old, demonstrates the good an institution can do. Long may it continue to do so.

September 2019

Autumn

Deep divide: Kavanaugh confirmation fight exposes America's bitter fault lines

DAVID SMITH

In the phrase of the journalist Carl Bernstein, this is what a cold civil war looks like.

A group of ageing white male senators stand on a podium to defend a white male judge chosen by a white male president to sit on the supreme court. They are opposed by a group of senators that includes a black man and a black woman. Thousands of women stage a sit-in on Capitol Hill and chant their belief in the woman who accuses the nominee of sexual assault. If this were a movie, the casting director would be fired for being too obvious.

The struggle over Brett Kavanaugh's ascent to the supreme court has brutally exposed fault lines across age, gender, geography, media, party and race. The only thing everyone agrees on is that the division runs deep.

For some, Kavanaugh has come to embody white male privilege. He was nominated by Donald Trump, a 72-year-old who has stoked racial division and is seen as a vehicle for white nationalism. His enforcer is Senate majority leader Mitch McConnell, a 76-year-old white man born in Alabama under Jim Crow.

When Christine Blasey Ford appeared before the Senate to testify against Kavanaugh, Republicans could not hide the dire spectacle of 11 white men sitting in judgment. The Arizona Republican Jeff Flake was confronted in an elevator by two New

Yorkers, both survivors of sexual assault: Maria Gallagher and Ana Maria Archila, the latter born in Colombia and active in mobilising immigrant voters.

At almost every turn, the battle lines are drawn. Black against white, college-educated against not, hipster against hunter, liberal against conservative, pro-choice against pro-life, secular against Christian, urban against rural, woman against man, young against old.

The groups are not monolithic. There are men who oppose Kavanaugh and women who back him. There are black, female and young Republicans. But the fact that such groups are newsworthy shows how the exception proves the rule.

In his book *The Red and the Blue*, Steve Kornacki traces a 'new kind of tribalism' to the rancorous showdowns between Bill Clinton and Newt Gingrich. It culminated in the 2000 election, he writes, where for the first time the electoral maps fixed Democrats as blue and Republicans as red. America had become 'a nation of two political tribes, each with its own value system, its own grudges and resentments, its own world-view'.

The parties' demographic makeup is becoming more and more polarised. In November's midterms, record numbers of women and people of colour are running for the Democrats. It will be more of the same for the mostly male, mostly white Republican party.

Flake, apparently moved by the elevator encounter, called for the FBI to reopen its investigation: 'The country needs to feel better about this. This is ripping us apart, and there are enough things ripping us apart.'

But now he is poised to vote Kavanaugh on to the highest court in the land. It seems unlikely that the country feels any better.

8 OCTOBER

Saudi journalist Jamal Khashoggi criticised the regime – and paid with his life

DAVID HEARST

Jamal Khashoggi is not the first Saudi exile to be killed.

Prince Sultan bin Turki was kidnapped in Geneva in 2003. Prince Turki bin Bandar al-Saud, who applied for asylum in France, disappeared in 2015. Maj Gen Ali al-Qahtani, an officer in the Saudi National Guard who died while in custody, showed signs of abuse: his neck appeared twisted and his body was badly swollen. There are many, many others.

Thousands languish in jail. Human rights activists branded as terrorists are on death row on charges that Human Rights Watch says 'do not resemble recognisable crimes'. I know of one business leader who was strung upside down and tortured. Nothing has been heard of him since. In Saudi Arabia, you are one social media post away from death.

A Saudi plane dropped a US-made bomb on a school bus in Yemen killing 40 boys and 11 adults on a school trip. Death is delivered by remote control, but no western ally or arms supplier demands an explanation. No contracts are lost. What difference does one more dead Saudi make?

Yet Khashoggi's death is different. It's right up close. One minute he is sitting across the table at breakfast, in a creased shirt, apologising in his mumbled, staccato English for giving you his cold. The next, a Turkish government contact tells you what they did to his body inside the consulate in Istanbul.

Last Saturday, Khashoggi told a conference in London that the kingdom realised it had gone too far in encouraging President Donald Trump's 'deal of the century' by promoting Abu Dis as the future capital of a Palestinian state, and has backed away from what is proving to be a burning issue in Saudi Arabia.

'This proves a very important point. It is only the Palestinians who will decide, not the Saudis, not the Egyptians. No matter how much they control the payroll of the Palestinian government, no one can decide for them,' he said. A week later, his voice is no more.

The Arab world refers to them as 'electronic insects', the trolls the Saudis deploy to create a blizzard of false news around the regime's routine crimes. Even before news of Khashoggi's presumed murder, they were gloating about the fate of a man they consider a traitor.

Prince Khalid bin Abdullah al-Saud sent a message to another Saudi dissident: 'Don't you want to pass by the Saudi embassy? They want to talk to you face to face.'

But Khashoggi's tweets and articles went completely over their grubby heads. He was concerned about absolutes such as truth, democracy and freedom. Khashoggi always considered himself a journalist, never an advocate or an activist. 'I am Saudi, but a different one,' he wrote.

As a journalist he hated humbug. The motto in Arabic on his Twitter page roughly translates as: 'Say what you have to say and walk away.'

He did just that to the fury of those who wanted to shut him up. And it's clear from his tweets why they went to such desperate lengths to do so. He laughed at the idea that Saudi Arabia under Mohammed bin Salman was fighting for 'moderate Islam'.

Khashoggi was reviled for being sympathetic to the Muslim Brotherhood. 'Tweet about freedom and you are a Brotherhood member. Tweet about rights, and you are a Brotherhood member. Tweet about your homeland, and you are a Brotherhood member ... Reject despotism, and, of course, you are a Brotherhood member ... To those who hate the Brotherhood, I'd say you have attributed to them all the virtues and have therefore made them the favour of the best promotion.'

Khashoggi was an unreconstructed democrat: 'Only with freedom of choice can religiosity reach the soul and lift the observant high up.'

He was unsparing on the issue that caused his final rift with Riyadh: Donald Trump. 'From time to time, Trump tweets that he is protecting us and that we must pay for such protection to continue. He protects us from what? Or he is protecting who? I believe that the greatest threat facing the Gulf countries and their oil is a president such as Trump who sees nothing in us apart from the oil wells,' Khashoggi wrote.

Khashoggi was right. None of what was about to happen to him could have happened without Trump.

On three separate occasions recently, Trump has gone out of his way to humiliate the kingdom, simply because he believes he can. No forum is too public. Trump told a campaign rally in Southaven, Mississippi last Tuesday: 'We protect Saudi Arabia. Would you say they're rich? And I love the king ... King Salman, but I said, "King, we're protecting you. You might not be there for two weeks without us. You have to pay for your military."'

Bin Salman responded, 'I love working with him', and it is all too clear why. He would not have been crown prince and one step away from the throne were it not for Trump. Trump knows this and therefore thinks he can say anything he likes. Trump is the bully, the master. And his slave can do whatever he likes, to whomever he likes, even to a journalist embedded in Washington, because ultimately Bin Salman knows that Trump has his back.

Khashoggi never really talked to me about the danger he was in. As an analyst he hated hypotheticals. He knew he had passed the point of no return with this regime and that he could never go back, so he set about creating a new life, with a new job as a *Washington Post* columnist in DC.

But he thought, too, that, wherever he was, it was his duty to continue to speak out.

'The Arab Spring did not destroy ... those who fought it and conspire against it are the destroyers, otherwise you, young man, would be by now enjoying its breeze, freedom, tolerance, jobs and welfare,' he wrote.

My bet is that nothing will happen as a result of Khashoggi's murder. Bin Salman has calculated that Turkey is too weak to reply, with about $700 billion in public and private debts that have to be repaid by a falling lira.

The millions of pounds the Saudi prince has just paid to PR companies to burnish his image in the west as 'a reformer in a hurry' have just been trashed by a killing that comes straight out of *Pulp Fiction*. Maybe he too will pay a price, when he absorbs the reaction of the media in Washington. Americans who cared nothing for Saudi Arabia now know who Jamal Khashoggi is.

'If a prince can pay $1 billion in return for his freedom, how much will a prisoner of conscience have to pay? How much will we all pay to get our freedom?' Khashoggi tweeted.

We now know the price one humble journalist had to pay so that Saudis can one day get their basic human rights. He paid with his life. May he rest in peace.

12 OCTOBER

When I was growing up, newspapers were deemed too boring, upsetting or costly

COCO KHAN

One of my earliest memories of reading a news article in print was a tabloid story about a woman who gave birth to a frog. Except she hadn't given birth to it, she'd gone swimming in a pond and, in my memory at least, a rogue bit of spawn attached itself to her – a horror she discovered when a trip to the bathroom resulted in a tadpole in the bowl. A perfect story, I thought in my 11-year-old mind. The twists! The turns! The drama!

I set about memorising the tale to retell it in the playground. I had it all planned out: I would build up the suspense ('She was just minding her own business'); add colour through mime (the swimming bit, maybe a frog jump); throw in some poor toad puns ('Surprised she didn't croak it!'). But when it came to delivery, my story was met with nonchalance.

'Yawn, already heard it,' one of my friends said. 'That story's three weeks old, mate.'

'Mum strikes again,' I thought.

You see, when I was growing up, there weren't many newspapers around – they were deemed too boring, upsetting or controversial. Plus, you had to pay for them, which in my perpetually skint family ruled out all broadsheets, no matter how much we kids begged.

I will never forget Eid 2004, when my Auntie B wrapped up a copy of the *Observer* and gave it as a gift to my cousin Amir. I can still see it now: Amir, confused, forced a grateful smile, while Auntie B declared proudly, 'It's got all the supplements!'

The best we'd get was the chance to read an old paper at the doctor's surgery or the hairdresser's, which Mum might bring home if they were throwing them out (hence the three-week-old frog pregnancy story). Perhaps my desire to get into journalism stemmed from this, a yearning not just to have pointless information, but to have up-to-date pointless information.

It's a quirk that has persisted. I recently appeared on the *Guardian*'s front page for the first time, and a number of friends messaged me to say that my mother must be proud. And she would be, if she had seen it. Let's just say it will be very big news in the Khan family in about three weeks, once Mum has been to the hairdresser's.

25 OCTOBER

Bolsonaro backers wage war on the rainforest

DOM PHILLIPS

The growl of a chainsaw and the howl of a tractor engine were enough to draw environment officials up a rutted track into the forest. In the clearing, three young loggers proffered their documents. They were paid in cash, they said – nearly four times the Brazilian minimum monthly salary of £200 ($260) – to ship out up to two truckloads a day of hardwood logs.

And like most people in the heavily deforested Amazon state of Rondônia on Brazil's western border, they are sure who they will vote for in Sunday's presidential run-off vote. 'It has to be Bolsonaro,' said Edivaldo da Silva, 22.

Polls show that Jair Bolsonaro, the far-right former army captain, has 78 per cent support in Rondônia, leaving his leftist rival Fernando Haddad in the dust. In the Amazon, Bolsonaro has promised progress instead of protection. And his radical proposals – to withdraw Brazil from the Paris climate deal, neuter federal environment agencies, back destructive hydro-electric dams, freeze the demarcation of new indigenous reserves and open up existing ones to mining – chime with voters here, including those breaking environmental laws. Loggers, illegal gold miners, and squatters on a protected reserve said they will vote for Bolsonaro because he will make their lives easier.

Environmentalists argue his plans will prove disastrous for the Amazon, and 33 non-government groups have said his proposals represent 'concrete and irreversible risks' to Brazil's forests, biodiversity and even the reputations of its agribusiness producers.

His allies rubbish such concerns – his proposed chief of staff and his candidate for governor of Rondônia both criticised foreign 'interference' in the Amazon and said they harboured doubts over global warming science.

Such views are common in a state where smallholders say they are unjustly penalised for breaking environmental rules and argue that the responsibility for climate change should be shared globally.

The three loggers showed the environment officials documents which, they said, proved their work was licensed under a plan permitting 'sustainable' tree cutting.

But the officials later concluded the papers referred to another patch of land 400 metres away – a common ploy, said Sebastiana Almeida, a forest engineer in Rondônia's environmental development agency.

People in Rondônia – 43 per cent of whose territory has been deforested – largely agree on two things: that they will vote for Bolsonaro, and that the state is getting hotter and drier.

Average annual temperatures in the northern part of the region averaged 26–28°C (79–82°F) in 2017, two degrees higher than five years previously. Annual rainfall has also fallen across the state.

Onyx Lorenzoni, a congressman tipped to become Bolsonaro's chief of staff, disputes that global warming is a problem.

'There are things that are solid and there are things that are ideological,' he said, before criticising Greenpeace for meddling in the environment. 'Brazilians will be in charge in the Amazon, my brother, not the Europeans,' he said.

Other Bolsonaro allies have called for more industry in the Amazon. Colonel João Chrisóstomo, a retired army engineer elected as one of the state's federal deputies for Bolsonaro's Social Liberal party (PSL), said the military should asphalt its dirt roads. Better roads would please residents such as Sheila Barros, 44, who lives inside the protected Lago do Cuniã reserve.

'There is no highway, no way to get our produce out,' she said. The reserve is just 70km (43 miles) from Porto Velho, but reaching it involves driving hours on dirt roads, two boat trips and a motorbike ride.

But paving roads brings development and destruction to forest reserves like Lago do Cuniã, run by the government's Chico Mendes Institute (ICMBio), which only allows fishing and sustainable farming for 400 residents.

Fisherman Mabel Lopes, 65, said that until the reserve was created in 1999, the lagoon was overfished by outsiders. Now, 'there are still plenty of fish'. 'Where else is there this much greenery?' he added.

Bolsonaro says he will end 'environmental activism' by ICMBio, and the environment agency Ibama, and may merge the environment ministry with the agriculture ministry, whose chief is chosen by the agribusiness lobby. He has also promised help for artisanal miners known as *garimpeiros*, some of whom work illegally, dredging mud from Amazon rivers in search of gold – and in the process dumping tons of mercury and poisoning fish stocks.

Rondônia's state governor, Daniel Pereira, and its state legislature are in judicial deadlock over 11 forest reserves created by his predecessor and overturned by state deputies. PSL governor candidate Marcos Rocha said people squatting on protected reserves should be allowed to stay.

Some of those squatters live on Jaci Paraná, a state government-run reserve around 100km (62 miles) from Porto Velho that only permits sustainable, small-scale agriculture by members of a co-operative.

Last week, a group of state environment officials toured the reserve with an armed police escort. They passed a motorbike whose pillion rider was carrying a chainsaw. Officers waved the bike over but the passenger made a dash for the undergrowth. One of the officers fired a shot and he was caught but later released.

Nobody pays much attention to environmental laws here. Ednesio Diogo, 51, and Jonas Dantas, 22, were cooking lunch beside the frame of a wooden house they were building as officials arrived.

When an environmental protection officer told them they were there illegally and would have to leave, Diogo just nodded. Both said they would vote for Bolsonaro.

On Saturday, Ibama vehicles were set on fire in Buritis, a day after ICMBio agents on an anti-deforestation mission were left stranded when locals torched a bridge in the state of Pará.

Brazil's new war on its forests and those who defend them has begun.

1 NOVEMBER

Feel the love, feel the hate – my week in the cauldron of Trump's wild rallies

ED PILKINGTON

There is no understanding Donald Trump without understanding his rallies. They are the crucible of his revolution, the place where his radical reimagining of the US constitution takes shape: not 'We the people', but 'We my people'.

As the US reels from a gunman killing 11 worshippers in a Pittsburgh synagogue, pipe bombs being sent to 14 of the US president's leading opponents and Trump declaring himself a nationalist and sending thousands of troops to the US border to assail unarmed asylum seekers, the most powerful person on Earth continues to rely on his rallies as seething cauldrons of virulent passions.

But that is not all. They are also a test run for his 2020 bid for re-election. Which is why I have crisscrossed the country, from Montana and Wisconsin in the north to Texas in the south, Arizona in the west to North Carolina in the east to attend five rallies in eight days. At each, I look at a different emotion that Trump uses to arouse his people's devotion, in an attempt to find from the inside that which seems so baffling from the outside – the source of his appeal.

RALLY 1 IN MISSOULA, MONTANA – LOVE
Attending your first Trump rally, you are confronted by an uncomfortable truth: love is very much in the air.

Twenty minutes into his speech in Missoula, Montana, Trump breaks off from his teleprompter and scours the crowd – 'Who said that? Who said that?' – until he locates the person who has just declared love for him. 'It's finally a woman,' he exclaims. 'So far, every guy that said "I love you", they're just not my type.'

Women cackle, men squirm. It is a lovefest.

Trump uses the word 'love' repeatedly. He loves Montanans; he loves the hangar where the rally is held; the people of Maine; his first lady; his hair; a couple of local Congress members; and hunting and guns.

His supporters repay his love with interest. They begin forming a queue well before dawn that by midday snakes around a giant field under the state's legendary big sky. Francie Bruneau, 58, has driven 200 miles from Spokane, Washington, and will stand in line for seven hours before Trump appears. 'He's like your friend next door, someone you can go to the pub with and drink beer.'

'He doesn't drink,' someone says.

Much has been written about the dark forces Trump rallies invoke. But today feels like a family outing. Phil Zacha, 82, is wearing a T-shirt that articulates what many people say to me: 'Trump: he says what I think.'

Tonight, there is more swagger in Trump's demeanour than there was in 2016 – and there was plenty then. Two years ago, he was the insurgent candidate; now he is the commanding victor. Here, in this sealed terrarium of 8,000 loving supporters, far from the multiple threats of Robert Mueller, legal worries over porn stars and debates over impeachment, he is in his element. The president entices his followers to believe he is lavishing his love on them. But it works both ways. The rally is where he goes to refuel his ego and his zealotry.

Tucked into the love, however, there is menace that has also grown. 'I love you people,' it seems to say, 'because you hate my enemy.'

Trump turns to Greg Gianforte, Montana's Republican member of Congress who, in 2017, physically attacked the *Guardian*'s political correspondent Ben Jacobs as he asked him a question about healthcare reform, throwing him violently to the ground. Trump praises Gianforte for being a 'tough cookie', and then acts out the motions of someone body-slamming another. The hangar explodes with delight. The slapstick display comes hours after evidence has emerged claiming that the journalist and Virginia resident Jamal Khashoggi had been killed by a Saudi hit squad to silence his criticism.

After the rally is over I call Robin Pedersen, a 56-year-old horse trainer from Florence, Montana, I had met at the hangar. She says of the body-slamming: 'He was joking. We read it as a joke.' Was it appropriate for the US president to joke about a violent assault on a fellow American? 'Probably not. But I'm not offended by it.' Did you laugh? 'I chuckled.'

RALLY 2 IN MESA, ARIZONA – FEAR

The peace Trump offers is twinned with fear. It is stamped on the sea of red hats: Make America Great Again. The slogan implies the country is going to the dogs, and that only one man can save it. As he steps out of his helicopter in Arizona, for a few precious moments Trump carries himself as president of the United States, with all the regalia of that office. Uniformed marines salute him, secret service agents scowl. Then he disappears into the mass of 5,000 devotees, transformed into a man of the people, the guy who puts your fears into words: 'The radical Democrats ... want to impose socialism on our country, turn us into another Venezuela, throw your borders wide open to deadly drugs and ruthless gangs.'

This is radioactive stuff for US conservatives, who, right across the country, fear illegal immigration more than anything else. It is especially incendiary in the border state of Arizona, where we are in Mesa, an outpost of Phoenix.

Rick Novak, 57, a retired building foreman and Harley guy, comes up to the press pen. What would happen to the US were Trump not on the case? 'We are going to get gang wars between white and black, whites and Mexicans. We could have our own little Vietnam, right here.' A full-blown war, in Arizona? 'We are under threat with Mexican people coming over the border. If we don't close it, we are going to let Isis come in with the Mexicans.'

A couple of days later, Fox News reports – without any evidence – that Isis fighters have infiltrated the caravan of 3,500 Central American asylum seekers heading towards the US border. A couple of hours after that, Trump warns that 'Middle Easterners' are hiding in the convoy. After my week of rallies has ended, Trump orders more than 5,000 troops to be sent to the border to intercept the caravan. Then he says he will end the right to US citizenship for babies born in the US – a violation of the 14th amendment from a president who claims to be a defender of the US constitution.

Back in Mesa, Trump snarls about 'kicking the criminals, the drug dealers and the terrorists the hell out of our country'. Outside this Arizona hangar, the world is a cruel and ugly place. Here, inside, his people are safe.

RALLY 3 IN HOUSTON, TEXAS – STRENGTH
When Trump began his rallies in 2015, he insisted on choosing his own music: the Rolling Stones, Elton John and Guns N' Roses. Three years on, in Houston, Texas, the sound system blares out Village People's 'Macho Man': 'Macho, macho man / I gotta be a macho man.' Is it irony? Is it bragging? As with so much of Trump's complex

aesthetics, if you had to guess, you would say both. There is no doubt he likes to present himself as a strong man. And strongman.

In Houston, the largest of the five rallies this week, 16,000 people are inside the auditorium, and several more thousand outside. With every wave of the crowd's affirmation, Trump's chest expands and his pose grows more martial: head back, lips puckered, shoulders square. 'I'm a nationalist,' he cries, fully aware of the storm he will provoke by using a term closely associated with US white supremacy. 'We are not supposed to use that word,' he tells his followers with a verbal wink.

Trump is all about strongman language. Where Barack Obama used philosophical acrobatics to wow his base, Trump is blunt. Democrats are evil, bad, lousy, sick, cuckoo socialists who produce mobs. Republicans are great, beautiful, tough, patriotic warriors who produce jobs. Occasionally, he will allow himself to stick two words together – fake news, crooked Hillary, radical socialism. But he will never place himself above his supporters. It is the root of his strength.

There is another source of Trump's strength: humour. He doesn't do gags or punchlines. What he does do is riff, a sort of free-form ranting. He goes on about 'Pocahontas', his pejorative name for liberal US senator Elizabeth Warren, and her Native American DNA test. He calls Maxine Waters, the black Democratic congresswoman from California, a 'low-IQ individual'. The way he tells it, with a cute 'don't blame me' look on his face, his arms outstretched, it comes across as funny, teasing. People laugh.

Stop and think about that: the systematic demeaning of women and the denigration of a person's IQ in terms Trump reserves exclusively for African Americans in front of a crowd that is 99.8 per cent white. Through laughter, everyone is made complicit.

I talk to three groups of Texan women of different ages. All three groups say Trump 'gets things done'. None believe that Brett

Kavanaugh, the US supreme court justice, sexually assaulted his accuser Christine Blasey Ford.

The only chink of light between the ages relates to Trump's vulgar sexual comments, such as calling Stormy Daniels, the adult film actor who alleges an affair, 'horseface'. The sixtysomethings think it's 'piddlin''. But one of the high-school students, Priscila Garcia, 17, doesn't like it. She recoiled at the *Access Hollywood* tape in 2016 in which Trump boasted that he would 'grab 'em by the pussy'. 'Him saying that makes me and other women uncomfortable,' she says. But there the disagreement ends. 'He's a better leader than he is a person,' she says. 'I don't agree with his personality, but he gets stuff done.'

RALLY 4 IN MOSINEE, WISCONSIN – HATE
On the morning of the fourth rally, the outside world blasts into Trumpland. Shortly after 10am, as CNN anchors are telling their viewers about a series of pipe bombs mailed to the Clintons, Obamas and Democratic billionaire George Soros, the network receives its own explosive device.

Jacob Spaeth and three buddies are lining up in a field in Mosinee, Wisconsin, for the latest rally, all wearing the same T-shirt with a cartoon sketch of Trump urinating over the CNN logo. Today, after the CNN pipe bomb became headline news, a merchant says he has sold about 15 of them in quick succession at $20 each. Spaeth, a 19-year-old college student, doesn't want to comment on the bombs, but says: 'It's not just CNN, it's the whole media. They are very unfair to Trump. They're manipulating kids, telling them that Trump is a horrible guy.'

Spaeth gets his information from *Infowars*, the website of Alex Jones. Jones is on the record as having said that 9/11 was a government set-up and that the 2012 Newtown school shooting, in which 20 children were gunned down, was fabricated. Within hours, he will be broadcasting that this week's pipe bombs are also a hoax.

Spaeth embodies one of the most puzzling aspects of my week in Trumpland. Throughout the five rallies, I talk to scores of welcoming and pleasant people. Yet, in the pressure cooker of the rally, they hurl insults at the press pen. Spaeth says it makes him happy to be able to express his feelings so openly among like-minded folk.

There is only one explanation: that Trump enables good, civil Americans to metamorphose into media baiters. 'Those people, fake news,' the president says sneeringly at almost every rally, pointing to the pen where reporters are cooped up during his speeches. As soon as he says it, the chants begin. 'CNN sucks! CNN sucks!' Many laugh. But CNN is taking no chances: it brings private security guards to every rally.

With the wound of the pipe bombs so fresh, tonight Trump refrains from the usual 'fake news' routine. He also holds back from personal attacks on Democrats, though in the other rallies I attend I hear him denigrate by name five of the 14 targets of the pipe bombs (Cory Booker, Hillary Clinton, Obama, Soros and Waters). Instead, tonight he talks about the need to 'bring our nation together'. It is an extraordinarily cordial message. But listen closer. He tells politicians to stop treating their opponents – for which read Trump – as 'morally defective', and references the 'mob' – for which read Democrats. He is mocking the very concept of national unity while calling for it.

The day after my week of Trump rallies ends, the consequences become fully apparent of a nation whose civilian population owns vastly more guns than any other being led by a man who whips up racial fears and mocks national unity. On Saturday 27 October, two hours after he had posted a rant against 'invaders that kill our people', Robert Bowers enters a synagogue in Pittsburgh, pulls out an AR-15 style assault rifle and at least three handguns, and massacres 11 Jewish worshippers.

Within a few hours, Trump is back, at his next rally in Illinois, promising 'strong borders, no crime and no caravans'. Within 48 hours, he has renewed his unfounded claims that 'very bad people' are mixed in with the caravan and that the 'fake news media' is the 'enemy of the people'.

But those events still lie in the future. Tonight in Wisconsin, the crowd includes Steve Spaeth (no relation), 40, who runs a home exteriors company. I ask him who he regards as his political enemies. He rattles off CNN, Soros, Clinton, Waters, Booker, 'Pocahontas' AKA Elizabeth Warren and others. The other day, he talked to his sister, who is liberal and votes Democratic. He said to her: 'If there is a civil war in this country and you were on the wrong side, I would have no problem shooting you in the face.'

You must be joking, I say.

'No, I am not. I love my sister, we get on great. But she has to know how passionate I am about our president.'

RALLY 5 IN CHARLOTTE, NORTH CAROLINA – HOPE
To end an account of a week in Trumpland on a low note would be fake news. At the president's last rally, all you can see is smiling faces. To grasp Trump rallies, you have to accept how good he makes his people feel. They are buoyed up by hope.

It begins with jobs. Trump's base is convinced that he has turned the economy round. America is great again. A gravel pit worker in Montana said orders are up; a teenager in Texas is overladen with weekend shifts; Matthew Holt, 20, here in Charlotte, North Carolina, says his family-run gas station is doing great.

While the president berates the media for its lies, his own taste for mendacity has been on display all week. He has boasted falsely that the tax cut he enacted last December was the 'biggest in history' (it is the eighth largest since 1918); that Asian-American unemployment is at a historic low (it was 1 per cent lower under Obama); that at least eight new steel plants are opening (only two existing plants are being expanded).

Katy Tur, the NBC News reporter who was targeted by Trump during the 2016 election, begins her book on the experience with a revealing quote from him: 'I play to people's fantasies. People want to believe that something is the biggest and the greatest.'

That is a perfect summary of how the rally ends. Thousands of supporters carry with them a renewed love of their leader, reawakened fears about the threats all around, conviction in the rightness of their crusade, hate towards those they call 'un-Americans', and hope that their worldview will prevail.

The doors are flung open, air rushes into the Trump terrarium, and they step outside into the dark night.

5 NOVEMBER

'Chunks of my tongue came off – you could see the tastebuds': Ross Edgley on swimming around Great Britain

ELLE HUNT

Ross Edgley, who has just become the first man to swim around Great Britain, is trying to describe what it feels like to have your tongue disintegrate. 'I realised something was bad when I woke up with chunks of it on my pillow,' he recalls. The flesh was translucent, but otherwise a lot like beef stroganoff or slow-cooked pork. 'It's that tender, you're just pulling strips off,' says Edgley energetically. 'You could see the tastebuds on it, it was that thick.'

Endurance swimmers call it salt mouth – the effect of seawater build-up in your mouth and throat. Edgley's was at its worst as he passed Dungeness in early June, about 85 hours of swimming after setting out from Margate harbour. 'Even a week in, it went from being a swim as most people consider it, as a sport, to being a survival exercise,' he says.

That 'exercise' lasted 157 days, during each of which Edgley swam for six hours, then slept for six hours (often less), in twice-daily cycles.

Alongside him was his support crew, husband and wife Matt and Suzanne Knight, on board their 16-metre (52ft) catamaran *Hecate*. The instant Edgley boarded the boat every day, its location was recorded, and it would return to that exact point when the time came for Edgley to return to the water, thereby ensuring a continuous circumnavigation of 1,792 miles – about the same distance as London to Moscow by road.

In the course of his five-month-long Great British Swim, Edgley raced ferries, stopped boats, braved storms, swam with countless dolphins, suffered hundreds of jellyfish stings, saw 'every single seal', and became a connoisseur of the nation's waters. 'Scotland tasted really nice,' he tells me. The Irish Sea, he says after consideration, was 'organic'. The Humber Estuary: 'straight-up fertiliser'.

Edgley – just turned 33, from Grantham, Lincolnshire – takes a perverse pleasure in pushing his body to its limits. A fitness expert and athlete, he played water polo for Great Britain as a teenager, before going on to study sports science at Loughborough University. He amassed a large social media following for his superhuman stunts, such as running a marathon while towing a Mini Cooper and rope-climbing the height of Mount

Everest, devised to both fundraise for charity and test his own theories about physical performance. He has no superpowers, he said in an early instalment of his weekly video diary – just the right combination of enough naivety to start, and enough stubbornness to finish. (He has since added a few caveats to that slogan, lest his followers – many of whom have already told him his feat has inspired them to sign up for ultramarathons and Strongman competitions – endanger themselves in their enthusiasm.)

Looking back, he had an overabundance of naivety, Edgley cheerily admits now, on the penultimate day of his journey. It is Saturday morning and we are drinking coffee in the cockpit of *Hecate*, moored off Margate pier ahead of his final leg. He shows me a 5-kilogram bucket of petroleum jelly, nearly hollowed out. 'At the start, I was like, there's no way we're going to get through that. We've done almost a kilo a month.'

Edgley himself is barely recognisable from the sleek body-builder of his first vlog. Then he had resembled a superhero who shared DNA with one of those giant river otters, or a pedigree bull terrier. The bearded man sitting opposite me, wearing a bobble hat and a fleece-lined hooded cloak, is more reminiscent of Bilbo Baggins towards the end of his unexpected journey.

In five months, Edgley has put on 8kg to weigh 100kg, gaining muscle in his shoulders, losing it in his legs, and developing a 'seal-like bulk' all over. 'My body's completely changed. I've got hairier, I've got fatter.' Fitness is a slippery concept, although he tried to pin it down in his 'eccentric and comprehensive' best-seller, *The World's Fittest Book*. 'There is no definition. Right now, I'm really fit if you want me to swim around Great Britain, but awful if you want me to run a marathon.'

After swimming 12 hours a day for five months, he has adapted 'to the point where I'm really going to be bad on land'. He has been doing balance and leg-strengthening exercises in readiness. His feet have entirely lost their arches, he tells me, though their purply-yellow colour is apparently no cause for concern. His trench foot ('pretty bad, at one point. Yeah, you can lose them') has cleared up, as has a 'sea ulcer' on his heel. 'It's not as bad as it sounds!' he says, seeing my expression. 'If you got a tiny cut, it would never heal, it would just get deeper and deeper. It would start going through to the bone, essentially.'

Edgley's achievement, it quickly becomes apparent, is compelling not just as an unprecedented feat of mental and physical endurance, but in a similar way to those lurid quasi-documentaries about medical anomalies. At the same time as his tongue was disintegrating, chafing from his wetsuit created a raw wound, inspiring the viewers of his weekly vlogs to give him the nickname Rhino Neck. Efforts to protect it with layers of Sudocrem, plasters, Vaseline, bin bags and duct tape were time-consuming and only partially successful.

'Imagine having an open wound and rubbing it with sand-paper for 12 hours a day – that's what it was like,' says Edgley. 'I woke up the next morning and my bedsheets were stuck to it. I was like, "Oh, for God's sake", ripped it off, then got in and swam.' His girlfriend, Hester Sabery, was fortunate enough to be visiting him on board *Hecate* at the time. 'Oh yeah, that was horrific,' she says later, wincing at the memory. 'He just had blisters all over his shoulders, his neck, his chest. And when he moved, they were all just there on the pillow.'

But he never thought of giving up, he says. He took to heart the advice of Alexei Janssen, a performance coach to the Royal Marines, to focus on the process – then the outcome would become inevitable. 'Never did I think about arriving at Margate, or quitting. I stopped counting up or down.' There was no time to feel sorry for himself, anyway, with his precious few hours out of the water spent sleeping or eating. With a daily target of 15,000 calories, Edgley has described his endeavour as a 'giant eating competition, with a bit of swimming in between'.

'ROSS EDGLEY'S BANANA TALLY', crudely scrawled on the cockpit roof in permanent marker, stands at 649. While in the water he ate one every 20 minutes, with the occasional break for fortified porridge or noodles. Between swims he ate breakfast – a proper fry-up, with four slices of toast, two or three eggs, baked beans, the lot – lunch and dinner: a full day's meals every 12 hours. 'It was like double time,' says Suzanne Knight, who took charge of Edgley's nutrition. 'The thing is, when he started the swim, he carried no fat at all, he was all muscle. That's why we went crazy and bulked him up so much.'

For Edgley, who co-founded a fitness supplements company, food needed to be dense not only in calories but also in nutrients digestible in the mix of what else he had eaten that day and palatable, given his current state of physical degradation. ('Can you imagine your salt tongue hanging off, then trying to eat granola?') He took an intuitive approach to his diet, which allowed for emerging from the ocean to wolf down two Domino's pizzas, back to back.

But the challenge was as much mental as physical. 'When you add it all up, I've probably spent a month on my own, staring at the bottom of the seabed,' he says. 'There were times when I wasn't thinking about surviving, when I could coast – that's when you can go into this moving meditation and mull over everything. But people ask if I've come to any amazing epiphanies, whereas I get out and go: "Have we got any cheese left? Can I get a cheese toastie?"'

In his cabin he was reading Marcus Aurelius's *Meditations* on Stoic philosophy ('It's been brilliant, this psychology in the face of adversity'), which he says dovetailed with sports science. Edgley knew that revving himself up, or swimming angry, could stress his immune system and jeopardise his endurance for the rest of the journey. His MO, as he explained in a vlog, was to 'swim with a smile', even through clouds of jellyfish. (Part of the reason he grew a beard was to serve as protection.) 'That was easier said than done, and sometimes I was putting on a brave face – for the crew as well.'

His lowest moment, he says – worse than the salt tongue or his 'neck hanging off' – was when he was kept awake for six hours by a serious sting while crossing the Irish sea. He mimes feverish scratching of his arms: 'I looked possessed. I was walking around naked on deck because the wind was the only thing that soothed my skin.' It sounds like King Lear on the moor, I say, by now in my own heavy-weather robe. 'Yeah, it was! Eventually, I went to bed and from my cabin saw day turn to night and night turn to day. The tide changed, and Matt knew I hadn't slept. He said: "Mate, I'm so sorry – you have to go in." It had literally just stopped itching.'

It seems paradoxical that someone so dedicated to fine-tuning the body 'as an instrument, not an ornament' – a phrase by which he repeatedly condemns the aesthetics-led approach of the wider fitness industry – would cause himself so much physical damage. 'I think sports science – and medical science – quite rightly errs on the side of caution and would be like: "You need rest, you need to take antibiotics, or *something*,"' Edgley agrees. But he sees his own body as not just an instrument but an experiment – a willing subject on which to test his theories of athletic performance 'in the lab that is the Great British coastline'.

He was inspired by the Hungarian-Canadian endocrinologist Hans Selye's work on general adaptation in 1936. By gradually increasing lab rats' tolerance to poison, Selye was able to prove that stress and stimuli were the key to adaptation, says Edgley.

'What I'm saying is, yes, I absolutely am worried about long-term damage. But what if I am becoming one of Hans Selye's indestructible rats? You don't know.

'In the fitness community, we're all told, "Lose a stone in the week", "Get fit in five easy steps" – no one wants to say, "Get fit through stress and stimuli according to Hans Selye's work in 1936." That's not going to sell anything. No one wants to say: "If you want to get fit or lose weight, it's going to be hard – you're going to suffer."'

Is he a masochist? 'That's a good question.' Five months ago, he would have said no; now, he is not so sure. 'In this small bubble, with Matt and I both so driven towards the same goal, I'm like: "Why wouldn't you swim with your tongue hanging off?" I would say I'm not a masochist, but maybe a month from now, I'll go: "What was I doing?"'

So what will he be doing a month from now? 'Well, genuinely learning to walk again' – and then a marathon by Christmas. 'I think that might be quite a good litmus test.'

12 November

'A political choice': UN envoy says UK can help all who hit hard times

PATRICK BUTLER

What tells you most about a society is how it treats its poor and vulnerable, the UN special rapporteur on poverty and human rights, Philip Alston, told a packed public meeting held in the UK's poorest neighbourhood on Sunday.

He said a wealthy country could decide to help all those who hit hard times, ensure that they don't slip through the net and are able to live a life of dignity: 'It's a political choice.'

Alston was in Jaywick, a tiny village by the sea in the south-east corner of Essex. It has found itself at the top of official indices of deprivation since 2010, and in countless articles and TV documentaries has come to symbolise the kind of bleak and gaudy poverty fuelled by chronic economic neglect and social breakdown.

The UN rapporteur heard an hour of often moving testimonies from local people describing their stories of being pitched into hardship and despair through what Alston called the 'human condition': best-laid plans derailed by unexpected life-changing events such as serious illness, job loss or marriage breakdown.

The clear message from this proudly patriotic area, with its Conservative-run council and Tory MP, was that in an age of austerity and spending cuts, the state was choosing not to help; instead it was stealthily withdrawing and casting people adrift with only an overstretched voluntary and charity sector to support them.

Several themes resurfaced throughout: the stress and humiliation of poverty and debt, the loneliness and feelings of worthlessness that brought on suicidal thoughts and the 'hostile environment' of the benefits system and bureaucratic nightmare of universal credit.

Erin, a former journalist from Colchester, described how birth defects had triggered a neurological collapse at the age of 30, a crisis that had rapidly escalated to the point where she and her family, once comfortably off, were now at risk of becoming destitute. 'Suddenly we were not a two-income middle-class family, we were living on disability benefit.'

Her partner had to give up his job as an NHS manager to care for her full-time. Then they were told by their landlord that he wanted them out in eight weeks as he needed to sell the house. Twelve years of paying rent on time counted for nothing: as soon as estate agents discovered they were on disability benefits they refused to even consider letting to them. 'I do not know where I will be putting my 12-year-old to bed soon. Will we be made homeless, because of my birth defects?' she told the meeting.

'We have paid our taxes, we are hard workers, we are active in the community ... and we face the real prospect of being made homeless.'

Steve, a former jobcentre worker, told how he was driven to the brink by the stress of living on the breadline and being unable to provide for his family. He ran up debt and they became reliant on handouts and food banks. At one point he felt so despairing he considered stepping in front of a speeding car. 'I thought, if I were to die no one would miss me.'

Rob, a nurse from Clacton, had been struck by chronic illness and was on long-term sickness benefit. He spoke of the 'failing' disability system. He had been found 'fit for work' by an official benefits assessor, despite presenting evidence from his GP and hospital consultant that he was unable to. Subsequently he was told he had to reapply for his disability benefits. The claim took seven weeks to be processed, leaving him without any income. He had to rely on friends for handouts, and made trips to the food bank. 'It makes you feel worthless. The whole thing is a disgrace.'

Alston told the meeting the testimonies reflected those he had heard throughout his two-week tour. Last week he visited Newcastle, Edinburgh, Glasgow, Cardiff, Belfast and Bristol. His tour continues on Monday in London. On Friday he will issue his interim report on how far the UK government is meeting its international human rights commitments on the right to housing, food and a decent standard of living. Earlier, Alston had met the Rev Sean Fountain, minister at Pier Avenue Baptist church in Clacton, a few miles up the coast from Jaywick. 'People are in crisis,' Fountain said, 'and there is very little in the way of support.'

Faith and community groups were picking up the pieces as local government, schools and policing budgets shrank, he said. Volunteers from his church ran a drop-in centre, a small homeless project, and helped run a food bank. But in the face of rising poverty, homelessness and youth crime, it sometimes felt like an unequal battle. He said they got no financial help from the council 'and there are only so many volunteers to go round'.

Giles Watling, the Conservative MP for Clacton, held a private meeting with Alston on Sunday. His message was that places like Jaywick were 'on the up' and that recent investment in roads, housing and drains had 'changed the place dramatically'. Asked by the *Guardian* whether he thought austerity was over, he replied: 'There's light at the end of the tunnel. But you can't just turn it off like a switch.'

Fountain is not so sure that things will get better. 'The government has not been interested in the community. They have been obsessed by the Brexit agenda and they have taken their eyes off what's happening to ordinary people.'

'Macron's arrogance unites us' – on the barricades with France's *gilets jaunes*

ANGELIQUE CHRISAFIS

On the grass verge of a village roundabout north of Toulouse, Céline stood at a barricade built from pallets of wood and old tyres, a bonfire burning behind her. French flags were flying alongside signs calling for Emmanuel Macron's resignation.

'I'm prepared to spend Christmas protesting at this roundabout with my children – we won't back down and we've got nothing to lose,' said the 41-year-old, who voted for Macron in last year's presidential election. 'He gave good speeches and I really believed his promises that he would change France. But not any more.'

Céline, a classroom assistant for children with special needs, earns €800 (£710) a month. She cannot afford rent so lives with her four children in a relative's house in the suburbs of Toulouse, in the south-west of France.

'Macron's first move in office was to slash the wealth tax for the mega-rich while cutting money from poor people's housing benefits,' she said. 'That is a serious injustice. The country is rising up and he's staying silent, he's hiding in an ivory tower, that's what disturbs me, he's not taking responsibility.'

At the roundabout barricade in Lespinasse, 20 people from surrounding villages – builders, nurses, workers in the local aviation industry – protested near a crucial fuel depot, wearing the yellow high-visibility vests that define France's *gilets jaunes* movement. Passing trucks and cars beeped in support. Drivers leaned out of their windows and shouted, 'Don't give up!'

This grassroots citizens' protest, which began as a spontaneous revolt against fuel tax rises last month, has morphed into an anti-government and anti-Macron movement, and is now the young centrist president's biggest crisis.

The demonstrators say Macron is an arrogant would-be monarch. He presents himself abroad, they say, as a progressive hero who can hold back the tide of nationalism, but at home he symbolises a distant political elite, stoking distrust and pushing people towards populism.

'I always feared that there was an element of dictator in the way Macron did things,' said Robert, 64, a left-wing Toulouse carpenter and cabinetmaker. 'He's well-presented and he speaks nicely – but he misread these protests because he thought he was the saviour of France. He wasn't listening, he forgot the human factor.'

Last Saturday saw the worst street unrest in central Paris in decades, as fringe elements of the otherwise peaceful protesters fought running battles with riot police and set cars alight. Tourist attractions and museums in Paris will be closed today, and the government has warned that thousands of rioters might come to the capital to 'smash' or even 'kill'. Yet *gilets jaunes* across France are determined to march in towns and cities this weekend anyway.

Crucially, the government fears violence outside Paris. Local government offices were torched in the small central town of Le Puy-en-Velay last weekend. In Toulouse, there were battles with riot police with several injured. Motorway tollbooths have been burned down and vandalised in southern France, and when secondary-school students staged protests this week against university and school reforms, police fired teargas at several demonstrations. The entrance hall of a school in Blagnac, outside Toulouse, was burned to the ground.

One transport worker in his 20s who took part in a street march in the small country town of Montauban in the south-west said he was shocked by the teargas. 'Things will kick off for sure again this weekend, there could be violence anywhere in France,' he said.

The roundabouts and motorway tollbooths that *gilets jaunes* continue to blockade are often near small towns and villages that do not normally make the news. Main cities are often far away, meaning residents cannot work or take children to school without a car – hence their fury at fuel tax rises.

Demonstrators of all backgrounds and political views seem united on one point – a personal disgust with Macron, whose 'arrogance' they cite from televised examples, including the time he told an unemployed person to just 'cross the road' to find a job, or when he wagged a finger to tell pensioners they shouldn't complain. Then there is the outrage over refurbishments to the Élysée Palace and the construction of a holiday pool in the presidential summer retreat. One poll this week showed Macron's approval ratings down to 18 per cent.

Isabelle, 41, a single mother, had never taken part in a protest movement before. She works at a sandwich stand at Toulouse airport for the minimum wage – less than €1,200 a month – and her daily shifts begin at 3am. She was among many who had deliberately spoiled her ballot paper in last year's presidential election final round, unwilling to choose between Macron or the far-right Marine Le Pen.

'This is now about so much more than fuel tax,' she said. 'We seem to live in a world gone mad where the rich pay next to nothing and the poor are constantly taxed. We've had enough of the elite.'

The *gilets jaunes* movement is unlike any other seen in postwar France because it sprang up online without a leader, trade union or party behind it. Along the barricades there is a broad mix of people, some apolitical, some on the left who feared nationalism, some who had voted for the nationalist Le Pen, some environmentalists. Many were against the EU, feeling it enshrined rampant capitalism.

One 24-year-old philosophy student said: 'This feels like a historic moment in France. I'd liken it to the Arab spring – a kind of revolution that started online.'

Although the demonstrators have complained that poor people bear the brunt of France's high taxation, they are still attached to public services. A banner on a building in Lespinasse read: 'We want a railway station.'

Across France, rural areas have complained about depleted public services. 'Hospitals are understaffed and underfinanced,' said a 39-year-old nurse from Toulouse. 'But what has united everyone is Macron's arrogance. He has made the tension worse, like a little king pitching himself against a whole nation. Macron has held us to ransom saying he was the only one who could hold back nationalism and Le Pen, but he has no credibility at all in France.'

Fabien Mauret, a self-employed builder, was cooking sausages on a barbecue for the protesters.

'I think we've got to the point of no return,' he said. 'Before, there were the rich, the middle and the poor. Now it's the very rich and the poor, nothing in between.' He used to vote socialist but now he votes Le Pen.

Raymond Stocco, 64, who used to work in aircraft maintenance, suggested the mega-rich should be forced to pay back the tax breaks they had enjoyed over the past four years. 'Macron's big mistake was treating people in France as if we were stupid,' he said.

In this corner of rural and suburban south-west France, protesters planned to blockade hypermarkets as a way to force people back to small local shops.

Many said the movement would last, in part because of the community feeling it had engendered. Alexandre, a retired trucker who lives in a caravan, was spending his 63rd birthday at the barricade. 'I'm less lonely when I come here to talk politics to everyone,' he said.

11 DECEMBER

The best gift for your ageing parent is the gift of your time

RANJANA SRIVASTAVA

A colleague is scrolling distractedly through images on her phone as we wait for a meeting to start.

'What do you get a mother in her 70s?' she whispers.

Leaning over, I examine cardigans, scarves and purses by the dozens, holding back on commenting that they all look the same.

'The problem is they all look the same,' she sighs.

The meeting starts, and I never ask her what she got, but I think of her dilemma a few months later as I wonder what birthday gift to get my father.

He is a man of letters, a retired Indian academic. His favourite pastimes are to read and write, especially in retirement when he sits at the dining table for hours on end, crafting deep essays and sublime poetry. I have bought him writing pads and elegant pens but there are only so many of those a writer needs and lately, knowing my penchant for pens, he has been giving them back to me to 'use in the meantime'.

His computer is ageing – you could comfortably make a cup of tea and drink half by the time it stirs. Recently, some hackers cunningly singled out all his Indian contacts to be notified that he had an urgent illness that required a financial bailout. Their consternation was nothing compared to my dad's. It turned out that his back-up system for five years of writing had been his brain. My husband and a shop managed to retrieve the data but my faith in his computer was forever lost.

'Let me buy you a new laptop for your birthday,' I say.

He frowns. 'Why? My old one is fine.'

The next week, the birthday a bit closer, I offer to replace his smartphone, which could really be a great deal smarter, but he is not convinced: 'My phone makes calls, sends texts and fetches mail. What more would a new one do?' I can't say.

Leaving me contemplating the infinite possibilities, my children do what they can. They bake him their favourite chocolate-chip cookies. Since they steal away some of the raw ingredients, they manage only 10 finished products, which turn out just right – large, golden and chewy. One cookie mysteriously crumbles, and they keep one each for their brilliant effort. This leaves six cookies hastily wrapped in a used plastic bag and placed into their grandfather's hands. He is gratified and thrilled beyond words. For the next few days, he savours his grandchildren's cookies bit by bit, ignoring his daughter's protestations about sugar hits for breakfast.

Which still leaves me short of a present – and, now, competing with my own children!

I go to work hoping to find inspiration. Every pre-Christmas clinic brings up a similar set of anxieties for a different set of people. Is it OK to have a break at Christmas? If I skip a dose, will my cancer grow faster? Can we give Dad a glass of wine at lunch? Could this be Mum's last Christmas?

I try to answer each question with honesty and consideration, regarding the disease in the context of the person. The majority of patients are reassured to hear that skipping a treatment will not jeopardise their wellbeing and, in fact, a convivial family gathering may be the most therapeutic intervention of all. I witness people's expression turn to joy at the thought of a Christmas unfettered by the toxicities of treatment – and as I sign the orders, I secretly can't help feeling a tiny bit like a magician.

But no closer to finding the perfect gift.

Later that day, I meet an elderly man who has resolutely denied my interpretations of his illness, insisting that he feels fine. Worried at the fatal toxicities that chemotherapy can impose, I hope that Christmas will tempt him to take a break. But to my surprise, he wants to know why we close for a public holiday. Sensing my frustration, he reluctantly offers an explanation.

'If I stop treatment, I may not see my son. He drives me to chemotherapy and takes me home – it's our time together. It's the nicest thing about having treatment.'

Then he sits back and looks out of the window as I let his simple and devastating reason wash over me.

Did he really see toxic chemotherapy as the price to pay for seeing his son? Had it taken a terminal illness for father and son to talk regularly? I don't know for sure, but I can see that he believes it and that's what matters.

'Tell me about your son,' I say, so that my chaotic thoughts might settle.

When he has finished, I realise that he has told me nothing about who his son is or what he does, only the times they have spent together that mean so much. They are mundane too – trips in the car, buying groceries, picking up a grandchild, going to the carwash.

He knows everyone is busy but, still, he can't deny that his son's company is his greatest consolation and his nicest reward. So, if that means having some extra chemotherapy, so be it. I listen to him, moved and humbled, and a little lost for words.

I find myself thinking of a friend who gave his mother 60 walks for her 60th birthday. Each week's walk was a great commitment but far more meaningful than any wrapped present. And another friend who visited her mother every single week for the years she spent in residential care, dementia chipping away at her core. In the end, there was no gift to give her save that of a familiar presence that could expect no return. It must have been a heart-rending gift to give, but, at the same time, priceless.

And it dawns on me that in searching for that elusive gift for an ageing parent, we are neglecting the one that is most obvious: the gift of our time. In an age where we live and work in far-flung corners of the world, spending time together isn't always easy or practical but we deceive ourselves by thinking that it doesn't matter. The antidote to an epidemic of loneliness doesn't lie in sending a bigger gift but in exercising our imagination. If the stories of my patients are anything to go by, our imagination would tell us to show up a little more, to call a little more and to simply be more attentive. A sorrow shared is a sorrow divided. No medical advance, and no wrapped gift, could ever compete with this.

I tell my patient that I will talk to his son and we will figure something out. He says thank you for not judging him. Then I stop looking for a gift for my dad and call him to say I will pick him up and we will go for a drive. I'll be ready, he says.

Ranjana Srivastava is an oncologist based in Melbourne, Australia.

12 DECEMBER

Theresa May is now a lame duck – too weak to take back control of her party

MARTIN KETTLE

So, Steve Baker, Jacob Rees-Mogg and the rest of you, was that really worth it? After the day of folly it doesn't look that way. In the end, the interminably long-discussed Conservative leadership challenge to Theresa May has come to nothing. When it came to it – even in a secret ballot where MPs could set their public protestations of loyalty to one side – it proved to be more mouth than trousers, a brief distraction from the serious business of Brexit. Tomorrow, grownup politics, damned difficult politics, resumes after today's hiatus.

The result showed what we knew already. The Tories are a very divided party, of whom a clear majority supports May as leader even in a bad Brexit crisis. The critics went for the kill, but May's 200–117 victory is a decisive one. It's a better result for May than when she won the leadership against Andrea Leadsom and Michael Gove in 2016 (she got 199 back then; against their 130). To coin a phrase, nothing has changed.

The echo of 1995, when the same part of the Tory party (and some of the same individuals) forced John Major to put his leadership on the line – Major won by 218–89 over John Redwood – is very strong. May will know, though, that Major's victory was entirely pyrrhic. May's victory could be pyrrhic too. The Tory party's chances of winning a working majority that would last a full term were certainly not helped by today's challenge.

Many groups should learn a lesson from the non-event of 12 December. First in the queue, obviously enough, are its immediate authors, the delusional Tory backbench plotters who thought that a leadership challenge would somehow transform the politics of delivering Brexit in a hung parliament, turning an intractable national standoff into an easy shoo-in for the nationalist Tory fanatics. It was never going to happen. The Thames would be more likely to flow backwards.

A period of silence would be welcome, also, from the superficial political culture of much of the wider Tory party. There is no party in British politics that is so obsessed with leadership navel-gazing as the Tories. Websites such as *ConservativeHome* are forever conducting beauty contests about the succession, deciding who's up and who's down. There is something fundamentally unserious about this.

The media, too, should eat some humble pie this Christmas. We talk up leadership contests at the slightest excuse. We have spent months bigging up a possible challenge to May when a few minutes' serious reflection would have shown its strict limits. We gave so much publicity to Rees-Mogg and the rest that it went to their heads. And in the end?

The truth is – and always was – that the implacable anti-Europeans were never going to muster the votes to get rid of May. The numbers were clear. So was the lack of realistic options. Above all, as Kenneth Clarke put it earlier today, a contest was 'unhelpful, irrelevant and irresponsible'. May would have had to have been found drunk in the gutter before most Tory MPs would have voted her out at a difficult time like this. And May would probably have been an even-money chance to survive if that is what it took to stop Boris Johnson.

So, why did it happen? One problem is that too many Tories are too easily beguiled by their own imaginary version of history. The anti-May plotters probably thought that real backbench discomfort with May's Brexit deal – which caused her to delay the Brexit deal vote this week – would translate seamlessly into the wish to oust her. They were wrong. They looked back to 1990 and perhaps remembered that although Margaret Thatcher won enough votes to beat Michael Heseltine, they weren't enough to save her leadership. Perhaps they thought the same would happen today. They were wrong. Perhaps they looked back to the ousting of Iain Duncan Smith in 2003 – the only other time that a confidence vote has been called against a recent Tory leader – and imagined that May could be got rid of the same way. They were wrong about that too.

More profoundly – much more profoundly – this vote was a wake-up call about the terminal sterility of a certain kind of Conservative vision. It's a kind of Conservatism that is a confluence of two different traditions, and the Tory party is too respectful to both of them. On the one hand, there is a white establishment tradition, largely English rather than British in mentality, that has not come to terms with the loss of empire, dislikes foreigners, and which somehow equates Brexit with the restoration of British superiority and power. On the other, there are Thatcher's children, often self-made, self-confident, petit bourgeois, anti-foreigner and anti-state, flirting with Ukip, beguiled by the Great in Great Britain and irreconcilable to any European engagement.

May's critics are genuinely hopeless at politics. They can cause a lot of trouble. But they cannot, will not, take responsibility for practical action in government. They appear to believe that there is a Commons majority for their faith-based, crash-out, free-at-last, ourselves-alone Brexit if only they can install a true believer and bring the DUP back onside. The vote confirmed that is not true. The naivety is breathtaking. Such a Tory leader would lose any Brexit bill or confidence vote. Luckily for the Tory party, most MPs proved today they are not so foolish.

In the end, it's the recklessness over Ireland, an instinct that lies deep in the DNA of part of the Tory party, that is the most frightening piece of foolishness. These fanatics, playing footsie with a DUP clique that puts sectarianism above the wider needs of a Northern Ireland that voted remain, are the direct political descendants, though with half the talent, of people such as Lord Randolph Churchill in the 1890s, FE Smith in the 1910s and Enoch Powell in the 1970s. All of them tried to play the Orange card. All of them did so with awful results for Ireland and Britain alike. As Talleyrand said of the Bourbons, they have learned nothing and forgotten nothing – and they proved it again this week.

It would be interesting to think that the Tory party will learn from what happened today. But that's hard, when the retro-right has boxed in every Tory leader from Major on. May is no exception to that rule. Her leadership survived – but at a price. She had to confirm that she will not lead the Tories into the next election in order to ensure it. That makes her too weak and too preoccupied with Brexit to take the Tory party decisively away from the people who tried to bring her down. Nevertheless, these are unique times. The prime minister is a lame duck, it is true, but she remains a remarkably resilient lame duck.

18 December

Mourinho and United ended up like a loveless celebrity marriage

BARNEY RONAY

Farewell, then, José. It's been fun. Or if not exactly fun then fitful, tedious and wreathed in a familiar sense of entropy. Either way,

José Mourinho's abrupt departure from Manchester United on Tuesday morning completes a familiar three-year cycle of doomed hope, doomed decline and, by the end, simply doom.

There was at least an inevitability about the end. It has been clear since the summer that Mourinho was preparing for this moment, using his public pronouncements to shift blame, distance himself from the squad of players assembled, and tend to the one element that really matters: his glorious but increasingly distant legacy.

In the event, United's struggles through the autumn proved irresistible. Mourinho has seemed to be fraying a little in recent weeks, resembling in his post-match interviews a particularly haggard and doomed minor European aristocrat hurled up against the palace wall by a cabal of Bolsheviks and asked to explain his extravagant misuse of the public purse.

But then, let's face it, the glorious red dawn of José Mourinho was only ever a chimera, someone else's misguided daydream. At times José in Manchester has felt like a loveless celebrity marriage, two fading stars of the last decade clinging to one another in the hope of some mutual rekindling, a Queen reunion tour fronted by Rick Astley.

And so here we go again, glancing around the jerry-built structures of another doomed post-Ferguson era. There will of course be an immediate urge to pile in on Mourinho, to attach all blame to the manager. This is the easiest and, indeed, most attractive option. It is also the option Manchester United's directors and owners would much prefer.

This is, in part, why football managers exist. One of the key functions of the first ever managers was to stand out front and assuage the ire of the Victorian crowds, straw men hoist into place to create a layer of padding between angry customers and the keepers of this fevered new form of public entertainment.

Not that Mourinho doesn't deserve his share. At United, he failed in the most basic task of creating a coherent high-level team out of the players at his disposal. Indeed, it is hardly controversial to suggest Mourinho is basically done at this level, that his methods and his persona simply seem out of time. Mourinho's deep block, the idea of crouching behind your guard and letting an opponent punch itself out, has given him some of his finest moments. But nobody really plays like this any more at the top end. Even nihilistic team defence has moved on and left Mourinho behind, becoming more complex and nuanced in other hands.

There has always been a basic paradox in Mourinho's presence at Real Madrid and Manchester United, club football grandees with a certain romantic entitlement about their own style, their own way of winning. Here is a manager who got so good at coaching underdog teams that he got to coach the overdog teams, employed by clubs where his strangulating methods no longer hit the right note.

Along the way his key early superpower, the ability to inspire undying loyalty in his star players, has been replaced by constant gripes about the youth of today. Mourinho has become managerial gammon, bleating on about the snowflakes and millennial narcissists, these kids with telephones and haircuts. Which is all very well. But Frank Lampard has retired. And while Paul Pogba may have plenty lacking in his game, he is also what you've got, José old boy.

In the end his failings at United were prosaic and even quite dull. Mourinho was unable to coach greater solidity into some average but serviceable defenders. As a result, he never trusted his most skilful players, never conceived any workable set of attacking rhythms against stronger opponents. Worse, he just seemed to lose heart, to lose the basic fun of inspiring players and building the vital units of a team. By the end United had become something they can't be, not just a poor team but a boring one, trapped within their own muscular limitations.

The most startling thing about the sacking of José Mourinho by Manchester United is still the appointment of José Mourinho at Manchester United in the first place.

The 30 months since tell us a great deal more about United's current state. It is easy enough to suggest what they really need is not a new manager but new owners, or at least owners who don't see this great sporting institution as just another business to be wrung out and stripped down, squatting upon its noble old shoulders like vampiric corporate homunculi.

Look closely enough and club owners are often a wretched spectacle. But what is most striking here is the lack of expertise and basic care in the grass-based football-facing side of the business. It is here that strange feeling of emptiness starts to creep in. Just enough is being done, corners cut, funds directed elsewhere. At the very least United require a coherent structure in place to fill that vacuum around the manager, a director of football to provide a layer of ballast between football and marketing departments.

There is no coherence to United's recruitment, style of play or managerial succession. David Moyes, Louis van Gaal, José Mourinho: what do these people have in common? Those with first-hand experience wince over the scouting and coaching structures. Even the stadium is starting to rattle a little compared with the best around Europe.

There is still a remarkable quality of deathlessness to the United brand, marching off around the world like a red and black zombie army. But how much longer can this momentum sustain itself?

Above all, in the dog days of the José era, this has felt like a club without direction, but also without love, without warmth, without someone in there taking absolute care over the details of what happens on the pitch. Mourinho may have gone. But it will take a great deal more hand-wringing, a great deal more leverage to shift the people who put him in place, and who remain at the rusting wheel of this grand old sporting supertanker.

29 DECEMBER

In the depths of despair, a journey on a night bus brings me solace

HANNAH JANE PARKINSON

I apologise for starting a column about the joy of small things with the doom of depression, but it was in the middle of a quagmire of ennui, nocturnal sleeping patterns and the cold winds of increasing isolation – familiar to many who experience mental health problems – that this particular delight was discovered. It's a slim delight, but a critical one. A delight that, when I am most well, I do not experience. It is riding buses at night.

Night buses are synonymous with drunken, rowdy revellers; takeaway food in polystyrene containers; the stink of skunk; amusing group banter overheard. But night buses midweek, when the sky is the colour of plums and the only other road users are council maintenance workers – those night buses are a different prospect altogether.

When I am deeply depressed, I sleep a lot. The opposite of the usual. I can sleep for 20 hours a day when at my most despairing. I'll wake up at midnight or so, when all over the country novels are slipping from the grasp of married couples propped up by pillows, glasses are removed, bedside lights snapped off. I wake up hungry and alone and pathetic.

In London, in the heart of Soho, there is a cafe that's open 24 hours a day. I pull on jeans and a jumper, close my flat door behind me – a slow, quiet click. Catching the bus at circa 2am, you can almost hear the wheels turn on the road. The driver will nod and perhaps wonder at your story. Mostly, the buses are empty. Many times, an entire journey has, start to finish, accommodated me as the only passenger. Occasionally, on the back seat, the hidden homeless sleep, or medics alight, bleary-eyed.

I head, always, to the front seats. Either I read (I read the entirety of Sally Rooney's *Conversations with Friends* on the 24 bus) or, more often, track the deserted streets while listening to music. Bowie; Cat Power; James Blake; Johnny Cash. Wondering what it would be like to shoot a man in Reno just to watch him die. Thinking about the turns that life takes. Turning the corner at the hospital where you yourself almost died, but didn't; appreciating the buildings that have survived all that technology has thrown at them. The bus waits at red lights for ghosts.

I have done some of my best thinking on night buses. The feeling of going from A to B, of having some kind of destination, when all else has ground to a halt. At the cafe, the waiters greet me warmly, as a regular who has the cover story that she works nights, but is almost certainly lying. I eat pancakes in a moat of syrup and sip at tea. I chat to them when I haven't really seen friends in weeks. And after, the drivers of the night buses see I get back home safe.

Winter

The *Guardian* view on Brexit: the government has failed – it's time to go back to the people

EDITORIAL

Next week the House of Commons will take what is probably the most consequential vote of our era. Unless the government again gets cold feet, key aspects of this country's economic model, social cohesion and international future will be shaped in the so-called 'meaningful vote' over Theresa May's Brexit deal. It will define what Britain is more than any other political event in modern times. It poses questions and choices that cannot be shirked.

This newspaper supported Britain's entry into the European Community in the 1970s. We opposed Britain's departure from the European Union in 2016. We took these positions on the basis of the same long-term principles. Britain is a European nation by virtue of its geography and history. It shares enduring economic and cultural ties and values with the rest of Europe. Above all, Britain has a direct interest, born from the suffering of our peoples in decades of war, in the peace and harmony of Europe from which all can prosper. In the era of Donald Trump and Xi Jinping, Britain's engagement in Europe is freshly urgent.

However, the *Guardian* has never been an uncritical supporter of the EU. It has warned against the delusion of a United States of Europe. It has upheld the centrality of democratic nation states within the EU and stressed the enduring reality of national borders. It was enthusiastic about the epochal re-engagement between eastern and western Europe after the collapse of communism, but measured about the practicalities. It was critical about the reckless way that European monetary union was launched in the 1990s and, after much thought, preferred that Britain should keep its distance from the eurozone and its rules. These concerns have been vindicated by events.

Although we opposed Brexit, it is essential to understand why a majority voted for it. Leave's victory cannot simply be dismissed as nostalgia for empire or dislike of foreigners, though these were factors. Many leave voters felt abandoned and unheard in an increasingly unequal Britain marked by vast wealth in parts of south-east England and austerity and post-industrial abandonment elsewhere. Income levels in London have risen by a third since the financial crash – but have dropped by 14 per cent in Yorkshire and Humberside.

A CRY FOR CHANGE
In June 2016 all this came together in the belief of a majority of voters that the EU did not offer the right solution to Britain's problems. Those of us who disagree need to show humility about what happened, respect the majority, understand the swirling dissatisfaction underlying it, and address it with sustained and practical answers. Ever since the referendum, the *Guardian* has tried to follow that approach in these columns. We accepted, without enthusiasm, that leave had won. We saw the vote as a cry for change. We hoped that Brexit would therefore be negotiated in the best way open to Mrs May's government. We took the view that a 'soft Brexit' would be the least bad outcome because it would prioritise jobs and the economy, maintain important links with the rest of Europe, not least in Ireland, and help to bind the wounds of 2016 by ensuring that the concerns of the 48 per cent who voted to remain were taken into account alongside

those of the 52 per cent who voted to leave. If the government had produced something along these lines, there might have been a pragmatic consensus around a soft Brexit. We awaited Mrs May's detailed proposals. This was the fair approach. Yet the Brexit process fell vastly short. Ministers did not say what they wanted before invoking article 50. The government took a hard approach, not a soft one. Mrs May misread the public mood in the election of 2017. Her ministers proved incompetent negotiators. They were dismissive of parliament instead of seeking to build a majority there. Nothing substantial was done to address the social causes of the vote. The prime minister prioritised holding the Conservative party together over uniting the country – and failed in both. Her government was contemptuous of genuine concerns about everything from the economy to civil rights. It took little notice of Scotland and Wales. It failed to see that the DUP's sectarian interests in Ireland are a world away from the interests of Northern Ireland or modern Britain. Instead of producing a deal which could command a majority in the Commons, it produced one that doesn't even command a majority in the Tory party.

COLLECTIVE FLOUNDERING

This outcome is not the fault of the remainers, the opposition parties or political elites. The government's failure is squarely its own responsibility. Brexit has never been a properly worked-out policy prescription for Britain's problems. For many Tories, it is an attitude of mind, an amorphous resentment against the modern world, foreigners, and Britain's loss of great-power status. This explains more than anything else why hardline Brexiters reject all compromise, refuse responsibility for the practical options, and continue to fantasise about a no-deal outcome which would make things far worse and hurt poor people most of all. It also explains why Mrs May's deal – which leaves almost everything about the future relationship with Europe up in the air for two more years – is a leap of faith, and scarcely more acceptable than no deal at all.

There has been a larger collective floundering across the political spectrum, including in Labour. We are living through a period of national democratic failure. We are deeply divided in many ways, not just over Brexit. Long-term comprehensive reform of Britain's concentrations of economic, social and political power is essential. Inequality must be tackled in a radical way, from the top as well as the bottom. There must be innovative, sustainable plans for towns, for the north, for the many areas that feel excluded from progress and success. There is no single magic answer to this national need. The past is no solution. That is partly why the *Guardian* has been and continues to be cautious about advocating a second referendum on Brexit as the solution to this wider failure of politics-as-usual. It may, in the end, be the only practical option facing MPs on Brexit. But badly framed referendums are a crude way of making democratic decisions, especially because referendums empower those who shout loudest.

Parliament's role is crucial, but parliament is not perfect. Brexit has exposed the decrepit nature of our political system's hardware (its constitutional arrangements) as well as its software (the way we do politics). We need to open up to new forms of power and politics – better distributed, more diverse, more strongly integrated, and more modern. Parliamentary sovereignty needs to be better rooted in the people. Other forms of deliberative debate are essential buttresses of the parliamentary process. Ireland found a reasoned route through its own long and divisive argument over abortion through such a mechanism. A citizens' assembly of voters – a representative group of voters selected at random – held a dignified and detailed civic conversation over several weekend sessions about the practical way forward. Its reasoned conclusions formed the basis of the proposal approved by the Irish people last May and passed into law last month. The contrast between this form of political dispute resolution and Britain's argument in and since 2016 is humbling. This lesson must be learned and applied in the reopening of the Brexit question.

PLAUSIBLE ALTERNATIVES

There is no outcome on the table this month that will not be divisive for years to come. That is true of a no-deal Brexit, which would be disastrous for the vast majority, especially younger people. It is true for Mrs May's deal, as it sets the terms of the UK's departure but not the nature of the future relationship with the EU, leaving the door open to more venomous debate. And it is true of a second referendum, because leave voters will fear that this is merely a device to rob them of their voice and restore a failed form of politics which has done little or nothing for them.

No one creates division lightly. But divisions can be mitigated and rationally resolved in significant ways if the perils are recognised and the anxieties that underlie them are determinedly addressed. If Mrs May's deal is rejected, as it should be, Britain should pause the article 50 process and put Brexit on hold. Parliament should explicitly reject no-deal. MPs should then open up the debate to the country: first, by establishing a citizens' assembly to examine the options and issues that face the nation; and second, by giving parliament the right, if it so chooses, to put these alternatives in a referendum this year or next. Such a vote should not be a repeat of 2016, but a choice between new options for Britain's future relationship with Europe which are spelled out and which parliament can implement. This would require a set of clear and plausible alternatives, and the time and political support for the assembly to deliberate. Given the schisms that we are seeking to heal, the medicine is not less democracy but more.

A NEW AND FAIRER DEAL

This newspaper wants to see a reformed Britain within a reformed European Union. Neither part of this will be better achieved with Britain outside the EU. The issue facing the country this month is not simply Brexit. It is the kind of Britain in Europe we seek to be. All the major parties have, in different ways, let the country down on Brexit. That is why any parliamentary vote for a second referendum must also be rooted in a more radical approach to political economy, in actively reducing the inequality between regions and communities, in a practical debate about immigration control, and ultimately in reform of democratic institutions. The correct relationship with Europe is inextricably linked to the need to invest in future-focused industries and work, and to a whole-nation redistribution of investment and power to the English regions, Wales, Scotland and Northern Ireland.

This is a movement that, in the current parliament, can only be achieved if Labour wants it to happen. The responsibility on the Labour party to rise to the occasion is very great and will define its future relevance. The overarching purpose must be to bind Britain together, not force it further apart. This intent must be realised in long-term national promises, strategies and programmes, aiming at leave and remain voters alike and across the political spectrum. The message must be that this country needs a new and fairer deal, and that this is best guaranteed by a better Britain in a better Europe. The government has failed, so we must go back to the people.

8 January

Half-baked: what Greggs' vegan sausage roll says about Brexit Britain

ZOE WILLIAMS

It is the controversy that nobody understands, while at the same time understanding it utterly: the Greggs vegan sausage roll. Launched on 3 January, presumably to coincide with Veganuary, it got off to a flying start thanks to the ire of Piers Morgan, who tweeted: 'Nobody was waiting for a vegan bloody sausage, you PC-ravaged clowns.' There is quite a lot packed into that tweet, if we want to go psychoanalytical on his ass: he has replaced 'I wasn't waiting for ...' with 'nobody was waiting for', signalling an ego out of control, then elided a dietary choice with political correctness. So, in Morgan's world, you can police what other people eat by accusing them of trying to police what you think, which arse-on-backwards argument distils almost everything that is obnoxious and distinctive about our current politics.

It was a culture-wars classic overnight: Angela Rayner, the MP for Ashton-under-Lyne, agreed with Morgan, as did the writer and activist Julie Bindel. Greggs sent a salty reply, a lot of people went on Twitter to despair of other people wasting their time on Twitter, and a few vegans asked: 'Why do people hate us?' It was all so hotly contested that two things happened: first, a conspiracy theory that, since Greggs was represented by the same PR agency that once did a book with Piers Morgan – Taylor Herring – it was probably all a concoction (it wasn't – the PR for the roll was handled in-house); the second was that the vegan sausage rolls sold out. All over the place, from Brighton to Manchester. I had to walk a mile and a half to get one this morning, nearly a week in. You have to conclude it is creating a deliberate scarcity: you don't get to be Greggs by failing to adapt to pastry demand from one day to the next. But here I go again, with the conspiracies.

It pushed some buttons, this delicious flaky-pastry ersatz meat product, and they weren't so much about veganism – or if so, only indirectly – as they were about politics and class. Greggs occupies a very specific place on the British high street, partly because it has a mission. I remember going to a meeting about the future of work – it was off the record so I couldn't quote Mr Greggs Rep even if I could remember his name, but the gist was that it always tries to employ young people from the area of the shop, if it can. It wasn't an insular or xenophobic point; it wasn't about anyone driving or not driving down wages and conditions. It was that locals tended to be a bit younger, and it's actually really hard, if you're 18, to go up against a 22-year-old. But you still need a job, and you could still do a job, if someone would give you one.

You can look at high streets from Eastleigh to Rotherham, which large chains have vacated, leaving nothing but charity shops selling nothing but secondhand fleeces, and there will always be one Greggs, sometimes two within 50 yards of each other. The company has become associated, not with corporate social responsibility, with all those nannyish and whitewashing connotations, but with the more ineffable quality of still giving a shit. McDonald's has launched a vegetarian Happy Meal, but could never spark a controversy like this; it is too global, too disembodied, a citizen of nowhere in the true, rather than Theresa May, sense. It helps that Greggs' roots are in the north-east of England (though don't delve too deep into its history, since you'll turn up the predatory paedophile Colin Gregg, the son of the founder, who somewhat interrupts the EDL narrative that only foreigners harm children).

Set against the prevailing line on obesity – people who eat cheap, processed food are a burden on the NHS and should be ashamed of themselves – and you have the perfect storm of a divided nation. On one side is a company that still cares, on the other a faceless, finger-wagging elite who don't understand anything about people's lives or how delicious those sausage rolls really are. Every meaty controversy, from George Osborne's pasty tax to David Cameron's pretend pasty-eating, from the cancer scares of bacon to the blanket meat tax proposed by Oxford University at the end of last year, has a bead of this conflict in it: 'Why don't you poor people take better care of yourselves?' v 'Why don't you rich people just get permanently out of my face?' Then some right-wing antihero – Morgan, or Nigel Farage – rides to the rescue, saying: 'We don't judge! We're team mind-your-own-business,' when in fact it was their wealth-supremacist worldview that created the division in the first place.

Meanwhile, of course, pork is off on its own mission as the incendiary device in what has now been a long wave of Islamophobia (note: the pork is rarely delicious in this context, but it still tends to be processed). This is no flash in the pan – in 2012, a man was arrested in Crawley, West Sussex, for throwing ham at a mosque, while another man was arrested four years later for throwing a bag of rancid meat at a mosque in Finsbury Park, north London.

All of which is why the confusion last week about a protest outside Greggs – mistaken for a demo against the vegan sausage roll, actually a demo in support of Brexit – is understandable. That EDL contingent is heavily invested in pork as a kind of toxic talisman, capable of defiling the enemy while at the same time expressing everything that is great about Britishness. As a product that also offends vegetarians and probably feminists, it's win-win. It is a perfect case study of the new tactics of the far right: take something that most people like; ascribe to the people who don't like it feelings far stronger than they really have; roll it into a symbol of hard-nationalism and bigotry; then, with magnificent syllogism, declare that everyone who likes bacon ergo hates Muslims, and also, everyone who likes Muslims probably hates bacon.

Gammongate, too, exploded from this tinderbox. On paper, the insult 'gammon' was aimed at any angry red-faced man because his face was red like a big ham. The imputation professional offence-takers chose to hear was that it was any working-class man, which it wasn't (it wasn't confined to a class, although it was confined to men). But it did mean more than 'red-faced'; it meant anyone overinvested in ham qua national identity.

If a sausage roll and a vegan sausage roll could exist quite happily side by side, if honest, hardworking meat eaters and self-righteous vegans could all go to the same shop, that would be disastrous for this zero-sum worldview in which obliterating the other is entirely justified by the notion that, otherwise, you yourself, your identity, your honour, your right to brown sauce, will be obliterated. In which case, this may well have been a beautiful, devilish, vast political act by Greggs – never forget how total its sausage roll dominance is (1.5 million sold a week). If it could dominate the vegan market like that, we might be looking at phase one in national healing: we can all think different things but like the same stuff. Who knew Arcadia was a diverse selection of baked goods?

I did a taste test, by the way: the Quorn ones taste fleetingly like sausage but have a different texture, a bit firmer and less greasy. Truthfully, both are delicious. The steak and cheese roll, in counterpoint, is totally disgusting.

12 JANUARY

'I left my knickers at a house party we crashed'

BLIND DATE

JOANNE ON MORGAN
What were you hoping for?
A fun evening on the
Guardian's dime!

First impressions? Cute, chatty
and early.

What did you talk about? I can't
really remember much after
four negronis and wine but:
books, scumbag Tories,
coming out.

Any awkward moments?
Probably when we got kicked
out of the house party we
crashed. And leaving my
knickers behind. I think I also
fell over at some point.

Good table manners? Excellent,
we both spoke with our
mouths full.

MORGAN ON JOANNE
What were you hoping for?
Someone to break up the week.

First impressions? Super-tall with
really nice eyes.

What did you talk about? I can't
wholly remember. Maybe,
failing sex education in UK
schools and her fairly ugly but
sadly estranged cat.

Any awkward moments? I walked
into a glass wall at one point
and my head still has a bump.

Good table manners? Who really
cares?

Best thing about Morgan? Her energy, intelligence and sense of humour. And she was up for getting pissed.

Best thing about Joanne? She is obscenely fun.

Would you introduce her to your friends? Absolutely.

Would you introduce her to your friends? Yes, asap.

Describe her in three words Fun, interesting, fit.

Describe her in three words Tactile, funny, engaging.

What do you think she made of you? Maybe that I talked a mile a minute and was a bit over-excited. Also that I am 'cool and hot', because that's what she said in a text to her friends, sent when I went to the loo.

What do you think she made of you? I think she thought I was really great, because she said she texted her friend that while she was in the bathroom.

Did you go on somewhere? Yes, to that fateful house party.

Did you go on somewhere? Yes, to a house party we weren't invited to.

And ... did you kiss? We did. A lot.

And ... did you kiss? Sure did.

If you could change one thing about the evening, what would it be? Wear better shoes for a quick getaway.

If you could change one thing about the evening, what would it be? I'm struggling to come up with anything.

Marks out of 10? 10.

Marks out of 10? 10.

Would you meet again? Yeah, next week.

Would you meet again? Yes.

14 January

'I don't trust the government to look after me or my dog': meet the Brexit stockpilers

SAM WOLLASTON

Jo Elgarf doesn't look like you would imagine a prepper to look.

She's not a swivel-eyed libertarian, camouflaged and armed to the eyeballs, crawling around the woods in Montana, skinning a squirrel for breakfast and fuelling up for the apocalypse. She lives with her husband and three young children in a sleepy suburb of south-west London.

Elgarf is happy to call herself a prepper. She is a member and a moderator of one of a growing number of prepper groups on social media. Hers – an anti-Brexit Facebook group called 48 per cent Preppers – gets between 100 and 200 requests a day to join. Everyone wants to be ready for a no-deal Brexit.

The stockpiling is not too extreme in Elgarf's case; it just means the kitchen cupboards are stuffed full of pasta, sauces, rice, tins, milk powder and washing powder. There are a few things she wouldn't normally get – such as tinned vegetables – which can go to a food bank if they're not needed. Otherwise, it's just a bit more of the usual. Elgarf reckons they have got enough to last the family from a month to six weeks.

The group is not about scaremongering, she says. It's about calming down like-minded people and promoting an old-fashioned larder mentality. 'Have a look in your cupboard; if you got snowed in for a month, could you cope? We're not predicting you won't get anything. What we're saying is: you may walk into a shop and can't find any rice. Have you got something at home to replace it?

'In Switzerland, they tell people to have, I think, two weeks' stuff,' she says. People are vulnerable there, not just because they're more likely to get snowed in, but also because they have a hard border. Elgarf's degree was in European studies. And she worked in the food industry; she knows how just-in-time it operates. Chris Grayling's little lorry exercise didn't reassure her. Nor the chief executive of the Association of the British Pharmaceutical Industry saying that a no-deal Brexit 'should be avoided at all costs'.

Because it's not just about food for Elgarf and her family. One of her four-year-old twins, Nora, who has been sitting happily on her mum's lap as we talk, has a rare brain condition called polymicrogyria. She has lots of prescriptions, but without two of them – Epilim and Keppra – for her epilepsy, she would have multiple seizures a day. Both Epilim and Keppra are imported.

If she could stockpile these medicines, she would. But they are controlled, and she can only get a month's supply at a time. 'It should be all right,' she has been told by doctors and the pharmacists. But when it's your daughter's life that's at stake, 'it should be all right' isn't good enough.

Many of the people who join the Facebook group have concerns about medicines, Elgarf says. There are a lot of diabetics and coeliacs among them. 'We need to know for certain they have got a proper plan in place for anybody who depends on meds.' She has heard rumours that the most critical medicines may have to be collected from central hubs, which would be stocked on the basis of lists provided by GPs. It's clearly something she has given thought to.

Elgarf is also clear about why she is talking to me. 'So come April and there's no Epilim in the country, I'll say: "Where's that

Guardian man?" And you guys are going to be interested because this little child you saw in January now has no meds.' Nora has fallen asleep on her mum.

And so to another unlikely prepper, and member of the same group, in Cardiff. 'I don't identify as a prepper, but I am prepping,' says Helena, who doesn't want her surname published. 'I always thought preppers were a bit batshit crazy and am quite surprised to find myself in this position.'

Helena, who has a politics degree and works for a charity, doesn't come across as crazy. None of the people I speak to do. Informed: tick. Cautious: tick. Organised: tick. Very organised, in Helena's case: she has – and shares with me – a spreadsheet, colour-coded according to what is fully purchased (e.g. tinned tomatoes and loo paper, alongside a note that the average person uses 110 rolls a year), part-purchased (e.g. cereal), waiting delivery (powdered coconut), or pending testing (dried falafel mix). Falafel! I'm going straight round to Helena's. She also has booze and biscuits. Brexit party in Cardiff on Friday 29 March, everyone. And she's got makeup! We're going to be looking good as the good ship Britannia goes down.

Helena is not just prepping for herself. She is doing it for her dog, Charlie, too. And while she has about three months' worth of supplies for herself, she is looking at more like a year for the dog, as she doesn't see that pet food will be a priority. 'I don't really trust the government to look after me; I certainly don't trust them to look after my dog,' she says. As well as dog food, there are treats and toys on the spreadsheet. Charlie is going to enjoy a hard Brexit.

Helena sees it as an insurance policy. 'Unless there's enormous panic buying, I don't think there's going to be nothing on the shelves at Asda,' she says. 'But I do think there's a very good chance that choice is going to be limited.'

Helena's dad agrees. He thinks he should be doing the same, but just hasn't got round to it yet. Her mum – who is 'nearly as keen on Brexit as Nigel Farage' – has accused her of gullibility, ignorance and spreading fear. 'I don't think it's scaremongering to protect your family, and because people are doing this earlier it means that, when we get to 29 March, there's going to be more left for people who haven't prepped, and the supply chains will have had the chance to catch up.'

She hopes she is being overcautious. 'I don't want to be proved right at all. I'd be super-happy if, a year from now, I'm sitting here thinking: "Bloody hell, I've still got tinned potatoes on the shelf." I hope that my mother is right and Brexit is a fantastic success ... the land of milk and honey.'

As opposed to the land of powdered milk and ... 'golden syrup', she says. Actually, there's honey and golden syrup on the spreadsheet.

In Cambridge, Diane says she is also stockpiling, though she doesn't want to go into too much detail. 'I'm a bit cautious about being presented as an idiot who has a cupboard full of stuff,' she says. She's OK about using her surname, though: she is Diane Coyle, OBE, FAcSS. She's an economist, the Bennett professor of public policy at the University of Cambridge, former adviser to the Treasury, vice-chair of the BBC Trust, member of the Competition Commission, winner of the Indigo prize ... in short, really not an idiot.

'The point about supply chains,' she explains, 'is that the things you buy in the supermarket today were on the road last night. Supermarkets now don't have warehouses full of stuff. If we have a no deal and the delays go up even by 12 hours – although I see there's a new report saying it is going to be much more – then things will stop being put on the shelves. They will run out. And it's not just stuff we buy from the EU, and it's not just fresh produce – it's quite a lot of things.'

Coyle knows that she can't get by without a cuppa and doesn't want to run out of teabags or coffee because she didn't get any in before a no-deal exit. 'It's things that matter to me, that we import, and it's a bit of insurance.'

She did the same with cash before the financial crisis. Lending rates were going off the scale. 'The message was the banks don't trust each other with their money overnight, so why should I trust them with money overnight?' She took out some cash and stashed it away just in case; in the end she didn't need it, but it emerged later that the cash machines were close to stopping working.

Does she really expect empty shelves this time? 'I don't know – it's completely uncertain. There are serious people saying the chances of a no-deal exit are significant. And even if they are only 10 per cent, and it's 90 per cent we'll have a deal, why would you not have that extra bit of insurance? It's perfectly sensible.'

Coyle worries that a lot of people don't get the point about supply chains and the modern economy. 'And, of course, it's not just things we buy in supermarkets – it's all the things companies use in making stuff, all of those imported components they use. It's a just-in-time economy. This is a source of a lot of efficiency gains and improvements in productivity ever since the 1980s, and it means that people don't hold stocks of stuff any more. So you're very vulnerable to delays in imports getting into the country.'

Surely the government realises this? 'Well, I'm sure the civil servants appreciate it, and I'm sure some of the ministers appreciate it, but I don't think all of them do, at least not from what they're saying in public.'

In north Cornwall, Nevine Mann believes we will leave the EU without a deal, and that's what she is preparing for. 'We're expecting it to be pretty horrendous for at least a couple of months, hopefully settling down and becoming less horrendous over time,' says the former midwife. 'Long term, we expect what's available to be more expensive and different.'

She and her family (five in total) are as ready as anyone. 'We've done it early and slowly, so it's not making a major impact on what's available for others. We're pretty much done. I've got a very short list of items I want to add.'

They have supplies to last from four to six months, stored under the stairs, in the loft and the garage. Food, for them and for the cat ('The cat is fussy enough to starve herself if she doesn't get what she wants'), and paracetamol and ibuprofen for kids and adults. And vitamin tablets in case there's a shortage of vegetables.

Mann has also been trying to stockpile a prescription antihistamine her younger son takes for his allergy to grass pollen. 'I've always had my prescriptions once every two months rather than monthly anyway, so what I'm doing is just ordering them early and gradually building up a supply.'

So far, they have only got a few weeks' worth. It's less of a worry than Nora's Epilim and Keppra, perhaps, but concerning nonetheless: without it, he can't go outdoors between March and October.

For the Manns, it's not just about stockpiling food and a bit of medicine. They are probably the best prepped of the preppers I speak to. They were planning to put solar panels on the roof anyway, but with the threat of no deal they have done it sooner, and they are trying to set up a system that stores energy on a big battery. They have a 1,100-litre water collection tank in the garden. And they're hoping not to be needing those vitamin tablets because they will have their own fresh veg. They're no experts ('Actually, I have a bit of a reputation for killing everything,' says Mann), but they have got vegetable patches in the garden, and they're giving it a go, trying to grow overwintering varieties from seed.

The results are mixed so far. Slugs and snails have had most of the purple sprouting broccoli, the winter lettuce and the chard, but the Manns have been more successful with broad beans, mangetout, shallots and garlic. I'm thinking the garlic may go with the snails, with a mangetout side ... but maybe that's one for further down the line.

Mann and family also have some mature fruit trees and bushes, and are trying to learn what to do with them. They're picking the brains of greener-fingered friends, they have bought a couple of idiots' guides, they're hoping they may have a little extra. 'We're planning, actually, to create a few little Brexit boxes for friends and family, who we know can't manage to prepare for themselves, so they've got something at least,' says Mann.

Brexit boxes! Isn't that lovely? Who says it's all about hatred, division and polarisation? And could this be the beginning of what may, one day, be known as Brexit spirit?

Lastly, and briefly, to Dollis Hill, a sleepy suburb of north-west London. Vicky, a nosy teacher, picks from the printer a draft of her boyfriend Sam's article about stockpiling for Brexit. It's all so bloody stupid, she says, and she means that it's come to this – a wartime mentality in what's supposed to be peacetime, not that people are stockpiling. 'I'm going to do a bit,' she announces. 'But where shall we put it? And we're definitely having dried falafel mix.'

15 January

'No way to live here': new Honduran caravan sets off north as Trump blasts warnings

TOM PHILLIPS

Rosa López was six months pregnant with her seventh child when the killers came for her husband – unnamed assassins acting on orders she cannot, or dares not, explain.

Ten months later the 30-year-old Honduran sits on a muddy embankment outside the San Pedro Sula bus station with her eldest son, Sergio, 12, getting ready to flee their homeland on the latest migrant caravan north.

'It's not easy. I leave half of my heart here,' López said of her decision to leave her other six children – including seven-month-old Josué Alexander – behind, in the care of a sister. 'But there's no going back.'

'We don't envision becoming rich,' said López, from Santa Cruz de Yojoa, a city 86km (53 miles) south. 'We just want the basics – a job to survive.'

It is a plan Donald Trump says he is determined to thwart.

On Tuesday morning, as hundreds, possibly thousands of Honduran migrants embarked on a punishing and highly politicised march towards 'El Norte', the United States president launched what promises to be a protracted Twitter war against the caravan and Democratic opponents on whom he blames the ongoing government shutdown.

'A big new Caravan is heading up to our Southern Border from Honduras,' Trump tweeted.

'Only a Wall will work. Only a Wall, or Steel Barrier, will keep our Country safe!'

In the days leading up to the caravan Honduran airwaves have filled with government propaganda adverts striking a similar tone. 'Honduran brother – don't be fooled!' a narrator warns would-be travellers in one. 'Just listen to your brothers who have come back from previous caravans and say it was all lies and pain.'

But there was no sign those warnings had been heeded on Tuesday morning as the sun rose over San Pedro Sula and migrants trudged out of this notoriously violent industrial hub towards the Guatemalan border.

'Lies. Pure falsehoods,' scoffed Leonel López, an unemployed factory worker who was setting off on the 5,000km odyssey alone.

'God will open the doors to the United States for us,' predicted the 24-year-old, who said he was abandoning his country because it offered too few jobs and 'so much death'.

When the last Central American caravan set a course for the US last October Trump painted it as an invading force filled with gangsters and 'some very bad people'.

But as scores of young families set off from the bus terminal, the caravan appeared to contain more pushchairs than drug pushers.

'We want a future for our son,' said Ramón Cruz, 31, a jobless motorbike mechanic, as he pushed his three-year-old son, Joshua, down the hard shoulder, container trucks rattling past. Hanging from the back was a Buzz Lightyear backpack with a carton of juice tucked into its side pocket.

'Our dream, like everyone here, is to make it to the United States because here there's no way to live,' said Cruz's 22-year-old wife, Ingris, who was wearing a blue and red Superman T-shirt. 'There are so few work opportunities, so much violence. We have to leave our country practically fleeing.'

Another family, including a three-month-old baby girl and her 16-year-old mother, said they were literally fleeing for their lives after being forced from their homes in the northern department of Colón by gangs of armed gunmen with ties to the military.

'The whole department is virtually at war,' complained the baby's grandfather, who said he had decided to get his six-member family out on the caravan after his daughter was raped and two of his homes burned down. 'I'll have to ask for political asylum. I can't go back ... they'll kill my whole family.'

Tears rolled down his teenage daughter's cheeks as she considered their sudden decision to take flight. 'I want a good future for my child. I don't want her to have the same destiny as her mother,' she said.

Dennis Matute, a 43-year-old travelling with his 11-year-old son, said poverty had forced them from the same region, a cocaine trafficking hub on Honduras's Caribbean coast.

'We are looking for a place where we can see a future for our children,' said the rural worker, a devout Christian who had spent four days fasting before setting off in order to ensure his God's support. 'Here, things just go from bad to worse.'

Matute, who had left his wife, Dalila, behind, believing she was not up to the gruelling journey, admitted the trip was 'a dramatic adventure', not least for someone who was leaving Honduras for the first time.

'It's a bit overwhelming because it's a tough journey – and there are risks,' he said of the caravan, which members expect to last up to a month.

'But,' he said, 'there's a [Honduran] expression that goes: "Who wouldn't give up on a boat to get to know a port? It's worth risking everything for the sake of a dream."'

Like most of the wanderers, Matute was carrying just one small black backpack containing a single change of clothes for him and his son.

An estimated 5,000 people eventually joined last October's caravan as it snaked northwards through Guatemala and then Mexico towards the US border, where many of its members remain in camps and shelters.

How many will join the latest expedition remains unclear, as does the exact route it will take.

But Bartolo Fuentes, an opposition politician and radio presenter told the *Guardian* he expected it to be larger than the previous one.

Up to 3,000 people had set off from San Pedro Sula between 10pm on Monday and 5am on Tuesday, by bus and on foot, Fuentes claimed.

Fuentes laughed at the idea that Trump's bluster – or his Great Wall – would succeed in halting the daily exodus from his country.

'It is madness for Trump to keep insisting on this wall. It's a show, it's a spectacle, it's propaganda,' he said as a column of pilgrims filed past him through the hills south of San Pedro Sula and, slowly, towards the southern border.

'These migrants aren't a threat to anybody, not even Donald Trump.'

'Change in people's hearts': anti-Bashir protests put Sudan at a crossroads

ZEINAB MOHAMMED SALIH
AND PETER BEAUMONT

Surrounded by brown hills close to the Ethiopian border, the town of El-Gadarif is an unremarkable place. A centre for sorghum and sesame trading, it is dominated by its huge Russian-built grain silos.

But four weeks ago the eastern Sudanese town was thrust into the spotlight when it became a hub for protests against the near-30-year rule of President Omar al-Bashir.

Locals say those initial protests consisted largely of school pupils who converged on a market to voice their anger over a cut to the subsidy for bread. 'Hungry people!' they chanted, and 'You dancer!' – a mocking reference to Bashir, 75, who often gambols at public occasions. Their voices were soon drowned out by gunfire as security forces shot 10 protesters, three of them children.

What followed would be significant not only for El-Gadarif, but for the entire nation. Inflamed by the regime's response, demonstrators turned their fury the next day on the offices of the ruling National Congress party and the intelligence services. In under a week, the protests had spread from rural centres to Sudan's major cities, exposing a widespread desire for an end to Bashir's harsh rule.

'The murder of innocent people and children turned the anger against the government,' said Jaafar Khidir, a member of the opposition in El-Gadarif. 'People came out to protest spontaneously.

'There was change in people's hearts,' added Khidir, who has been arrested four times since the protests began. 'I expect to be taken into custody at any time because the authorities think I am inciting people to take to the streets.'

Since the first protests in December, more than 40 protesters have been killed nationwide, human rights groups say – some reportedly shot by the Rapid Support Forces, a government militia. Hundreds more have been injured. Activists have also been detained across the vast country, often by the intelligence services, notorious for documented abuses and use of torture.

Yesterday, security forces were out in force in Khartoum, as demonstrators marched on Bashir's palace to deliver a written request that he step down. Simultaneous protests were held in 11 other towns and cities, including Atbara, another cradle of the current movement. Activists said a child and a doctor were killed in clashes in Khartoum as they called for Bashir to go. The protests marked some of the most widespread disturbances since unrest began on 19 December.

In the most violent clashes, police in Khartoum's Burri neighbourhood fired rubber bullets and teargas, and chased protesters with batons, witnesses said. Several people were exposed to teargas, while some were bruised by the bullets or beaten.

Hundreds of young people blocked streets and alleyways with burning tyres, and some hurled stones at security forces. Many chanted 'Down, that's it' – a call for Bashir to quit.

The protests may appear to have come from nowhere, but Sudan's current instability has been a long time growing. Bashir, who took power after leading a military coup in 1989, has survived conflict, protests, years of US-led sanctions and even pursuit by the international criminal court for alleged genocide in Darfur. But this time the plethora of problems facing Sudan is having an impact even on the elites who have backed him.

Two million people are internally displaced, and corruption and mismanagement are rife. The country's long-running economic crisis has its roots in the secession of South Sudan in 2011 and the loss of oil reserves to the southern state. Spiralling inflation has hit Sudan's middle classes. The cut in the subsidy for bread was the spark that ignited deep-seated anger.

Bashir faces mounting discontent within his own party as well as in areas of the country's north, once considered his strongholds.

Another feature is the use of social media. Activists have actively documented confrontations and posted footage that they claim is 'exposing' Bashir's government.

Observers say the protests have also managed to unite people from different tribes and ethnicities. Women have joined in; dressed in headscarves, they can be seen in nearly all the social media footage.

All of which has led some, including Hafiz Ismail, an analyst at Justice Africa Sudan, to argue that the current demonstrations are likely to continue. 'The protests won't stop,' Ismail said, 'because the regime doesn't have any solution for the problem, which is as much political as economic.'

Particularly problematic for the regime has been the involvement in the protests of the Sudanese Professionals Association, a new and broad movement representing middle-class professions.

Mohammed Yousif al-Mustafa, a relative of the president and a professor at Khartoum University, who is a spokesman for the association, described the moment he realised the movement had created a new reality. 'We can't be behind the people,' he said. 'People would laugh at us if we stuck to our position of handing a memorandum to parliament and asking for a rise in the minimum wage. Our position is opposing the regime and its policies.'

Which raises the question: what next? 'The longer the protests go on, the more violence and abuses we might see the government use,' said Jehanne Henry of Human Rights Watch. 'They use the same sorts of tactics every time there are protests. The risk is that it will get bloodier. People are already dying and getting tortured and detained.'

Experts are divided about likely outcomes. The International Crisis Group suggested three potential scenarios in a recent briefing paper.

'One is that the president survives, though – without funds to offer protesters significant reforms – he will probably have to subdue them by force. A second scenario could see protests gathering pace and prompting his ousting by elements within his party or security elites ... A third scenario would see him resign. This would allow for a leadership change that could mollify protesters,' it said.

For Henry, much hinges on Bashir. 'The key question is how much the government feels it is facing an existential threat. That's hard to predict.'

England's rebel spirit is rising – and it wants a no-deal Brexit

JOHN HARRIS

In my innocence, I didn't expect many people to be in a central Portsmouth Wetherspoons at 10.30 on a Friday morning. But there they all were, in their droves: passionate supporters of Brexit, there to hear the pub chain's founder and chairman, Tim Martin, make the case for Britain leaving the EU with no deal. Martin has been on the road since November, with the aim of visiting at least 100 of his boozers. The day we crossed paths, he was traversing the south coast: given that it has whetted the appetite of what remains of the local press, drawn large crowds and shifted huge amounts of food and drink, the whole thing looks to have been an unlikely success.

Martin's case was unconvincing to the point of tedium: a half-argument that ignored what a no-deal Brexit would mean for British exports, and too blithely dismissed all those concerns about supply chains, and chaos at UK ports, let alone what a no-deal scenario would mean for the island of Ireland. But on the level of political sociology, the spectacle presented was compelling: the hardest of the Brexit hardcore, many of them on the pints and riled to snapping point before the speech even got going, and then taken into incandescence by the posse of local Liberal Democrats interrupting Martin's speech at every turn.

It is quite an experience, watching people repeatedly yell at each other about trade tariffs before they have had their lunch. Meanwhile, very familiar mutterings punctuated the argy-bargy, and took the argument out of the realms of politics, into a mish-mash of culture and history: the second world war, the supposedly perfidious Germans, the idea that if we prospered before 1972, why can we not do so again?

Last Thursday, the BBC's *Question Time* was broadcast from Derby, where an endorsement for no deal from the writer Isabel Oakeshott triggered mass whoops and cheers, and yet another explosion of Brexit noise on Twitter. Whatever the warnings from politicians, many people currently support the nightmarish prospect of the UK leaving the EU without any formal agreement.

It seems pretty clear that many people say they would opt for no deal if pushed, but do so in the midst of disconnection and bafflement. Nonetheless, an inconvenient truth remains.

Whereas I have never heard any member of the public make the case for what politicians call Norway plus, and belief in a second referendum still seems to be largely the preserve of a certain kind of middle-class person, no deal is the position that scores of people have recently expressed to me without prompting: 'We should just get out'; 'We have to leave, now'; 'Why can't we just walk away?'

At its heart, I suppose, is a terrible logic, combined with a certain stubborn ignorance, which results in an insistence that the only thing that matches what millions of people thought they were voting for in 2016 is a clean break. Some support for no deal closely echoes the specious stuff repeatedly uttered by leading Brexiters, about the EU needing Britain more than we need them, a country set free from Brussels diktats and trading again with its former colonies. But the most fascinating element of popular no-dealism is altogether more complicated, and built on a defiant rejection of all the warnings about falling off a cliff edge, so passionate that the refusal of advice feels more relevant to what people think than what the most reckless kind of Brexit actually might entail. In that sense, supporting no deal amounts to the same performative 'fuck you' that defined a reasonable share of the original vote for leave.

The gender aspect of Brexit is still too overlooked. Of the people gathered in that Wetherspoons, 90 per cent were men. In a recent YouGov poll, support for no deal was put at 22 per cent, but whereas 28 per cent of men were no-dealers, among women the figure was a paltry 16 per cent. There is something at play here similar to the belligerent masculinity channelled by Donald Trump: a yearning for all-or-nothing politics, enemies and endless confrontation, and an aggressive nostalgia. Some of the latter is shamelessly misogynistic, part of a macho bigotry that harks back to hierarchies of privilege that linger on, and blurs into racism. But there is also an element that ought to attract empathy: a yearning for a world in which men were steelworkers, coalminers and welders, and a desperate quest for something – anything – that might allow their successors to do the same.

The politics of no deal betrays an urge for drama and crisis that a lot of us ought to be humble enough to recognise in ourselves. Not that long ago, a high-profile supporter of Jeremy Corbyn looked ahead to Labour taking power, and wondered: 'Have we prepared the people who chanted for Jeremy at Glastonbury for the fact that, at some stage, they may only be able to withdraw 50 quid a day if the credit runs dry? If there is a very British coup, will they hold the streets?' A comparable romanticism surrounds the idea of a besieged post-Brexit Britain nobly trying to make its way without the interference of Brussels. It is, perhaps, one of the great failings of mainstream politics that it has been unable to project anything similar on to issues that cry out for public attention: imagine, for example, if people were as worked up about climate change.

Finally, there are questions about no-dealism that are bound up with England, and national traits that go back centuries. One is a tendency to indulge in futile, inexplicable gestures, evident in everything from 18th-century riots to 1970s punk rock, and perfectly summed up in a sentiment mewled by a young man named Johnny Rotten, in the midst of a hit single titled 'Anarchy in the UK': 'Don't know what I want, but I know how to get it.' These things explode from time to time, but what never seems to go away is the self-image of an island nation, the seductive myth of Britain standing alone, and an eternally mistrustful attitude to the EU, now intensified by the bloodless functionaries – Tusk, Barnier, Juncker – apparently calling the shots on Brexit.

At the moment, mainstream politics operates on the understanding that if no deal came to pass, queues of lorries and thinly stocked shops would spark public outrage, and cause huge political damage to the Conservative party. But if the current complexities surrounding Brexit give way to starker realities of what the EU calls a 'disorderly withdrawal', I would not be so sure. Somewhere between the Wetherspoons spirit, a mass desire to simply get Brexit over with and the mirage of a wronged country fighting for survival, there might lie the key to why no-dealism is proving more popular than some people would like to imagine. A no-deal exit would confirm that politics has entered the realms of the darkly surreal, and that 23 June 2016 was only the start.

26 January

Diana Athill's story was remarkable, and its end serene

IAN JACK

Diana Athill had lots of confidence. She understood the social class she came from and could stand outside it, looking in, whenever she chose. As she wrote in *Stet*, her memoir of her years in the publishing trade, she was a member of a caste: 'one of the London-dwelling, university-educated, upper-middle-class English people who took over publishing towards the end of the nineteenth century from the booksellers who used to run it'. But she was also a white woman who had several black lovers in an age when that kind of relationship could be seen as a political statement and she despised the 'self-consciously beautiful writing' of the 'quintessentially caste writer' Virginia Woolf. To her, 'caste standards – it ought not to need saying – have no right to be considered sacrosanct'.

Her confidence helped her to be a writer, of course – it stands somewhere between 'talent' and 'connection' in the list of useful attributes – but it made her a fine editor, too. She was clear in her judgments and certain in her encouragement. We first met in the early 1980s, when a book I was allegedly writing for her publishing firm, André Deutsch, had long passed its delivery date. I took the work-in-no-progress to the office, where Diana read some of the first chapter aloud with such elegant enunciation that I was almost (though not quite) persuaded to carry on with the rest. At that time I didn't know she'd been a writer, but then I read her two books of memoir, *Instead of a Letter* and *After a Funeral*, and was struck, as many others have been, by her frankness and clarity and the wonderful rhythm of her prose.

Then our roles changed. At Granta, I was the editor and she was the writer. Via a mutual acquaintance, she sent in a piece for the magazine about her professional friendship with Jean Rhys. She mentioned it had been taken from a book she was writing. I asked to see the whole typescript of the book, which turned out to be *Stet*. She was 82 and about to embark on her Indian summer as a writer. Several other books and a magazine piece or two followed, and we republished her backlist. Very little editing was ever required. I could begin reading at any point on one of her typed pages and never want to stop, impelled by the delightful force of her narration, as though she was speaking to me.

Very occasionally, I suggested a change. There was too much sex, I thought, at the beginning of what turned out to be her most successful book, *Somewhere Towards the End*. That seemed an odd thing to say to a writer who was then close to 90, but I thought we didn't need as many pages to establish the author's pleasure in sex as a mechanical rather than psychological or emotional activity. Diana agreed and the book was adjusted. My second suggestion had more interesting results.

I wondered to Diana if, towards the book's close, her tone sounded too complacent. 'Let me have a think,' she said, and soon after submitted a new passage that began: 'Not long ago a friend said to me that I ought to be careful not to sound complacent, "because" he added kindly, "you are not".' She disagreed with her anonymous friend (I guessed it was me). She declared she was complacent. She had started out, she wrote, 'wrapped warmly in my family's belief that we were the best kind of people short of saintliness: a belief common in the upper levels of the English middle class and confirmed by pride in being English'. And though that 'tribal smugness' and 'wicked nonsense' had been smashed when her first and most important lover jilted her, self-satisfaction of another kind had returned with her late success. If this was smugness, and she couldn't help feeling that it was, then she had to report that 'though repulsive to witness, it is a far more comfortable state to be in than its opposite'.

So she was happy to be smug – you might say smug about it – because comfort was what one needed on the 'downhill journey' of advanced old age. Disguised in her attractive and thoughtful sentences, there was sometimes the brisk approach of a governess who wants to settle her brood's every question by being sensible. What was sex? What was death? What was the point of moping after the first or fearing the second? She knew her nature – she confessed to a 'nub of coldness' at her centre – but it still gave me a jolt when in conversation she might scoff ('Ridiculous!') at the memory of a dying old man crying with fear in his hospital bed or other evidence of irrational human behaviour. She could be tough. You didn't want her to think of you as 'sentimental' or your writing as 'saccharine'.

Though she was a partner in a publishing firm, and often rightly described as one of London's best book editors, she never made much money. She lived in a flat rented from a cousin in

Primrose Hill, and drove a small car. We paid mean advances for her books, and the approach of dependent old age loomed without the benefit of children or a big bank balance. But *Somewhere Towards the End* won a prize and became a bestseller. Diana could scarcely believe it: a book about being old was going to make it easier for her to be old. She had discovered a retirement home that was 'astonishingly acceptable', and with her new income she could afford to move in. As she wrote to me, it was 'Bye-bye geriatric ward!!!' And it was.

I went to see her on Wednesday at a hospice in Belsize Park. Her final room – there she lay, aged 101, head back on the pillow and mouth open in a frozen yawn. Her silver hair had thinned but her skin was as clear as ever. We drew chairs to the bedside and talked, as people surrounding the apparently unconscious tend to do, hoping that she could hear even if she couldn't speak. The talk was about her. Her nephew Phil remembered that she'd got frustrated with the lack of attention during a recent hospital visit and, unusually for her, pulled rank. 'I write for the *Guardian*, you know,' she had said.

She breathed on. I took her hand briefly, and then Pru Rowlandson from Granta took it for the rest of her life. Diana made three or four sounds in her throat, and her eyes opened a little. Her breathing paused. Pru said her hand was cold. Dead or alive? It was hard to be sure, for a few minutes, and then it was certain. Phil closed her eyes.

Diana always remembered that her mother's last words, having been asked about a visit to a nursery garden in Norfolk, were: 'It was absolutely divine.' She hoped she would end her days with something similar in her mind's eye. And it seemed that she had. It was the most serene transition: a small bird would have made more fuss.

2 FEBRUARY

'Sweet Shop'

AMIT CHAUDHURI

The whole universe is here.
Every colour, a few
on the verge of being barely tolerable.
Every shape as well as minute flourishes
created in the prehistory
of each sandesh by precise pinches.
The horizontal trays
brim (but don't tremble) with mass and form.
The serrations are near-invisible.
You'd miss them if they were deeper or clearer.
The soft oblongs and the minuscule, hard
pillow-shaped ones are generated
so neatly that instinct alone
could have given them shape, and no mould.
In the harmony shielded by the glass
is an unnoticed balance of gravity and play.

Ignore the free-trade evangelists. Brexit can create a fairer economy

LARRY ELLIOTT

It all seemed so simple back in the 1990s. Barriers were coming down, the free market was advancing to all corners of the world, and in return for production being shifted to low-cost countries, consumers in the west were getting cheaper clothes and gizmos. Globalisation was said to be unstoppable. The end of history was nigh.

The financial crisis and its aftermath have changed the political weather, with a decade of low growth, unevenly distributed pain and business as usual prompting a backlash. Voters in the west have started to focus on globalisation's dark side: the multinational companies that avoid paying tax; the towns hollowed out by de-industrialisation; the loss of democratic control over market forces; the uneasy sense that the entire edifice is poised precariously on a mountain of debt.

Somewhat belatedly, the politicians and officials who are responsible for running the show have woken up to the threat. As Mark Carney, the governor of the Bank of England, rightly noted earlier this week, trade tensions and Brexit are manifestations of fundamental pressures for a different form of globalisation, perhaps even deglobalisation. Britain's departure from the EU, according to Carney, is 'an acid test' of whether a way can be found to broaden the benefits of openness while enhancing democratic accountability. Put simply, can you have your globali-sation cake and eat it?

The answer is that cake-ism won't be remotely feasible until the basic assumption that has underpinned economic policy for the past four decades – freer markets are always better markets – is challenged, and there is no real evidence that it has been. The direction of travel in trade deals, for instance, is for governments to press for the things that business groups want – protection of intellectual property rights and inves-tor-state dispute settlement clauses that allow companies to sue governments for alleged discriminatory practices – rather than changes that benefit workers.

Consider, too, the way in which MPs of all stripes have been obsessing about the need for frictionless trade with the EU after Brexit, to ensure that there is no disruption to the supply chains of multinationals. The benefits of just-in-time production are seen as more important than the environmental costs of ship-ping parts and semi-finished goods backwards and forwards across Europe. Frictionless is good.

It is curious to hear centre-left politicians talking in these terms, because progressive politics for the past two centuries has traditionally been about the need to inject friction into markets, in order to soften the impact of capitalism and make it compatible with democracy. The economy of the early industrial revolution was as close to frictionless as you could get. There was no collec-tive bargaining, so wages were set by the interplay of demand and supply of labour. There was no welfare state, so those who fell on hard times went to the workhouse. There were no health and safety regulations to protect workers or the environment, so industrial injuries and pollution were rife.

It eventually became apparent that this model of capitalism was sowing the seeds of its own destruction, and that there would have to be reform if the revolutionary outcome predicted by Karl Marx was to be avoided. The century from 1850 to 1950 saw the birth of the trade union movement, public provision of education, the development of a redistributive tax system and the creation of a welfare state. Social democracy, Keynesian demand management and full employment all interfered with the workings of the market, and when James Tobin first proposed a financial transaction tax in the early 1970s to curb currency speculation, he talked explicitly about throwing sand in the wheels of the foreign exchange markets.

Generally, though, reformers talked about injecting fairness rather than friction into the system – and were wise to do so. Language matters a lot, which is why, when the counter-revolution began in the mid-1970s, the talk was of economies becoming freer. Frictionless sounds so much more attractive than friction, in the same way that flexible sounds preferable to inflexible.

But the past decades have shown what frictionless or flexible markets are like in practice, and it's really no surprise to find that voters don't like them very much. Abolishing the Glass-Stegall Act – which separated investment from commercial banking in the US for more than half a century – removed friction from the financial markets but at the expense of an orgy of speculation that led to the biggest economic crisis since the 1930s. The neutering of trade unions and the decline in collective bargaining made labour markets more flexible by allowing firms to hire workers on zero-hours contracts, to fire them more easily and to secure a bigger share of the gains of growth for themselves. Employers' organisations are the biggest champions of free movement of labour because it allows them access to an unlimited supply of labour, holding down wages.

The quest for a frictionless economy has its supporters, and they like to cite the fact that, since the current era of globalisation began in the early 1990s, a billion people have been lifted out of poverty. What they don't say is that most of them live in China, which has grown rapidly because it has chosen a development path that is far from frictionless.

Carney is no free-market utopian, but it is a lot easier to talk about a new form of international cooperation built on a better balance of the local and the supranational than it is to bring it about. A good starting point would be to rediscover the joys of managed markets, to recognise that a frictionless economy is like a car without brakes, and that the right amount of friction makes countries fairer, safer and happier.

18 FEBRUARY

I backed the SDP. But this Labour schism makes no sense at all

POLLY TOYNBEE

The great Brexit crisis slices through both parties, dividing families, friends, neighbours and colleagues. It may yet break apart the moribund political system. But that seismic rupture didn't happen today when seven MPs walked out of the Labour party.

Seven is a pitifully small number. The timing is monstrously badly judged and the reasons the MPs give are oddly scattergun, lacking political punch and focus. To be sure, they are not alone in thinking Jeremy Corbyn a weak leader with many failings: his poll ratings show most of the country agrees, as did the 172 Labour MPs who voted no confidence in him two and a half years ago, as his 'kinder gentler politics' turned poisonous.

But whether born of despair or vanity, this walkout is a damaging distraction, because right here, right now, there is only one cause that matters – Brexit. That's not one issue among many, it is the great question that has the nation's future hanging by a thread. It is the debate that contains within it all the other arguments about Britain's ideals, identities, ideologies and insanities.

Those other MPs who tried to oust Corbyn still think much the same of him now as they did then. But they have not quit, not at this catastrophically inappropriate juncture, diverting attention from the supreme task of this generation of politicians. The best of them, such as Peter Kyle and Yvette Cooper, are stuck deep into battle to rescue us from calamity: Labour will again back Cooper's amendment next week to prevent a no-deal crash-out and delay withdrawal. Some of those 35 Labour MPs who failed to back it last time are being brought round, giving it a good chance of success.

It does of course madden many Labour MPs that foot-dragging Corbyn has been almost absent from the fight against this Tory Brexit disaster. With him surrounded, if not held captive, by a cabal of Len McCluskey's people, you only had to listen to the Unite leader's infuriating pro-Brexit views on the *Peston* show last week to suspect he spoke the Labour leader's mind too. Their views are deep-frozen in the 1970s. But what matters is less what Corbyn privately thinks than what he does when it comes to crunch Brexit votes – and, so far, there has been no misstep.

Labour MPs walking away at this point only give succour to those Labour pro-Brexiters, such as Caroline Flint, who caricature those in favour of reversing Brexit as members of 'metropolitan elites'. Paradoxically, their defection hardened the resolve of scores of Labour MPs to stay, those who in the past considered splitting. They are the ones most angry at the defectors, accusing them of failing to work hard enough in their constituencies, failing to build around themselves loyal teams to fight off marauders. The one who has their sympathy is Luciana Berger, bombarded with antisemitic abuse and forced to fight off deselection when about to give birth.

This walkout comes as a head of steam is building up within Labour at Corbyn appearing to dodge his party's conference policy to back a referendum. Corbyn's own Momentum movement has been expressing its frustration at their leader's reluctance to get behind a people's vote. Labour has been haemorrhaging members, old and new, over Brexit. Wherever I go, Labour people tell me they are struggling to persuade members not to tear up their cards. 'Don't do it!' they say. 'Stay and fight for Labour to take the right stand on Brexit. Corbyn won't be there much longer: stay to select the next leader, don't abandon us.'

Does this feel at all like 1981 and the creation of the Social Democratic Party (SDP), which broke away from Michael Foot's Labour? Not a jot. I was there and there is no comparison. These seven lack anyone of the stature, public recognition or intellectual heft of the SDP leaders. The Gang of Four between them had all held serious government office – between them they had occupied the roles of chancellor, home secretary, foreign secretary, education and transport secretary. This grouplet does not have that kind of weight and it lacks ideological substance and ideas. Corbyn's failure to stamp out antisemitism is a just cause, but why not stay to fight it?

Remember, the SDP defectors left not out of irritation with an inadequate leader, but because they could not and would not stand on – among other things – Labour conference pledges that a future government would abandon nuclear weapons and take Britain out of the European Economic Community. (Labour went on to entrench these pledges in the manifesto under which Foot fought the 1983 election.)

Compare that to Corbyn and John McDonnell's last manifesto, which was widely popular, with no ideological deal-breakers for a broad-church party. Some might query costings or priorities – why billions for middle-class students, not for needy toddlers in Sure Starts? Some might niggle at the practicalities of utility renationalisation – but these were popular policies. Nothing there felt like an updated version of the notorious 1983 manifesto, dubbed the 'longest suicide note in history'. These seven defectors were vague on reasons for jumping ship, beyond wishing for a better leader.

Philip Collins, a former speechwriter for Tony Blair, has written a good manifesto for a putative new social democratic party, entitled *Start Again*. But since almost any Labour MP would back almost all of it, that suggests less need for a new party than for one better led. Brexit could still destroy Labour. The 2017 manifesto got away with promising 'the benefits of the single market and the customs union'. Since then, Keir Starmer has deftly led the party to vote the right way on every Brexit division. So far so good.

But now Corbyn needs to back the Peter Kyle/Phil Wilson clever compromise. Their plan is for MPs to agree to pass Theresa May's bad deal, but only on condition it is put to the voters for a final decision. People on both sides of the divide are gathering round this option as the best chance of resolving Brexit, once and for all, whenever May finally holds her meaningful vote. The plan lets MPs in Brexit-voting seats obey their electorate by voting for May's Brexit – but frees them to campaign to remain in a referendum. The good signs are that McDonnell and Starmer are warming to the plan. This will be Corbyn's vital test: in the end he will have no choice but to do the right thing.

If the Labour leader ends up in any way enabling Brexit; if as a modern-day Ramsay MacDonald he makes Labour complicit in this historic Tory catastrophe, then expect all hell to break loose in the party. If he goes against the will of his party, the great majority of his voters and his MPs, the party will break apart – and so it should. But that hasn't happened. These seven are jumping a gun that may never be fired. They will find it cold out there. I know that from experience. So deep was the SDP/Labour split that sitting in the *Guardian* canteen, Labourites picked up their plates and walked away from us SDP-ites. Schism is bitter and personal. And, in this particular case, needless.

19 FEBRUARY

A British girl has asked to come home. We must meet our responsibility to her

CHITRA RAMASWAMY

Imagine this: a British teenage girl is groomed online at the age of 15. Stay with her nationality for a moment. She is British. She is indoctrinated by one of the world's most brutal terrorist cults and within 10 days of fleeing her home country is married to an extremist fighter. Stay with her age for a moment. She is 15. Four years later, two of her children have died and she has escaped across the desert, nine months pregnant, to a refugee camp. There, aged 19, she gives birth. And now she is asking to come home.

Remove the inflammatory dog-whistle references to Isis brides and jihadi runaways and how much more likely is

Shamima Begum to incite our pity and mercy? How much more likely are we to prioritise our duty of care to her as a British citizen? To treat the question of whether she poses a terrorist threat as one to be settled by the rule of law rather than trial by tabloid?

But this is not how it's playing out. The home secretary, Sajid Javid, for starters, has vowed that he will not hesitate in preventing Begum's return. We could be discussing how to meet our responsibility to a vulnerable citizen. Instead we are deciding whether a traumatised teenager who claims not to be fazed at the sight of a severed head in a bin is sorry enough for our compassion to kick in. Or worse. One newspaper proudly announced Begum should 'expect no sympathy from Britain'. That same newspaper ran a column that read: 'Sorry my heartless little jihadi bride, but you made your bed and now you can lie in it.' Begum may have compared the Manchester Arena bombing to western airstrikes (she also said it was wrong that innocent people were killed), but is it really a surprise that a woman who fled to Syria at the age of 15, has spent the last four years living alongside extremists and may still be radicalised, is not saying the things we would like her to say? Meanwhile, others are spouting precisely the kind of poison we would expect, like Piers Morgan whose message to Begum is simply to 'go f*ck herself'.

When the three schoolgirls fled to Syria in 2015 (Begum is the only known survivor), the reaction was to 'other' them so absolutely that neither the girls nor their actions could have anything to do with Britain or its values. They were evil; they knew exactly what they were doing; they deserved what was coming to them. But listen to what Begum said when asked what attracted her to Isis in the first place. 'The way they showed how you can go and they will take care of you,' she replied. 'You can have your own family.' That Begum sought such seemingly benign and uncontroversial values is a damning indictment of this country. In every sense, we are responsible for her.

This disturbing case holds a mirror up to Britain. In it we see a reflection of the racist, vengeful and weak society we are, as opposed to the strong, stable, tolerant, humane, or even baseline-functioning one some, unbelievably, still claim us to be. Begum has asked to come home. She is right to ask this of the country where she was born, raised and radicalised.

19 FEBRUARY

Karl Lagerfeld sent me 50 roses – I don't think he'd ever met a large Brummie

ADRIAN CHILES

Many years ago, I made a film for the *Money Programme* about Chanel. We were taken by a fragrant phalanx of PR people to Coco Chanel's apartment just off the Place Vendôme in Paris. We were told it was exactly how Mademoiselle, as they always referred to her, had left it. Her spectacles were lying there on a little desk. It felt as if we were at the still-beating heart of a personality cult.

Later on, we had an interview booked nearby with the great Karl Lagerfeld. He was fashionably late, and then unfashionably late and then, as the hours passed, the eternal wait came to feel rather fashionable all over again.

Eventually he appeared and the phalanx collectively drew breath. I don't think he had been interviewed by a large Brummie type before. We got on rather well. All I remember clearly is the moment I asked him about Coco – pardon me, Mademoiselle – and he said: 'Huh! I tell you what kind of bitch she was!' One of the phalanx made a slight screaming noise.

That night, I stayed in a very small, cheap hotel room. At around 10pm there was a knock at the door from a chap bearing a huge bouquet of roses. There may well have been more than 50 stems. The card read: 'Adrian. Love from Karl.'

I slept badly, mainly because the pollen in that tiny hotel room was overwhelming. In the small hours, gagging, I had to put the bouquet outside.

Come morning, I had a train to catch. Not really being the type to carry roses on trains, I gave them to a startled woman at the patisserie across the road.

'*Pour moi?*' she asked. '*Oui*,' said I. I'll never know if it was his or a PR's idea – but thanks anyway, Karl. May you rest in peace. We'll always have Paris.

25 FEBRUARY

This Time with Alan Partridge review – an excruciating white-knuckle ride

LUCY MANGAN

Impossible though it is to do justice to Alan Partridge with only the written word at our disposal, we must try. Because after his years in the wilderness, Linton Travel Tavern and North Norfolk

Digital radio, the monkey-tennis pitcher is back. Almost. Well. To be clear. The exquisitely excruciating creation of Steve Coogan and Armando Iannucci (and others at *On the Hour*, where Partridge made his first appearance) 'Alan Partridge' is definitely back, in *This Time with Alan Partridge*.

It's the character's first proper run-out since his 2013 feature film *Alpha Papa*, and is co-written and directed by twin brothers Neil and Rob Gibbons, who have become – since 2010's *Mid Morning Matters* – not just keepers of the flame but fuel and bellows for it too. They have accomplished the feat of finding new layers in Alan, somehow allowing him growth without change, development without enlargement of that definitively constricted soul.

But is Alan himself – as it were; good God but we live in complicated times – back? He has returned to the BBC proper, standing in, dry mouthed and periodically stricken, for the co-presenter on a current affairs programme (a parody of *The One Show*, with a dash of most of the others to season) who has fallen ill. But he is not the broadcasting behemoth he once – if only in his ceaselessly self-deluding mind – was. Still, it's a start. And as he says in the opening scenes, 'I am here to give of my best.'

Oh, the fractional excess of it. The infinitesimal flinch it causes in everyone around him. That ineffable blend of neediness and arrogance that infuses every word. He is back. He is back.

All of Partridge life is here. The dogged pursuit of the wrong path, becoming irretrievably mired in the wrong tone that sucks him down like quicksand (a lighthearted piece about leopard seals finds him describing how they 'toss penguins around like rag dolls ... for fun'). The desperate, conscious arranging of his face into the right expression. The attempts at banter or just simple conversation that always circles back to the subject of Alan. The endless compounding of errors that makes any time he speaks a white-knuckle ride to potential disaster; realising, for example, that referring to 'bosomy' downs is Not Right, he corrects his description to 'or like a smooth, fat teenage boy'. You know you are in the presence of Partridge when you wish to flee as you laugh. And all the while, his co-host Jenny, portrayed with consummate brilliance by Susannah Fielding who plays off Coogan in about seven different dimensions, fights the conversational fires he sets as she strides unblinking on to the next link.

The differentiation of *This Time with Alan Partridge*'s layers and escalation of every exchange is precision-engineered: beautiful things and a joy forever. There is the bedrock in the perfect replication of such a show's set, energy and topics. Then comes the skewing and skewering of the show, its format's absurd swinging between the frivolous and the heavyweight with occasional curve balls, with Alan reading lines from his autocue that could almost be pasted directly from a script nicked from Eamonn Holmes or (presuming they still bother supplying him with such things) Richard Madeley. Where in 'Bedroom-based do-badders known as "hacktivists"', Alan's introduction to a piece on internet dangers, could real life be said to leave off and invention begin?

And from there, his creators modulate smoothly, seemingly effortlessly although it cannot be, into Partridge. Through the overconfidence, let the neediness poke, then the rage that lies beneath that thin, thin skin and let the moment go to hell in a handcart. Watching Alan is to watch his creators let him give enough rope to hang himself, watch him choke then cut him down just before he starts to go blue.

This Time brings Alan back, in all his glory and his tragedy, at just the right time. He surely voted leave but, as a man of no convictions or courage, must now want to remain. He has always been little England made flesh, while also embodying the tortured monster of insecurity and discontent that lives unchanging inside us all. We get the heroes we deserve, and as you finish writhing in agony and lie limp from laughter, hatred, panic, despair and/ or stilled in awe at the end of another half hour in his appalling company, you can only reflect that if Brexit means Alan then the whole business just got more complicated still.

25 FEBRUARY

What lunch with the PM taught me: her dullness disguises a dangerous power mania

SUZANNE MOORE

Have I told you about the very long lunch I once had with Theresa May? I was reminded of it as I watched a clip of her playing pool with the Italian prime minister at an EU summit at the weekend. The lunch went on for several hours – or so it seemed. All space and time came to a halt as I sat there, staring at my cutlery in a state of existential despair, failing, somehow, to communicate with her. I gave up the will to live between the starter and the main course and just kept glancing over at her security detail on another table, wishing I could be with them. Ordinary people talking.

This was when I worked at a right-wing newspaper and would often be taken along as a token woman to meet Tory grandees. Some of them were quite a laugh. Some sort of fun and gossip could be had. Some were incredibly dull and thick. Some sent me into a trance, they were so boring. And some were just obnoxious. Ann Widdecombe, for instance, was, I felt, nasty to the waitress.

To me that breaks the 11th commandment. I remember asking her what star sign she was, just to annoy her.

With May, it was different. She didn't answer questions or make small talk, or big talk. She is present only in that she makes you feel her pain. Social interaction appears torturous for her, and so it is for all around her. Dancing, snooker, her endlessly repeating what we know are lies, walking into meetings where everyone despises her. I used to feel a bit sorry for her. But that lunch, when I stared into the abyss and saw someone who has no need to make anyone else feel at ease, made me understand she is a dangerous, power-crazed maniac. The dullness is a cover. That's all.

25 February

'We are now free': Yazidis fleeing Isis start over in female-only commune

BETHAN McKERNAN

Berivan runs over to join in the dancing, her traditional gold dress catching the winter sunlight. The 15-year-old Yazidi clasps hands with her best friend and stands among the line of women stamping their feet to a Kurdish pop song.

Berivan and her mother are from Sinjar in Iraq, the Yazidi homeland, but like thousands of other Yazidis they were kidnapped by Islamic State fighters in 2014 when the group stormed across the border from Syria.

Far from here, in the eastern desert, Isis has almost lost control of its last stronghold, Baghuz, but there are at least 3,000 Yazidi women and girls whose fate is unknown.

During the genocide, Yazidi men were rounded up and shot, then dumped in mass graves. The women were taken to be sold in Isis's slave markets. Many passed from fighter to fighter, who inflicted physical and sexual abuse.

Rights groups say that suicide among the captives is common. Even for those who manage to escape after years of enslavement and rape, many struggle to survive without an income or identity papers.

Berivan and her mother have lost the other members of their family. But at a new women's commune near Qamishli, in northeastern Syria, they have been given a chance to start again.

'I like it here,' Berivan says. 'I love going to school, I love mathematics. And I'm going to be a hairdresser when I grow up.'

Jinwar is a female-only community, set up by the women of the local Kurdish-run administration to create a space where women can live 'free of the constraints of the oppressive power structures of patriarchy and capitalism'. It opened in November and 12 of its 30 adobe brick houses are home to Kurdish, Yazidi and Arab families.

The women built their own houses, bake their own bread and tend to the livestock and farmland, cooking and eating together.

At a graduation celebration for a group of local women who attended a course on natural medicines at Jinwar's education centre, residents discussed how the newly planted apricot, pomegranate and olive trees were doing.

'We built this place ourselves, brick by brick,' says 35-year-old Barwa Darwish, who came to Jinwar with her seven children after her village in Deir ez-Zor province was freed from Isis, and her husband, who joined the fight against the group, was killed in action.

'Under Isis we were strangled and now we are free,' she says. 'But even before that, women stayed at home. We didn't go out and work. In Jinwar, I've seen that women can stand alone.'

Jinwar grew out of the democratic ideology that has fuelled the creation of Rojava, a Kurdish-run statelet in north-eastern Syria, since the civil war broke out in 2011.

The area has largely thrived, despite the presence of enemies on all sides: Isis, Syrian president Bashar al-Assad's troops, and Turkey, which regards the Kurdish YPG (an acronym whose translation means People's Protection Units) fighters as a terrorist organisation.

The women's revolution, as it is known, is a significant part of Rojava's philosophy. Angered by the atrocities committed by Isis, Kurdish women formed their own fighting units. Later, Arab and Yazidi recruits joined them on the frontlines to liberate their sisters.

But at home, many parts of Kurdish society are still deeply conservative. Some of the women now in Jinwar have left arranged marriages and domestic abuse. Those dynamics, as well as the legacy of Syria's brutal eight-year war, have to be unlearned at Jinwar.

'When the families first arrived, the Arab children wouldn't play with the Kurdish children,' says Nujin, one of the international volunteers working at the village. 'But even in just two months you can see the change. The children are already so much happier.'

Berivan's mother, Darsim, was mute when she arrived at Jinwar, a side-effect of trauma. Little by little, she has started to form words again. 'The village is the best rehabilitation for the things these families have suffered,' Nujin says.

Jinwar is not finished yet: there are gardens to plant and an empty library waiting for books. The community is still coming up with ideas. Behind the education centre there is a swimming pool that will be filled with water in the summer. Most of the residents will be able to use a pool – the preserve of men only in most of the Middle East – for the first time. The women have also voted for driving lessons and to start a sewing business.

There are plans for a second commune in Deir ez-Zor, an Arab province bordering Iraq that is still the scene of fierce fighting – but there is also a sense that what has been built at Jinwar is fragile and could be taken away. It is not clear what will happen when American troops leave the area in a few months. Renewed fighting is a possibility.

'This place is peaceful and a refuge from the war,' Nujin says. 'So how can we bring guns here if we needed to defend ourselves? I hope Jinwar never has to face that.'

26 FEBRUARY

If we're heading for a hard Brexit, then we're heading for a united Ireland

PATRICK KIELTY

The year is 2025 and the prime minister, David Lammy, has just phoned the Sinn Féin leader, Mary Lou McDonald, to congratulate her on victory in Ireland's unification referendum. The deputy prime minister, Nicola Sturgeon, tweets that she hopes Scotland will follow suit in the referendum she secured at the last election for taking the Scottish National party into coalition with Labour.

Gerry Adams gives the dedication as a statue of Jacob Rees-Mogg is unveiled in Crossmaglen. The Tory leader, Amber Rudd, refuses to publicly blame her predecessor Boris Johnson for the breakup of the union but, like the rest of what's left of the country, she knows the truth.

As anyone involved in the Good Friday agreement will tell you, principles guarantee no deal. It's why the current Brexit negotiations between the UK and itself are going so well. Theresa May has red lines, the European Research Group (ERG) has absolute red lines, the Democratic Unionist party (DUP) has blood-red lines, and Jeremy Corbyn has blurred lines featuring Pharrell. If they all hold firm, we're heading for a hard Brexit. And a united Ireland.

We were always going to end up here because Brexit has never been about Nissan X-Trails or the shape of your bananas. It's only ever been about sovereignty. For the gammons and bowler hats on the team, the final destination has always been the top of the white cliffs of Dover dressed as Dad's Army, straddling Dysons.

Northern Ireland has always been about sovereignty for a different reason – almost half of its population see themselves as Irish. How very rude. Yet as Brexiters preach about their precious union, Irish nationalists in the same country are meant to park the union they want and just work out how the chicken crosses the border.

Last week I was back in my home village of Dundrum, County Down. It lies in a constituency that in the past has elected both Éamon de Valera and Enoch Powell, but when talk in the pub turned to Brexit, the same truths were repeated again and again: nothing good can come of this for Northern Ireland. And: we knew this would happen.

Most people in Northern Ireland voted to remain in the EU because there have only ever been two options post-Brexit – customs checks at the Irish border or in the Irish Sea. Each would cause divisions just as we were bridging the gaps (in spite of our politicians). Depressingly, there's no way through this.

As the prime minister Maybots her way through the charade of alternative arrangements, there's only one thing you need to know – there are no workable alternative arrangements. If there were, you'd have heard of them by now. The details of this technological masterpiece would already be a double-page spread in the *Daily Mail* with Rees-Mogg mocked up as Alan Turing under the headline 'Enigma cracks Enigma – spirit of Bletchley takes back control'. If an alternative arrangement that worked actually existed (or was likely to exist in the next couple of years) Brexiters would have already accepted the backstop, knowing they could easily replace it with their idea during the transition. The fact that they won't bet on themselves tells you all you need to know about what they have in the locker.

Yet none of that matters when you've inoculated yourself against reality. It's why the ERG continues to cup its balls and cough while looking at a picture of Winston Churchill. 'Did you feel that, too? We need a clean break.' Meanwhile, Corbyn complains the clock is being run down, but knows his last hope of a general election is when time's up. To those outside the Labour party he's become the José Mourinho of Brexit, sticking to a system that has lost half the dressing room while a people's vote remains benched like Paul Pogba for daring to be more popular than the manager.

All of this could have been avoided if the majority in Northern Ireland had been listened to during the referendum campaign. But as Nigel Farage and Johnson trumpeted their migrant-free magic kingdom, we were Kevin in *Home Alone* – only remembered at the baggage carousel after the plane had landed. It's why the minutes of the first meeting between Michel Barnier and David Davis will never be released. 'So, what do you propose for your land border with Europe?' Polite laughter. 'We have a land border with you guys?'

Even at this late stage, it remains the unanswered question – how can you take back control of your borders when the only land border you have can't be put back in place? The fact that more than 70 per cent of people in Northern Ireland voted to give up control of that border via the Good Friday agreement so they could live in peace remains totally ignored.

When Conservatives say they care about Northern Ireland, they actually just mean the freehold. Like a stable block with planning permission, they know the extra square footage adds value but they've no intention of actually developing it. Just as long as they can see it from the big house, they're happy. As for those who live in the stable? If Brexit has proved anything, it's that many Tories don't give a stuff about the people of Northern Ireland – not even the unionists. If they did, they wouldn't dream of a hard Brexit because it only guarantees one thing – a border poll.

That's one that will be decided not by Sinn Féin or DUP votes, but by the moderates in the middle – nationalists who once felt Irish enough post-Good Friday agreement and those pro-European unionists applying for Irish passports. The inevitable economic downturn and border circus of a hard Brexit might just be enough to swing those floating voters and Northern Ireland out of the union. So, why would any member of the Conservative and Unionist party take that risk? Because no matter what they say in public, they've never honestly believed Belfast is just like Finchley.

All notions of a border poll could easily have been damped if, post-Brexit referendum, the DUP had accepted that Northern Ireland was a special case. Like they insisted it was when they asked George Osborne to drop Northern Ireland's corporation tax to mirror the Republic back in 2014. Or how same-sex marriage and abortion laws are different to the rest of the UK thanks to a veto by the DUP in the Northern Ireland assembly (apparently, it's also in a confidence and supply arrangement with the Lord Jesus). But that was never on the cards because, for the DUP, Brexit is about proving they're biologically British, not adopted. It means the party will always order what Johnson and Farage are having but, unlike them, actually eat it.

Of course, special status for Northern Ireland would mean some form of 'dreaded backstop' (pause, pearl clutch, continue), but when a country has more than 300 land border crossings and only five main ports to the mainland, where would you rather try to do the 'dreaded paperwork'? And, let's face it, any customs check that can take place in the middle of the Irish Sea while a lorry driver hoovers a fry-up on the ferry then has a snooze in his bunk has to be a good thing. Cue sash-shaking Brexiter rage. 'Don't you understand Northern Ireland would then become a rule-taker not a rule-maker?!' Because, apparently, it's all about rule-making – as the Stormont assembly, where rules should actually be made for Northern Ireland, remains in mothballs since 2016 because the DUP backed out of a deal with Sinn Féin to restore power sharing. So we've reached the fatberg in the sewer of principle. We're told that the DUP has the government over a pork barrel and unless the backstop goes, it will bring the house down. But as time runs out, it's actually the Tories who have the political wing of the Old Testament surrounded.

On the one side is May's deal (complete with backstop). On the other is the ERG and a hard Brexit. If the DUP buckles on the backstop, party members will walk away with their UK sovereignty between their legs. For those of us who have their early albums, this isn't going to happen.

Which leaves just one option. The DUP holds firm and jumps off the cliff with the ERG, knowing a hard Brexit is the only scenario that guarantees a hard border in Ireland, a border poll in Northern Ireland and the perfect economic storm where it could lose that vote. By trying to be the most British person in the room, the DUP could actually end up the most Irish.

Whisper it quietly, but the best outcome for the DUP is actually a people's vote. They'll scream red, white and blue murder if it happens but privately breathe a sigh of relief. Like Boris Johnson, they never wanted Brexit but wanted to be seen to support it. A second referendum offers an escape from their worst nightmare, while allowing them to reluctantly go along with 'the will of the entire country'. Very unionist.

For Northern Ireland as a whole, another EU referendum is also the only way out of this mess. Not to save face. But to save peace, prosperity and a shared future. It's wrong that Northern Ireland should take one for the team so that others can have their version of Brexit. It's now time to act, or Northern Ireland might decide the team is no longer worth playing for.

4 MARCH

Keith Flint: the neon demon who started a fire under British pop

ALEXIS PETRIDIS

Like virtually every successful 1990s dance act, the Prodigy were faced with a problem: their mastermind was a producer, not a pop star. Liam Howlett was prodigiously gifted, visionary enough to have turned the Prodigy from a joke into rock stars. By 1994, they were an original, eclectic musical force. But, like most dance producers, Howlett wasn't a natural frontman.

The standard answer to this problem was to retreat behind an overwhelming light show and dazzle the audience with visuals. The Prodigy had a more radical solution.

It was de rigueur for rave acts who performed PAs in night-clubs to have a few dancers on hand. The Prodigy had three – in contrast to the usual Lycra-clad women, they were all men: raving mates of Howlett's from back home in Essex, who added to the Prodigy's blokey appeal.

One of them, Keith Flint, was unexpectedly promoted to the role of frontman in 1996, adding vocals to tracks on their third album, *The Fat of the Land*. Once long-haired, he changed his look to something more striking, lining his eyes with kohl and shaving the centre of his head, leaving two spiked patches of hair either side, which he dyed.

What seemed like a remarkable leap of faith on Howlett's part turned out to be inspired: whatever qualities Howlett lacked as a performer, Flint had in abundance. He became a manic presence on stage, projecting an image that lay somewhere between threatening and cartoonish. He memorably described his revised dancing style as 'using my body to shout'.

He fitted perfectly with the music that Howlett was now making: increasingly dark and noisy. Critics started dubbing it 'electronic punk', a perception amplified by Flint's raw-throated vocal style.

Certainly, the impact of Flint's elevation on the Prodigy's commercial success can't be overestimated. Their first single with him on vocals, 'Firestarter', went straight to number one in the UK. More surprisingly, it went gold in the US.

Flint's persona fitted the moment perfectly: thanks to the Criminal Justice Act and a spate of high-profile ecstasy-related deaths, the British dance scene was enduring a folk-devil moment in the media. Here was a performer who seemed happy to own the moral panic, to look and behave – on camera at least – like middle England's nightmare.

He helped catapult the Prodigy to becoming the biggest dance act in the world. *The Fat of the Land* went on to sell 10 million copies.

In its wake, the Prodigy became a huge live draw. Perhaps tellingly, their next album, *Always Outnumbered, Never Outgunned*, which didn't feature Flint, was noticeably less successful. Clearly to a considerable proportion of the people who bought *The Fat of the Land*, Keith Flint *was* the Prodigy.

If they subsequently never scaled the same commercial peaks as they had in 1996–97, they never ceased being a vastly successful live band, a state of affairs that had a great deal to do with Flint's demonic stage presence. It is for the Prodigy's commercial zenith that he'll be remembered – a moment that proved that star quality lurks in the most unexpected places.

6 MARCH

Death of the high street: how it feels to lose your job when a big chain closes (extract)

HILARY OSBORNE AND SARAH BUTLER

It has been a terrible time for the high street. Since 2008, when the fall of Woolworths sent shock waves across the UK, 32 major retailers have closed their doors for good, with the loss of 115,000 jobs, according to the Office for National Statistics.

High street retailers have been hit by a combination of the financial crisis, competition from online shops and large supermarkets, belt-tightening by consumers and a feeling that we, as a society, have reached 'peak stuff'. And that is before considering rising business rates and rents.

The resulting job losses have led to some disquiet, but there is a feeling in some quarters that they have not attracted the same political action that is triggered whenever manufacturing posts are under threat.

We asked *Guardian* readers to tell us about losing jobs in retail; here are some of their stories.

JACQUI MARTIN, 43, WORKED AT ATHENA IN EXETER

Things started to go seriously wrong for the card and poster seller Athena in 1995, but some shops lived on as franchises. The last one closed in 2014.

Being in a big student city, Athena was the place to go. Freshers' week was like Christmas, and we'd sell a lot of film posters, especially *Harry Potter* and *The Lord of the Rings*. We still had the tennis girl and *L'enfant*, the one with a man holding a baby, right until the end. They were a bit of a cult thing.

Athena was big for its framing service, and people would bring in photos and pictures – things they had bought on their holidays – and we would talk to them about where they bought them and how the colours would fit in their home. My house is full of frames from Athena.

I had about six members of staff. We'd all go out at Christmas and on birthdays. It was very social.

It didn't come as a shock when we closed. Athena had become a franchise not long before I started, and they were gradually closing. We were the last one in the whole country to go.

The last day was awful. We used to have music playing in the shop, and we put on 'Everything Must Go' by the Manic Street Preachers just to add to the melancholy. I remember locking the door for the last time in tears. I don't want to sound overdramatic, but it was like a bereavement after such a long time.

I got redundancy pay as I had been there 15 years. I stuck with retail, and was assistant manager in a shoe shop for a while, but that also closed. Then I worked in another shop, but now I'm a bank cashier. It's still customer-facing, which I love, but I have been diagnosed with multiple sclerosis, so I needed a role where I wouldn't be on my feet all day.

We have seen more shops closing in Exeter recently. The high street is so different now, and shopping isn't as pleasurable because you don't have the variety to go and look at. The choice is online. Shoppers are so used to getting everything instantly at the click of a button. In my heyday, there was time to talk with customers and build a rapport, and they would come back because of your service.

MIKE MOSS, 51, WORKED AT VIRGIN MEGASTORE/ZAVVI
Music retailer Virgin Megastore became Zavvi in 2007 after Richard Branson sold the business to its management. It went into administration just over a year later.

I joined Virgin in 1997 as a store manager in Edinburgh. Then I set up a new store in Glasgow. It was a really big event. We put on a free concert for 6,000 people. Travis played, Richard Branson came up for the launch and opened the store with Mel C. We would put these huge hoardings round the shop that said: 'A gift to Glasgow,' and we literally unwrapped it.

We would put on all kinds of in-store events. We did a Coldplay show once before they were big – there were about 10 people watching, and we had to put some of our colleagues in coats to increase the size of the crowd.

I ran a store on Sunset Boulevard in LA, then I went to New York as an area manager, before coming back to be head of retail in the UK. We were taken over by Zavvi, and the business was flying – we were opening new shops and doing refits.

Things started to go wrong when Woolworths went into administration in November 2008 – our supplier was owned by them and all the Christmas stock was frozen. We were living hand-to-mouth, trying to get the latest games, DVDs and music from other suppliers into stores, but Zavvi was new, and we didn't have a lot of buying power. At the same time, the supermarkets were doing crazy offers where they were practically giving away new releases if you spent enough on other things.

I got the call at 9am on Christmas Eve to say we were going into administration. Boxing Day was when the misery started – people who had bought gift vouchers were streaming into stores, and we couldn't let them spend them; they were really angry.

After Christmas, it was my job to organise the weekly closures. I'd get a call with a list of shops to close that week, and I'd organise for a Zavvi representative and administrator to go in on a Thursday. Staff knew if no one came to the store then they were staying open for another week. Every week, I dreaded waking up on the Thursday, knowing I was about to shatter people's hopes.

I was made redundant on 23 February 2009. It was devastating. But you don't need a head of retail when there isn't any retailing. I spent the first weeks applying for roles that were clearly already taken, waiting for email replies or for the retail agencies to return calls.

Since 2013, I've worked for Topps Tiles – it's a terrific business. I don't think physical retail is dead, but there needs to be more support for it.

JULIA CRONIE, 59, WORKED AT COMET IN HUDDERSFIELD
The electrical firm Comet went bust in 2012, closing 240 shops in the UK.

I worked for Comet for 22 years. For the last eight years, I worked at the Huddersfield store as a senior administrator.

When Comet was bought for £1 [in 2011], things carried on the way they had been – the stock was always coming in, on time. There was no sign anything was wrong. The day we went into administration, I was having my breakfast and watching the news – that's how I found out. I was on a 12pm–8pm shift that day, but I went in at 9am.

We couldn't open for the first five or six hours because we didn't know what we could sell. We couldn't sell Dyson vacuum cleaners, we couldn't sell Hoover products. Big vans started to turn up at the back door to take away stock. The only company that seemed to still have faith that we would sell stock was Apple.

I don't think any of us were under the illusion it would be bought. We were told we would close on 18 December and what we needed to do before then. The first thing I thought was: 'I'm in my 50s. What am I going to do now?' I hadn't had a job interview for 20 years.

It was physically and mentally exhausting. We were packing things up all day, moving boxes, moving stock. And the exchanges with some of the customers were exhausting too. They were trying to haggle over prices. One man came in and wanted a refund for some batteries – there were signs everywhere saying we couldn't do refunds, but when I refused he said: 'I'm glad you've lost your job.' My reply wasn't very ladylike.

One of the saddest things was losing my colleagues. We were like family in the shop where I worked. Eight years is a long time, and we'd gone through a tragedy in my family, and these people were my rock. After a couple of months, I got a job at Card

Factory. I'm still there – it's a great place to work and I'm getting the trust back that it won't all be broken up again.

8 MARCH

Michael Jackson's trick was to groom an entire culture

EMMA BROCKES

It was hard this week – watching R Kelly claim his greatest problem was being 'big-hearted' and sitting through hours of Michael Jackson revelations – to hang on to the idea that the truth has implacable meaning. In both cases, the sense of outrage from the accused parties (in Jackson's case, his estate) was palpable and brought to mind another example of male-pattern entitlement: that of Brett Kavanaugh during his supreme court confirmation hearing.

'They are trying to bring us down,' Jackson was reported as saying to one of his victims, while asking him to lie in court. The double-think was part of the abuse. The narrative was only ever these men's to control, and one suspects that control was in large part what they got off on. Guilt or innocence seemed secondary to the fury generated by the presumption of those who dared to doubt them.

And the prominence of these men has traditionally been a part of their camouflage. It seemed to me, after watching *Leaving Neverland*, that the biggest grooming project was less of any one individual than of a culture as a whole. Most of us are primed to believe that a powerful man is more likely to be telling the truth than his nobody accuser. Revisiting child abuse allegations against Jackson from 1993 and 2004 brought on an almost out-of-body experience. All that footage of him holding 10-year-old boys' hands; the admission that he slept in a bed with them; the way he got older but the age of his 'friends' never did. It was hard to condemn the two mothers in the film when their faith in Jackson's innocence – or at least their doubt in his guilt – had been shared by the rest of the world.

One did blame them, though, of course. While the fathers floundered on the sidelines, it was the mothers Jackson zeroed in on. Both James Safechuck and Wade Robson's mothers talked of the separate relationship they thought they had with Jackson, how he courted them in their own right and, although they both spoke of it as a mother–son thing, it was clearly a matter of seduction. Meanwhile, Jackson was teaching their sons to hate their mothers and distrust women in general.

It was this that felt like the oddest reversal of received wisdom: that whether Jackson was a lovable weirdo or something darker, he was essentially guileless. In fact, it becomes clear that he was, like all abusers, deeply calculating. He went to huge lengths to set up the conditions for abuse. Large parts of his career – putting young boys in his videos and on stage with him – weren't artistic decisions but a means of furthering his aims as an abuser.

Another recent documentary, *Abducted in Plain Sight*, told the unbelievable story of a girl taken from under her parents' noses by a neighbour who'd seduced them both. This happened in 1974, and many of us said in response to the foolish credulity of the parents, 'Those were different times, it couldn't happen now.' I'm not so sure.

Greta Thunberg, schoolgirl climate change warrior: 'Some people can let things go. I can't'

JONATHAN WATTS

Greta Thunberg cut a frail and lonely figure when she started a school strike for the climate outside the Swedish parliament building last August. Her parents tried to dissuade her. Classmates declined to join. Passersby expressed pity and bemusement at the sight of the then unknown 15-year-old sitting on the cobblestones with a hand-painted banner.

Eight months on, the picture could not be more different. The pigtailed teenager is feted across the world as a model of determination, inspiration and positive action. National presidents and corporate executives line up to be criticised by her, face to face. Her *skolstrejk för klimatet* (school strike for climate) banner has been translated into dozens of languages. And, most striking of all, the loner is now anything but alone.

On 15 March, when she returns to the cobblestones (as she has done almost every Friday), it will be as a figurehead for a vast and growing movement. The global climate strike this Friday is gearing up to be one of the biggest environmental protests the world has ever seen. As it approaches, Thunberg is clearly excited.

'It's amazing,' she says. 'It's more than 71 countries and more than 700 places, and counting. It's increasing very much now, and that's very, very fun.'

A year ago, this was unimaginable. Back then, Thunberg was a painfully introverted, slightly built nobody. 'Nothing really was happening in my life,' she recalls. 'I have always been that girl in the back who doesn't say anything. I thought I couldn't make a difference because I was too small.'

She was never quite like the other kids. Her mother, Malena Ernman, is one of Sweden's most celebrated opera singers. Her father, Svante Thunberg, is an actor and author (named after Svante Arrhenius, the Nobel prize-winning scientist who in 1896 first calculated how carbon dioxide emissions could lead to the greenhouse effect). Greta was exceptionally bright. Four years ago, she was diagnosed with Asperger's.

'I overthink ... I remember when I was younger, and in school, our teachers showed us films of plastic in the ocean, starving polar bears and so on. I cried through all the movies. My class-mates were concerned when they watched the film, but when it stopped, they started thinking about other things. I couldn't do that. Those pictures were stuck in my head.'

She has come to accept this as part of who she is – and made it a motivating force instead of a source of paralysing depression, which it once was.

At about the age of eight, when she first learned about climate change, she was shocked that adults did not appear to be taking the issue seriously. It was not the only reason she became depressed a few years later, but it was a significant factor.

'I kept thinking about it and I just wondered if I am going to have a future. And I kept that to myself because I'm not very much of a talker, and that wasn't healthy. I became very depressed and stopped going to school. When I was home, my parents took care of me, and we started talking because we had nothing else to do. And then I told them about my worries and concerns about the climate crisis and the environment. And it felt good to just get that off my chest.

'They just told me everything will be all right. That didn't help, of course, but it was good to talk. And then I kept on going, talking about this all the time and showing my parents pictures, graphs and films, articles and reports. And, after a while, they started listening to what I actually said. That's when I kind of realised I could make a difference. And how I got out of that depression was that I thought: it is just a waste of time feeling this way because I can do so much good with my life. I am trying to do that still now.'

She discovered she had remarkable powers of persuasion, and her mother gave up flying, which had a severe impact on her career. Her father became a vegetarian. As well as feeling relieved by the transformation of their formerly quiet and morose daughter, they say they were persuaded by her reasoning. 'Over the years, I ran out of arguments,' says her father. 'She kept showing us documentaries, and we read books together. Before that, I really didn't have a clue. I thought we had the climate issue sorted,' he says. 'She changed us and now she is changing a great many other people.'

The climate strike was inspired by students from the Parkland school in Florida, who walked out of classes in protest against the US gun laws that enabled the massacre on their campus. Greta was part of a group that wanted to do something similar to raise awareness about climate change, but they couldn't agree what. Last summer, after a record heatwave in northern Europe and forest fires that ravaged swathes of Swedish land up to the Arctic, Thunberg decided to go it alone. Day one was 20 August 2018.

'I painted the sign on a piece of wood and, for the flyers, wrote down some facts I thought everyone should know. And then I took my bike to the parliament and just sat there,' she recalls. 'The first day, I sat alone from about 8.30am to 3pm – the regular school day. And then on the second day, people started joining me. After that, there were people there all the time.'

She kept her promise to strike every day until the Swedish national elections. Afterwards, she agreed to make a speech in front of thousands of people at a People's Climate March rally. Her parents were reluctant. Knowing Thunberg had been so reticent that she had previously been diagnosed with selective mutism, they tried to talk her out of it. But the teenager was determined. 'In some cases where I am really passionate, I will not change my mind,' she says. Despite her family's concerns, she delivered the address in nearly flawless English.

People with selective mutism have a tendency to worry more than other people. Thunberg has since weaponised this in meetings with political leaders, and with billionaires in Davos. 'I don't want you to be hopeful. I want you to panic. I want you to feel the fear I feel every day. And then I want you to act,' she told them.

She has been lauded at the UN, shared a podium with the European commission president Jean-Claude Juncker and has been endorsed by the German chancellor, Angela Merkel.

You may think this would put the weight of the world on the 16-year-old's shoulders, but she claims to feel no pressure. If 'people are so desperate for hope', she says, that is not her or the other strikers' responsibility.

'I don't care if what I'm doing – what we're doing – is hopeful. We need to do it anyway. Even if there's no hope left and everything is hopeless, we must do what we can.'

In this regard, her family see her Asperger's as a blessing. She is someone who strips away social distractions and focuses with black-and-white clarity on the issues. 'It's nothing that I want to change about me,' she says. 'It's just who I am. If I had been just like everyone else and been social, then I would have just tried to start an organisation. But I couldn't do that. I'm not very good with people, so I did something myself instead.'

She seems incapable of the cognitive dissonance that allows other people to lament what is happening to the climate one minute, then tuck into a steak, buy a car or fly off for a weekend break the next. Although Thunberg believes political action far outweighs individual changes to consumer habits, she lives her values. She is a vegan, and only travels abroad by train.

At its best, this sharpness can slice through the Gordian knot of the climate debate. It can also sting. There are no comfortable reassurances in her speech, just a steady frankness. Asked whether she has become more optimistic because the climate issue has risen up the political agenda and politicians in the US and Europe are considering green New Deals that would ramp up the transition to renewable energy, her reply is brutally honest. 'No, I am not more hopeful than when I started. The emissions are increasing and that is the only thing that matters. I think that needs to be our focus. We cannot talk about anything else.'

Some people consider this a threat. A handful of fossil fuel lobbyists, politicians and journalists have argued Thunberg is not what she seems; that she was propelled into prominence by environmental groups and sustainable business interests. They say the entrepreneur who first tweeted about the climate strike, Ingmar Rentzhog, used Thunberg's name to raise investment for his company, but her father says the connection was overblown. Greta, he says, initiated the strike before anyone in the family had heard of Rentzhog. As soon as she found he had used her name without her permission, she cut all links with the company, and has since vowed never to be associated with commercial interests. Her family says she has never been paid for her activities. In a recent interview, Rentzhog defended his actions, denied exploiting Greta and said that climate change, not profit, was his motive.

On social media, there have been other attacks on Thunberg's reputation and appearance. Already familiar with bullying from school, she appears unfazed. 'I expected when I started that if this is going to become big, then there will be hate,' she says. 'It's a positive sign. I think that must be because they see us as a threat. That means that something has changed in the debate, and we are making a difference.'

She intends to strike outside parliament every Friday until the Swedish government's policies are in line with the Paris climate agreement. This has led to what she calls 'strange contrasts': balancing her maths homework with her fight to save the planet; listening attentively to teachers and decrying the immaturity of world leaders; weighing up the existential threat of climate change alongside the agonising choice of what subjects to study in high school. But now that she is active on climate, she is no longer lonely, no longer silent, no longer so depressed. She is too busy trying to make a difference. And enjoying herself.

This Friday, when she takes her usual spot outside the Swedish parliament, she will be joined by classmates and students from other schools. 'It's going to be very, very big internationally, with hundreds of thousands of children going on strike from school to say that we aren't going to accept this any more,' she says. 'I think we are only seeing the beginning. I think that change is on the horizon and the people will stand up for their future.'

And then the activist slips back into being a teenager. 'I'm looking forward to it and to seeing all the pictures the day afterwards. It's going to be fun.'

Rioters flee tear gas during an anti-government *gilets jaunes* protest in January, one of a wave of protests across France this year. ALAIN JOCARD/AFP/
GETTY IMAGES

Swedish climate activist Greta Thunberg with her home-made sign at Davos in January. The 16-year-old inspired schoolchildren around the world to join the fight against climate change. FABRICE COFFRINI/AFP/GETTY IMAGES

Members of the Kurdish-led Syrian Democratic Forces stand guard in February as a woman and child leave the Islamic State group's last holdout in Baghouz. BULENT KILIC/AFP/GETTY IMAGES

New Zealand prime minister Jacinda Ardern comforts a mosque-goer in Christchurch after the right-wing terror attack that left 51 people dead in March. HAGEN HOPKINS/GETTY IMAGES

The steeple of Paris's Notre Dame cathedral succumbs to the flames after a huge fire engulfed it in April. GEOFFROY VAN DER HASSELT AFP/GETTY IMAGES

Demonstrators hold up lights from their phones during a rally against extradition laws in Hong Kong. The protests have been gaining momentum since the spring. HECTOR RETAMAL/AFP/GETTY IMAGES

In a year of turmoil for British politics, anti-Brexit protestors make their feelings known at the Put It to the People rally in March. DAN KITWOOD/
GETTY IMAGES

Former Tory MP Ann Widdecombe returned to politics in April, standing as an MEP for Nigel Farage's Brexit Party. The newly formed party went on to triumph in the European parliament elections. LEON NEAL/GETTY IMAGES

A tearful Theresa May resigns as prime minister on the steps of Downing Street on 24 May following a mutiny from her own party. DANIEL LEAL-OLIVAS/ AFP/GETTY IMAGES

Prime-minister-in-waiting Boris Johnson poses with a battering ram at a police training centre in July. A few months later, he was to take a similarly bullish approach to pushing through his Brexit policy. DYLAN MARTINEZ/REUTERS

'There are those that say they have never seen the Queen have a better time':
Donald Trump interviewed by Fox News after his state visit to Britain in
June. CHRIS JACKSON/AFP/GETTY IMAGES

'A victory lap for British rap': Stormzy in a Banksy-designed stab-proof
vest during his headline performance at Glastonbury in June. DAVE J HOGAN/
GETTY IMAGES

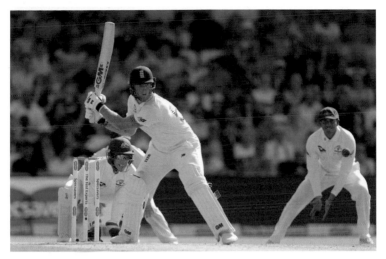

Ben Stokes was dubbed the 'hero of Headingley' after his dramatic innings at the Ashes in August. TOM JENKINS/GUARDIAN

'The physical embodiment of arrogance, entitlement, disrespect and contempt for our parliament': Jacob Rees-Mogg lounges on the front bench during an emergency Brexit debate in September. @ANNATURLEY

Amid dramatic scenes in August, the army were called to Whaley Bridge, Derbyshire to help shore up the local reservoir after it threatened to burst its banks. PHIL NOBLE/REUTERS

The Amazon rainforest was engulfed in a devastating series of fires over the summer, attributed to President Bolsonaro's anti-environmental policies. EPA/VICTOR MORIYAMA/GREENPEACE BRAZIL

Thank you, climate strikers. Your action matters and your power will be felt

REBECCA SOLNIT

I want to say to all the climate strikers today: thank you so much for being unreasonable. That is, if reasonable means playing by the rules, and the rules are presumed to be guidelines for what is and is not possible, then you may be told that what you are asking for is impossible or unreasonable. Don't listen. Don't stop. Don't let your dreams shrink by one inch. Don't forget that this might be the day and the pivotal year when you rewrite what is possible.

What climate activists are asking for is a profound change in all our energy systems, for leaving fossil fuel in the ground, for taking action adequate to the planet-scale crisis of climate change. And the rules we are so often reminded of by those who aren't ready for change are not the real rules. Because one day last summer a 15-year-old girl sat down to stage a one-person climate strike, and a lot of adults would like to tell you that the rules say a 15-year-old girl cannot come out of nowhere, alone, and change the world.

Sweden's Greta Thunberg already has.

They will tell you the rules are that those we see in the news and the parliaments and boardrooms hold all the power and you must be nice to them and perhaps they will give you crumbs, or the time of day, or just a door slammed in your face. They will tell you that things can only change in tiny increments by predict-able means. They're wrong. Sometimes you don't have to ask for permission or for anything because you hold the power and you yourselves decide which way the door swings. Nothing is possible without action; almost anything is when we rise up together, as you are doing today.

I am writing to you in gratitude and enthusiasm as someone who has lived for almost six decades, which has been time enough to see extraordinary change. To see what had been declared impossible happen over and over again. To see regimes topple when ordinary people rise up in non-violent direct action. To see dramatic expansions of rights in both law and imagination. To see what were once radical new ideas about gender and sexual orientation and race, about justice and equality, about nature and ecology become ordinary accepted ideas – and then to see people forget how our minds were changed, and how much that process matters too.

The world I was born into no longer exists. The role of women has changed extraordinarily since then, largely for the better. The entire Soviet empire collapsed suddenly 30 years ago, a few years after the eastern bloc of communist countries liberated themselves through the actions of people who were themselves supposed to be powerless to topple regimes backed by great militaries and secret police. I saw apartheid fall in South Africa, and a prisoner doing life become its president. I was born into a world where to be gay or lesbian or trans was criminalised, and I watched those laws and attitudes change in states, in my country, the US, and in many countries.

I saw wind and solar power go from awkward, ineffectual, expensive technologies only 20 years ago to become the means through which we can leave the age of fossil fuel behind. I have seen a language to recognise the Earth's environmental systems arise in my lifetime, a language that can describe how every-thing is connected, and everything has consequences. Through studying what science teaches us about nature and what history teaches us about social forces I have come to see how beautiful and how powerful are the threads that connect us. Here's one. Who did Greta Thunberg describe as a key influence on her actions? Rosa Parks.

That a black woman born in Tuskegee, Alabama, in 1913 would influence a white girl born in Sweden 90 years later to take direct action about climate change is a reminder that everything is connected and your actions matter even when the results aren't immediate or obvious. The way Rosa Parks broke the rules and lived according to her ideals still matters, still has power, still has influence beyond what she could have imagined, beyond her lifetime, beyond her continent, beyond her partic-ular area of activism.

The rules are the rules of the obvious, the easy assumptions that we know who holds power, we know how change happens, we know what is possible. But the real lesson of history is that change often comes in unpredictable ways, power can suddenly be in the hands of those who appear out of what seems to the rest of us like nowhere. I did not see Thunberg coming, or the Sunrise Movement or Extinction Rebellion or Zero Hour.

When I went to Standing Rock I never dreamed this indig-enous-led uprising against an oil pipeline would inspire Alexandria Ocasio-Cortez to run for office. Nor that she would go on to win a victory that broke all the rules and become the great spokesperson for a Green New Deal. I didn't dream it, but I knew that something powerful, magical, alive with possibility was happening. That's why I wasn't surprised when it did, and why I don't assume we have seen all of what that gathering in 2016 achieved, either. It is not over, any more than Rosa Parks's impact is over. Good work matters. Acting on your ideals matters. How it matters is not always immediate or obvious.

What I see all around me is what I call climate momentum: people from New Zealand to Norway stepping up their response to climate change. I see pipeline blockades in Canada and the US, I see investors backing off from fracking and coal, I see universities and pension funds divesting from fossil fuel, I see solar farms and wind turbines going in all over the world and engineers working to make the technologies better, I see lawsuits against oil companies and coal companies, I see politicians, newspaper editorialists, businesspeople and others who have power under the usual rules getting on board in a way they never have before. There is so much happening, in so many ways, to respond to the biggest disaster our species has ever faced.

It is not yet enough, but it is a sign that more and more are facing the catastrophe and are doing something about it. I don't know what will happen, because what will happen is what we make happen. That is why there's a global climate strike today. This is why I've started saying, Don't ask what will happen. Be what happens. Today, you are what is happening. Today, your power will be felt. Today, your action matters. Today in your individual action you may stand with a few people or with hundreds, but you stand with billions around the world. Today you are standing up for people not yet born, and those ghostly billions are with you too. Today you are the force of possibility that runs through the present like a river through the desert.

16 MARCH

Made in Swansea: at night I would be woken by the screech of stolen cars

JOE DUNTHORNE

Two sides of Swansea's personality glare at each other across the bay. At one end is Mumbles and the pretty coastline, a necklace of lights along the pier, Catherine Zeta-Jones's massive house. And on the opposite side, looking unimpressed, is Port Talbot and the steelworks: a knot of pipes and smokestacks filling the sky with yellow, blue and sometimes green flames. I grew up on the hill halfway between the two and, depending on my mood, I can see two completely different versions of my childhood.

From one angle, it was an endless summer spent swimming in Three Cliffs Bay, my sunburnt friends and I building fires, climbing rocks and trying to get off with each other. Looking the other way, I remember traipsing through a wet, grim city that could be genuinely frightening, a place that was famous for two things: car theft and football violence. I still can't quite believe that my father – a bespectacled history lecturer who was known to wear actual elbow patches – often took me to watch the match from the North Bank of the Vetch Field stadium, to stand quivering among the furious skinheads, praying that they wouldn't hear his English accent. At night, I would be woken by the stolen cars screeching down the steep road by our house. They had to install concrete bollards at the bottom of the hill to stop joyriders careering through people's bay windows.

Swansea thrives on its contradictions. Dylan Thomas, who grew up on the same hill, called it a 'lovely, ugly town'. Many years later the film *Twin Town*, which is about joyriding in Swansea, updated that phrase to 'pretty shitty city'. I've always felt that, in a sense, the shittiness protects the prettiness. The steelworks, for example, are a literal smokescreen to stop outsiders from noticing the most beautiful landscape on Earth.

Of course, when I was growing up in Swansea, I wanted to escape. I wanted to become a writer. I wanted to see the world. All my early, terrible fiction was set in exotic-sounding places I'd never been to: Santiago de Compostela, Tokyo, Oaxaca. It wasn't until years later when I finally wrote about my home town that my characters felt believable. It was exhilarating to discover that I had the whole of Swansea stored in my brain, like a multisensory Google Streetview.

Though the city's hard edges have softened a little over time, it's a relief that it has kept its cracked personality. You can still find perfect empty beaches. The steelworks still fill the sky with fire. And if you're lucky you might still see boys from the hill riding wild horses down into the city centre, trotting bare-chested past the big McDonald's. Though that's a detail you could never include in a short story. No one would believe it.

17 MARCH

'Like a war': the struggle for space that pushes young Londoners to violence

ROBERT BOOTH

'Round here we've got Third Set, in Shepherd's Bush you have 12 Anti, who are currently beefing Third Set. 12 World are beefing 12 Anti. Then you get into Ladbroke Grove and you got Ten Eleven. Then you've got Mozart.'

This is just one corner of a bewildering jigsaw of gang rivalries in west London, described by Colin Brent, a youth worker at the Bollo Brook youth centre in south Acton. 'You can have Acton beefing Acton, Bush beefing Bush. Bush beefing Acton. Young people don't even know whose side they're supposed to be on any more.'

Driven by the drug trade and amplified through social media, similar tensions are replicated across Britain's towns and cities where youth knife crime has been rising.

Knife crime convictions among 10- to 17-year-olds have surged by 51 per cent since 2014 in England and Wales, with the steepest rises in the West Midlands and the east of England. The number of under-18s admitted to accident and emergency units with stab wounds across England rose 76 per cent over the same period to 566 in 2017–18, according to NHS tallies. Eleven teenagers have been stabbed to death in England already this year.

Leon and Ayanna, 18-year-old friends, have seen enough of this to know they want out. Ayub Hassan, a 17-year-old who attended the Bollo with them, was that 11th youth fatality. So slight he was nicknamed X-Ray, he had been stabbed twice before. His family said he wanted to be a barrister. A 15-year-old boy has been charged with his murder.

'Thing is about Ayub,' said Leon, 'that could have been me or one of my friends. He was a normal kid.'

Leon is growing up poor in west London. He has seen three people stabbed, associates with gang members and is always on alert for a possible attack. Ayanna has been excluded from schools four times. Her ex-boyfriend often strapped a knife to his leg and wore a stab vest, and at 18 she found herself homeless, sleeping on buses. Ayanna behaved badly at school and ended up in a special unit, but because it was controlled and focused on her, she finally knuckled down and got six GCSEs, including an A in philosophy and ethics. They are thoughtful, vulnerable and angry, and over the last four months the *Guardian* has spent time with them listening to their views.

Amid a national debate focused on boosting police numbers and increasing stop and search, they reach deeper into the roots of the crisis. They highlight school exclusions, poor education, inflammatory social media, the lack of decent jobs, youth service cuts and racism. But one theme keeps recurring: the struggle for space, at home or on the streets.

'Overcrowding is from poverty,' said Leon. 'You don't have enough money to get a bigger house. It's not that violence is there for the sake of violence. People are being violent because they are pushed there.'

It is not unusual for children at the Bollo to come from eight-person households squeezed into two-bedroom flats. Ayanna lived with her mother, younger brother and boyfriend. She would want to eat after college, but her mum would be asleep in the living room, having worked at night. Her brother slept with her mum, so her mum couldn't get a boyfriend. Tensions mounted until she had to leave.

'You don't have space at home so you go to the Bollo, but they're trying to make youth clubs smaller,' she said. 'So then you don't have space at home, you don't have space there. What are you going to turn to? You're going to feel like you belong outside on the street, right?'

The squeeze has now reached the Bollo. Ealing's youth service budget has fallen from £1.9 million to £800,000, and it has been moved into smaller premises to make way for housing.

Street friends become family substitutes and once in and around a gang 'family', 'you're willing to fight for it', Ayanna said.

After sleeping on buses and a friend's sofa, she now lives in a hostel, but tension over space remains. She was recently beaten up by three other girls motivated in part by the fact that her room was slightly larger than theirs.

Her life would be different 'if I was middle class', she said, and her family had more rooms, and could eat, sleep and work better.

In Islington, where Nedim Bilgin, 17, was stabbed to death in January, council officials have assessed the common factors among the borough's 25 most prolific violent young offenders. Witnessing or being a victim of domestic violence, being detached from parents, and being excluded from mainstream education were the most common.

Once out on the streets, 'beef' makes life dangerous, said Leon. Caused by competition over drug-dealing patches or perceived slights, it is often exacerbated by cannabis-caused paranoia.

'[Customers] have got so many options of people to call, it comes down to quality,' he said. 'So now it's competitive. Now you're needing to up your game or you just choose the other option and take people out.' He once saw a dealer working a rival's corner slashed across the face.

One day 'it was like a war', he said. 'I saw a guy with a Mac-10 [submachine gun] running from the feds [police].' The stress of the streets can be so exhausting that 'a lot of people see prison as an escape ... [because] you're not going to get shot there'.

'I've had people tell me if I go there at least I will have somewhere to sleep and three meals to eat,' said Ayanna. 'Exercise, get to focus on the gym. It's a bloody leisure centre.'

Any perception that you are affiliated to a rival gang is dangerous. She explains how her ex-boyfriend is from area A and her hostel neighbour is from area B. The gang in area A is allied with a gang from area C. Gang C doesn't get along with gang B. So Ayanna has to be careful not to be heard listening to music made by gang C, because that could make her a target for her neighbour.

'Things do escalate quickly,' said Leon. 'Nobody wants to seem like a bitch [coward], especially with social media, because someone would [post], "Oh, you had your shank and you didn't stab me. You're wet."'

Brent said many of the youngsters at his club simply could not see a long-term future for themselves. 'A lot have seen their parents on crap wages for 20, 30 years and struggle to get by. [They] don't want to go into a minimum-wage job for the next 40 years and be a slave to the system. But they don't see an alternative. And so they get involved in drugs and in gangs, alternative systems of power where they can be powerful.'

For Leon and Ayanna, the staff at the youth club are 'like our parents' and 'a godsend'. But English councils have slashed 62 per cent from their spending on youth services – more than £700 million – since 2010.

Ayanna credits the Bollo with giving her the strength to seek a career in interior design. 'My future would be in prison instead of starting up a career that can probably get me £90k a year,' she said.

But the people in power are remote, they said.

'I think you need people from communities to represent their own community,' said Leon. 'The same way I don't know about the Chelsea garden festival ... you don't know about gang violence.'

18 MARCH

Until Christchurch I thought it was worth debating with Islamophobes. Not any more

NESRINE MALIK

If you have been paying attention, you will know that there is now a genre of response protocol that is followed after attacks on Muslims. It blows dog-whistles even as carnage is unfolding. A ghoulish routine has become established. It usually goes like this. Condemn the attack in the strongest terms, and then water down that condemnation. We mustn't get carried away, you see, and forget about the context. Attacks against Muslims must not stop us from continuing to criticise Islam and Muslims when it is warranted. The unvoiced subtext is that maybe these particular Muslim victims didn't have it coming, but such atrocities don't come out of nowhere. But, you know, thoughts and prayers at this difficult time.

Following the Christchurch massacre, there is an article I could write today to explain the danger of this forked-tongue response. An article that exposes the fallacy of thinking that extremist hate crimes can be separated and quarantined from the fact that western societies have become radicalised against Muslims. An article that tries again to show the link between mainstream, fashionable Muslim-bashing and its violent manifestations on the right. An article that fillets the semantic tricks played to stop Muslims ever being complete victims: the line that Islam is not a race; the use of women's and LGBT rights as a rhetorical stick to beat Muslims with; the cant about freedom of speech, political correctness and the danger of identity politics; the whataboutery and the strawmanning.

I could detail the volume of anti-Muslim front pages and columnists forensically quoting from made-up news items, incendiary columns in the mainstream press and politicians' rhetoric. The article would provide evidence for the undeniable rise in hate crimes against racial minorities in general and Muslims in particular, buttressing the argument with statistics. It would be an article similar to those I have written many times – after the Muslim travel ban in the United States, for example. I could plead that something even more horrible will happen if we do not find a way of reversing this juggernaut, of tempering language and applying the same sensitivity filters when talking about Muslims that we do when talking about other minorities.

I am not going to write that article today, or ever again. The reason is simple, and it is this. I used to write on the assumption that people didn't quite fully see the danger and ubiquity of casual hate speech against Muslims, and how it has been racialised and associated with immigration. Naively, I used to think it wasn't necessarily an obvious danger, because people had been subjected to Islamic terrorism and were coming to terms with that, sometimes sloppily and irresponsibly, but understandably.

I no longer believe this to be the case. Politicians and the media know exactly what they are doing. They know that hating Muslims sells, whether it is for votes or for clicks or for profile-raising. They know that there is a sweet spot where prejudice against Muslims and anti-immigration sentiment intersect, and that the former is a good way of legitimising the latter. They know that there is a market for racism, but one that isn't simply based on skin colour – that's too difficult to justify openly – and so 'Muslim' became a good shorthand for the unwelcome other.

They have perfected the techniques, the tools, the winks that mean they can always walk it back and turn it back on their critics as censors and race baiters, out of touch with the real people just concerned about their way of life. The very act of responding to them is co-opted into their narrative of Muslims asking for special dispensation, used as evidence that you can't say anything these days without Muslims telling you to shut up, inventing words like 'Islamophobia' to 'shut down debate'.

There is no point in trying to explain to these people the damage they do. Because they know. They know that there is a way they can talk about the burqa without calling it a 'letterbox' or saying that they are 'just tired of Islam being thrust in their face day in, day out'. They know that they can criticise Muslims in the public eye without fabricating associations with terrorism. They know there is a way to address and accept that prejudice against Muslims exists without dissimulating endlessly about how it is, however, not as serious as, or comparable to, antisemitism. There is a way to critique Islam and Muslims without falling into mockery, dehumanisation or the language of the invading non-integrating horde. They know this. I am done explaining how it could be taken, and accept that this was how it was always meant to be taken.

It is too late to ring the alarm bells once again. Events have overtaken that approach. The warnings have failed and the world has changed. Because the message about Muslims, unchecked, has morphed into something far bigger than one that results in sporadic hate crimes. It has become incorporated into a white supremacist narrative that has borrowed successfully from the playbook of legitimate concerns, weaving anti-Muslim hate into a tapestry along with antisemitism and anti-immigration.

If there was ever a point at which anti-Muslim prejudice could have been staved off by any effort, journalistic or political, it has now passed. This new, militarised white supremacy nexus is global. It has adherents in the White House, and its representatives grace our news programmes and debating shows, explaining that their positions are nothing to do with race, of course: they are just worried about the white race being replaced.

To carry on explaining these associations – between populist politics, the complacency of the debate-hosting media and the activity of its anti-Muslim wing – is to assume that these associations are not obvious and already forged in strong, established ways. To still think that there is some productive debate to be had, some way to successfully challenge these views by inviting them into the mainstream and 'exposing' them, is to be lulled into a false sense of security. The horse hasn't just already bolted: it is armed with intent and livestreaming its rampage on Facebook.

It is time to face the jeopardy. Near an old home of mine in Cairo, there is a beautiful Coptic church – old, perfectly preserved and almost constantly attended for masses, weddings and funerals. But the scene is marred by large concrete blocks that stand outside it, the patrolling private security forces, and the bomb-detection machine that desecrates its entrance. It is time to accept that a mosque in the ostensibly civilised, non-sectarian west is now as vulnerable as a church in Egypt, and raise those blocks.

It is time to stop pleading. It is time to call things what they are and not temper or apologise for the strength of the allegations, to call people racists, opportunists and complicit hatemongers even if they do grace our prestigious publications and seats of governance. It is time to do what they always accuse you of doing anyway, and 'shut down the debate'.

22 MARCH

How the media let malicious idiots take over

GEORGE MONBIOT

If our politics is becoming less rational, crueller and more divisive, this rule of public life is partly to blame: the more disgracefully you behave, the bigger the platform the media will give you. If you are caught lying, cheating, boasting or behaving like an idiot, you'll be flooded with invitations to appear on current affairs programmes. If you play straight, don't expect the phone to ring.

In an age of 24-hour news, declining ratings and intense competition, the commodity in greatest demand is noise. Never mind the content, never mind the facts: all that now counts is impact. A loudmouthed buffoon, already the object of public outrage, is a far more bankable asset than someone who knows what they're talking about. So the biggest platforms are populated by blusterers and braggarts. The media is the mirror in which we see ourselves. With every glance, our self-image subtly changes.

When the BBC launched its new Scotland channel recently, someone had the bright idea of asking Mark Meechan – who calls himself Count Dankula – to appear on two of its discussion programmes. His sole claim to fame is being fined for circulating a video showing how he had trained his girlfriend's dog to raise its paw in a Nazi salute when he shouted: '*Sieg heil!*' and 'Gas the Jews'. The episodes had to be ditched after a storm of complaints. This could be seen as an embarrassment for the BBC. Or it could be seen as a triumph, as the channel attracted massive publicity a few days after its launch.

The best thing to have happened to the career of William Sitwell, the then editor of *Waitrose* magazine, was the scandal he caused when he sent a highly unprofessional, juvenile email to a freelance journalist, Selene Nelson, who was pitching an article on vegan food. 'How about a series on killing vegans, one by one. Ways to trap them? How to interrogate them properly? Expose their hypocrisy? Force-feed them meat,' he asked her. He was obliged to resign. As a result of the furore, he was snapped up by the *Telegraph* as its new food critic, with a front-page launch and expensive publicity shoot.

Last June, the scandal merchant Isabel Oakeshott was exposed for withholding a cache of emails detailing Leave.EU co-founder Arron Banks's multiple meetings with Russian officials, which might have been of interest to the Electoral Commission's investigation into the financing of the Brexit campaign. During the following days she was invited on to *Question Time* and other outlets, platforms she used to extol the virtues of Brexit. By contrast, the journalist who exposed her, Carole Cadwalladr, has been largely frozen out by the BBC.

This is not the first time Oakeshott appears to have been rewarded for questionable behaviour. Following the outrage caused by her unevidenced (and almost certainly untrue) story that David Cameron put his penis in a dead pig's mouth, Paul Dacre, the then editor of the *Daily Mail*, promoted her to political editor-at-large.

The Conservative MP Mark Francois became hot media property the moment he made a complete ass of himself on BBC News.

He ripped up a letter from the German-born head of Airbus that warned about the consequences of Brexit, while announcing: 'My father, Reginald Francois, was a D-Day veteran. He never submitted to bullying by any German, and neither will his son.' Now he's all over the BBC.

In the US, the phenomenon is more advanced. G Gordon Liddy served 51 months in prison as a result of his role in the Watergate conspiracy, organising the burglary of the Democratic National Committee headquarters. When he was released, he used his notoriety to launch a lucrative career. He became the host of a radio show syndicated to 160 stations, and a regular guest on current affairs programmes. Oliver North, who came to public attention for his leading role in the Iran-Contra scandal, also landed a syndicated radio programme, as well as a newspaper column, and was employed by Fox as a television show host and regular commentator. Similarly, Darren Grimes, in the UK, is widely known only for the £20,000 fine he received for his activities during the Brexit campaign. Now he's being used by Sky as a pundit.

The most revolting bigots, such as Tucker Carlson and Donald Trump, built their public profiles on the media platforms they were given by attacking women, people of colour and vulnerable minorities. Trump leveraged his notoriety all the way to the White House. Boris Johnson is taking the same track, using carefully calibrated outrage to keep himself in the public eye.

On both sides of the Atlantic, the unscrupulous, duplicitous and preposterous are brought to the fore, as programme-makers seek to generate noise. Malicious clowns are invited to discuss issues of the utmost complexity. Ludicrous twerps are sought out and lionised. The BBC used its current affairs programmes to turn Nigel Farage and Jacob Rees-Mogg into reality TV stars, and now they have the nation in their hands.

My hope is that eventually the tide will turn. People will become so sick of the charlatans and exhibitionists who crowd the airwaves that the BBC and other media will be forced to reconsider. But while we wait for a resurgence of sense in public life, the buffoons who have become the voices of the nation drive us towards a no-deal Brexit and a host of other disasters.

22 MARCH

'It was not clear if she had a plan at all': how May's night at the summit unfolded

JENNIFER RANKIN AND DANIEL BOFFEY

Theresa May usually gets less than an hour to explain her Brexit plans to the EU's 27 leaders at regular summits. Finally, with only eight days to go until the original deadline, the British prime minister was granted a full 90 minutes in the multicoloured summit room in the Europa headquarters on Thursday night. For the EU, it was not time well spent.

'It was 90 minutes of nothing,' one EU source said. 'She didn't even give clarity if she is organising a vote. Asked three times what she would do if she lost the vote, she couldn't say. It was fucking awful. Dreadful. Evasive even by her standards.'

About a dozen EU leaders peppered the British prime minister with questions. Did she have a plan B? How was she going to gain a majority? When would she hold the vote? 'She very much dodged these questions,' a second EU source said. A third added:

'She was not convincing. It was not clear if she had a plan B; it was not clear if she had a plan at all.' May knew the EU's patience was at breaking point. In case she needed a reminder, Luxembourg's prime minister, Xavier Bettel, said Brexit was like waiting for Godot 'and Godot is never coming'.

Over coffee and biscuits, May thanked EU leaders for their patience and said it would be helpful if the UK could delay Brexit until 30 June.

Once she had left the room, leaders vented their frustrations. 'Maybe we should just let them go,' Bettel said, a remark made more in frustration than in earnest, according to one observer.

France's Emmanuel Macron said the British prime minister's presentation had led him to downgrade his prognosis of the deal passing Westminster from 10 per cent to 5 per cent. Donald Tusk, the European council president, replied: 'You are very optimistic.'

Even Hungary's prime minister, Viktor Orban, surprised the table with a rare intervention on Brexit. 'This is pretty grim,' he said, adding that he had lived in the UK during Margaret Thatcher's government and 'all Conservative party leaders care about is the Conservative party'. Germany's Angela Merkel responded: 'Viktor is right, this is really serious.' Another EU leader said the UK needed to be taken care of 'like a patient'.

Each leader was handed an A4 white envelope containing the draft decision on the Brexit extension – one copy in English, one in their own language.

And then the real talks began. In previous summits, it has been easy. EU leaders signed off pre-prepared conclusions in a minute with a round of applause. It soon became clear this would not happen.

Several EU leaders were angered by what they saw as an attempt to pin the blame on the EU for a messy no-deal breakup. 'That is why we had to change the plan, because her plan, it was a trap,' one diplomat said. The proposals in the envelopes were torn up.

Macron said the UK should get an unconditional extension until 7 May, but no later. The French president was determined not to be back in the Europa building in seven days for another Brexit crisis summit and warned EU leaders against a last-minute decision. But Merkel objected, pointing out he risked a no-deal Brexit on the eve of Europe Day on 9 May, which marks European unity. She called for realism to find a way out.

In a corridor, Europe's most senior diplomats and officials huddled together redrafting the text, as the scheduled 7pm finish came and went. Ireland's prime minister, Leo Varadkar, told the leaders how difficult a no-deal Brexit would be for his government to handle. Varadkar said that while the Irish Republic was prepared, Northern Ireland had not put anything in place in preparation.

'The British policy will make things difficult,' he added.

The leaders were deeply aware as a group that if they accepted 12 April as the new cliff edge, it could mean a no-deal Brexit. Macron turned to Varadkar and asked: 'What will happen if there is a no-deal Brexit on 12 April. Would you be fine?' He responded: 'We can cope.'

By now, rumours were swirling of different dates, while the Twitter commentariat proclaimed the first EU split over Brexit. Insiders said it was not like that, describing the meeting as a 'sleeves-rolled-up, brainstorming session', rather than rows.

The only thing the leaders found easy to agree was that there was 'no ideal date'. One of the EU sources said: 'It's a very, very unusual moment, because it is really leaders putting their arm in.'

May was holed up in the UK delegation room on the ninth floor. She declined the three-course meal that would be served to EU leaders, choosing something else instead. Two floors above her, the EU's 27 leaders were deciding her fate over a dinner of green lentils and langoustine terrine, roast duckling à l'orange and a dessert of chocolate variations.

Over the meal, the Brexit extension variations were whittled down. Eight hours after arriving in the room – with an EU debate on China pushed into Friday – the compromise emerged: a 'flex-tension' that will force the UK to make a choice by 12 April if the Brexit deal fails to pass.

May would not join EU leaders the following morning for a summit with the leaders of Norway, Iceland and Liechtenstein to celebrate 25 years of the single market. They smilingly pointed to her empty space on the podium, as the prime minister was already back in London crafting a last-ditch attempt to save her deal.

After saying goodbye to May, Tusk was asked at a press conference whether, if MPs refused to vote for her deal, more room would be made in hell – a reference to his earlier remark about where those people who promoted Brexit 'without a sketch of a plan' would go.

He replied: 'According to our pope, hell is still empty and it means there are a lot of spaces.' Juncker said: 'Don't go to hell.'

24 MARCH

The rise and fall of the Isis 'caliphate'

MARTIN CHULOV

THE LAST DAYS
On a midwinter night in early January, the most wanted man in the world entered a home in a forsaken town near the Syrian border for a rare meeting with his surviving aides.

Abu Bakr al-Baghdadi was down to a few dozen loyalists, all tested in battle and by the chaos of his organisation's scrambling retreat to the far eastern edge of Syria. The caliphate he had proclaimed four and a half years earlier had been whittled down to less than 50 square kilometres and was shrinking by the day. Gunfire crackled in the middle distance and bombs thudded nearby, just as they had for months as the last towns and villages held by Islamic State fell steadily to the advancing Kurds.

Above the small town of Baghuz, where the terrorist group's leader and his entourage were holed up, two US drones circled, searching for targets below. Several villages away, Kurdish forces were taking positions among the fresh rubble of still-raging battles, readying for a final assault on the last holdout, a place that until very recently few could find on a map. The most diehard Isis members were preparing for what increasingly looked like their last stand, a long and ignominious way from where it all began when its fighters swept into towns and cities across Iraq and Syria, capturing all before them and rendering the border between the two countries little more than a line in the dirt.

Baghuz, barely a speck on a bank of the Euphrates, was about to be etched into infamy. Inside the walls of the small home, Baghdadi, ailing, angry and paranoid, would face the biggest challenge yet to his authority. The small town would soon be known around the world as the place where Isis fought and lost its final battle, where the vainglory of the 'caliphate' finally crumpled in defeat. But according to three intelligence agencies and two sources with detailed knowledge, it was the place where foreign fighters close to Baghdadi's inner circle nearly succeeded in killing the leader.

Accounts of intelligence officers and people in Baghuz who spoke to the *Guardian* say Baghdadi and his guards were forced to flee when several men inside the small home opened fire. 'We are certain about this,' one European intelligence source said. 'We don't know about his condition, but we do know there was an attempt to kill him.'

According to regional and foreign intelligence officers, Baghdadi fled from Baghuz to the Syrian desert around 7 January. Outside his immediate circle and the men who tried to kill him, very few knew he was there and even fewer know where he has gone since. The best guess of those who have hunted him and known him personally is that he has crossed the border into Iraq's Anbar province, where the earliest incarnations of Isis gained momentum.

The enclave Baghdadi left behind finally fell over the weekend, after six weeks of gruelling battles and a seemingly never-ending departure of diehards who staggered from bunkers, rubble and tunnels in the ruins. Up to 50,000 people emerged from a corner of the town that was thought to hold no more than a few hundred holdouts, with the scale of the exodus both stunning the victors and overwhelming camps that had been set up to house less than a quarter of their number. Some of the war's newest refugees had news about the caliph who had left them to their fate, and now far more incentive to disclose what they knew.

Few in Baghuz knew what had happened when the gunfire erupted, but they later gained some sense of events when Isis members circulated a leaflet calling for the execution on sight of a leading foreigner, Abu Muath al-Jazairi. Locals who fled the town in February said something serious had clearly taken place. 'We could not go outside,' said Jumah Hamdi Hamdan, 53, who had retreated to Baghuz from the nearby village of Keshma. 'There were things we could not involve ourselves in. Baghdadi's men were fighting north Africans. The danger was too high.'

Other witnesses, including the US woman Hoda Muthana, who was with the Isis vanguard on its scrambled retreat, said the fighting had started several months earlier in Keshma, which lies in near-total ruin, along with every other village in the area. 'There were battles going on between the factions in Isis,' she said from a detention centre in eastern Syria. 'There were a lot of Tunisians and Russians and there were two sheikhs who were tortured and executed. One was from Jordan and the other from Yemen. Isis was trying to wipe out anyone who criticised them.'

Destruction had been a calling card of Isis's presence ever since Baghdadi proclaimed the group's existence. Nearly every town and city it had occupied was decimated, both by the extremists themselves and coalition jets above that relentlessly battered their hideouts. Raqqa and Kobane in Syria were laid to waste and, across the river in Iraq, Falluja, Tikrit, Ramadi and Mosul remain broken and dysfunctional years after Isis was driven out.

On the road to Baghuz, enormous craters dot both sides of roads leading in and out of every village. Ruined homes and factories are caked with concrete dust and trucks are scattered around like playground toys. Not one building appears to be intact.

Less visible, but even more significant, is the damage the Isis occupation has done to the local communities. 'Our homes may be broken, but the toll on our young and old is worse,' said Radwan Shamsi, an elderly man who ran a shop in the Syrian town of al-Bab before fleeing to the al-Hawl refugee camp. 'It is like trying to put an egg back together. May God damn them.'

EXPANSION AND OVERREACH

It wasn't always this way. From the moment Baghdadi announced the formation of Isis on 8 April 2013, unilaterally declaring that the al-Qaida-aligned Jabhat al-Nusra had been subsumed into the group he led, until his proclamation of a caliphate from the Great Mosque of al-Nuri in Mosul in mid-2014, his organisation's rise seemed unstoppable. The group had seized power through a classic Trojan horse act, sending senior members from Iraq to first infiltrate, then absorb communities in northern Syria. The rival jihadist group Jabhat al-Nusra was its first target, then any opposition group that stood in its way.

From Aleppo in Syria to Mosul in Iraq, Isis conquered its way. Five divisions of Iraq's national army fled as 700 jihadists in pickup trucks advanced towards Mosul, and the border with Syria was rendered redundant. As with the 13th-century Mongols who conquered cities, in modern-day Iraq and Syria, just the threat of Isis approaching was enough for tens of thousands of men to ditch their uniforms and weapons and leave. Kurdish peshmerga forces were soon in a race with Isis to secure the oil fields of Kirkuk, and only US airstrikes saved the Kurdish capital, Erbil, from an Isis incursion that could have changed the fate of northern Iraq.

Banks were looted and abandoned and US-supplied heavy weapons were seized in areas of Iraq under Isis's control as it became the most cashed-up and well-supplied startup in the region. It commandeered oil fields, sold crude to Damascus and Turkey and started levying taxes. Within months of Baghdadi's appearance in Mosul, foreigners from all over the world were flowing in to fight for the so-called caliphate. An estimated 50,000 arrived in its territory. The blowback was not long coming for Europe, where borders had already been tested by huge flows of migrants, and the savagery of terrorism hatched inside Isis territory was about to be carried home.

Nothing, it seemed, would ever be the same again. By late 2014, the very fabric of the region had been tested. Iraq's Nineveh plains, hailed as an ancient cradle of civilisation and a modern example of coexistence, were emptied of minorities as Turkmen, Christians, Shabak and Yazidis all fled for their lives.

As it expanded, however, Isis began to overreach. Its push into the Kurdish town of Kobane on the Syrian–Turkish border in late 2014 was one such moment. More a show of strength than a strategy, Isis sent thousands of its men to control the area. The US, in return, sent jets. 'I was one of the people preparing our guys for battle, and sending them,' said a former Isis member now living outside Syria. 'Every time I'd send people they'd be killed. Once I sent 30 Tunisians and they were all killed before they even got there. That was the time that people started to think twice.'

Isis lost more than 1,500 men in Kobane for no apparent gain. 'Kobane was the first real battle in which American air power was deployed to support a group, in this case the Kurds, on the ground,' said Shiraz Maher, the director of the International Centre for the Study of Radicalisation at King's College London. 'I think the number of people Isis threw into the campaign therefore reflected their desire to show the Americans they were prepared to fight hard. Ultimately, of course, the campaign was a very wasteful one.'

Throughout the rest of 2015, and into the following year, the organisation appeared to hold its ground. Turkey gradually sealed its borders, stemming the flow of foreigners, but the already large numbers of fighters on the ground posed a formidable problem. Worst fears were not far off being realised. Chilling executions were soon being showcased on cutting-edge cameras, their production values and widespread distribution designed for maximum impact.

High-definition horror became a prime component of Isis propaganda, all filmed and disseminated by foreigners, including a group of four Britons who sadistically tortured their captives and beheaded some on camera. In late 2015, suicide bombers attacked Paris. More hit Brussels airport. The UK was not spared, with Isis-inspired attacks at a pop concert in Manchester and at

Westminster and Borough Market in London. In their wake came intensified efforts to chase the extremists from the land they had seized but, as soon became clear, were unable to control.

'The caliphate as a go-to destination started to drop away from 2016 when the campaign to retake Isis territory intensified and the group began being pushed back in places like Mosul,' said Maher. 'The group's senior leadership told people to no longer travel to join them, but to instead conduct attacks at home. That change in emphasis was quite significant. After that, the group's loss of territorial control accelerated and its appeal was further diminished.'

In late 2016, Kurdish and Iraqi forces started an offensive on Mosul that succeeded, at great cost to the city and its residents, in pushing the extremists out of the city and into western Iraq. Another year of town-to-town fighting pushed it largely across the border towards Raqqa, the second and last of its centres of gravity. The Raqqa offensive started in mid 2017 and ended six grinding months later, with the city ravaged and the remnants of Isis allowed to flee in a deal struck with Kurdish forces.

From there, Isis members and their families gradually withdrew through eastern Syria, pursued by the Kurds to their final redoubt, which finally fell this week after a month of fighting. At least 15,000 jihadists and their relatives joined a caravan pushed into never-ending retreat, among them children born inside the 'caliphate'. Local women had sons and daughters with men from all around the world. Foreign women had also given birth to children fathered by Isis members. Inside the refugee camp, the US jihadist Hoda Muthana was carrying an 18-month-old son fathered by her second husband, a Tunisian fighter. British citizen Shamima Begum gave birth to her third child in February. It later died. Stateless, isolated and with few protections, children, along with many hundreds more in the camp, are among the most vulnerable people on the planet.

Those who made it out of Baghuz were the lucky ones. Many hundreds more remained in an elaborate tunnel network dug below the town, the Isis equivalent of a doomsday bunker. Among the organisation's rearguard were its most zealous devotees, those who refused to surrender even as death closed in. British families were among them, as were other foreigners, who mingled with Iraqis, Syrians, Russians and Tunisians, all of whom had stayed the course as Baghdadi's vision of utopia crumbled around them.

The two children of Bashirul Shikder, a US citizen from Florida, were among the last group in the rubble of Baghuz, held by British jihadists who refused to leave. Burned by an airstrike that killed their mother in January, waiting to learn of their fate became an agonising ordeal for their father, who flew to northern Iraq in the hope of being reunited with the children taken from him four years ago by a wife who left him to join the 'caliphate'.

As bombs rained down on Baghuz, a German woman, Laura Hensel, having surrendered to the Kurds weeks before, implored the women holding the children to hand them over to the Kurds. Her pleas appeared to go unanswered as the final assault on the last bastion of Isis pressed on. Those who had stayed this long appeared unwilling to leave now.

FEARS OF A NEW INSURGENCY

Once a juggernaut that posed an existential menace to Iraq and Syria and aimed to conquer three continents, the so-called Islamic State lies in ruins, its foreign legions decimated, many in its homegrown ranks dead or imprisoned and its remaining leaders again on the run. The precipitous fall has led the group to rebrand its *raison d'être*. Central to that is claiming that the losses are a result of an ongoing global war on Islam.

'Isis has explained away the loss of its caliphate in two ways,' said Maher. 'The first is by pointing to divine providence and saying that it is the will of God. Either God is punishing or testing the caliphate by afflicting it with trials, but either way, they tell their supporters, the only suitable response is to double down in your devotion because that's what God would want.'

Some holdouts who surrendered during the dying days of Baghuz had bought the new message. 'The Islamic State will rise again,' screamed two women, their faces covered in niqabs, as they were driven to detention centres by their Kurdish captors.

Baghdadi, meanwhile, appears to have slipped the vast net of the search for him that ran throughout the heights of Isis territorial power and into its dying days. Those close to him say that he always harboured fears that his most devout advocates would one day turn on him. Officials who have hunted Baghdadi for the past five years say he had become obsessive about the dangers of digital technology, and for good reason. The drones circling above were looking for technical traces that could pinpoint their quarry. No one who met the fugitive leader was allowed to carry a phone anywhere near him.

The best guess of officials on both sides of the border is that he has slipped back into the familiar terrain of western Iraq, where the rumblings of a fresh insurgency are beginning to trouble leaders in Baghdad and Syria. The spectre of a guerrilla war, this time on both sides of the river, looms large in their fears.

Masrour Barzani, the chancellor of the Kurdistan region security council, said: 'Taking away territory from Isis was central to the war. While the cost has been high, and the aftermath palpable in areas across Iraq and Syria, the underlying political and economic conditions remain just as unresolved. Unless regional governments address those grievances, Isis will remain one of many symptoms bound to re-emerge in a new form.

'Isis is about ideology, not fighters or territory. The group has already adapted to territorial defeat by returning to insurgency in areas with pre-existing sectarian fault lines. It has gained renewed momentum in recent months across Iraq's northern provinces using tactics it was always more comfortable with than holding territory. In areas freed from their terror, local sleeper cells have already reappeared to spread panic and fear.'

Spring

Fleabag has gloriously affirmed every woman's right to screw up in style

GABY HINSLIFF

It isn't just because of the hot priest. Although, to be honest, the hot priest does have quite a lot to do with it. But the other reason almost every woman I know is gripped by the bittersweet BBC comedy *Fleabag* is that there's something so exhilarating about its attitude to women getting things wrong. Its heroine leads an intensely interesting life but a faintly disappointing one, at least in the eyes of her well-to-do family: she is the classic underachieving younger sister, the screw-up, the damaged one always on the verge of doing or saying something inappropriate. Compared with older sister Claire – she of the hysterically uptight manner, creepy husband and tediously successful corporate career – she's a mess.

Yet nobody watching this really wants to be Claire. Fleabag's habit of needily seeking sex from all the wrong people looks significantly more fun than her sister's miserable compromise of a marriage, and even her financially precarious cafe business beats sitting in Claire's enormous office fretting about keeping the clients happy.

Like the author Elizabeth Day's new book *How to Fail* – which tells the story of her own failed IVF procedures, miscarriage and divorce, interspersed with tales of failure from the rich and famous and reflections on whose expectations she really wants to live up to anyway – *Fleabag* neatly inverts the idea of success. Phoebe Waller-Bridge, who wrote and stars in the series, once said that in drama school, where she wasn't particularly successful, she felt under pressure to get it right when what she wanted was to be surprising. The best drama comes, she argued, from getting it wrong – but in an interesting and unexpected way.

There are worse philosophies to put in front of a generation of overly anxious young women, under constant pressure to excel at things all the time; to jump through endless hoops without even questioning who put them there in the first place.

It is obviously a huge step forward that children's TV is now full of swashbuckling, can-do heroines for little girls and that publishers now fall over themselves to provide strong role models, churning out endless books by successful women about other successful women in history. These stories deserve to be recovered from obscurity, just as exceptional women deserve to be celebrated in wider culture.

Yet there's something slightly exhausting about it all, for by definition not everyone is going to be exceptional. We need role models for low-fliers too, reassurance that you can still have a perfectly nice life without getting A*s for everything. And even high-fliers need to know that things don't always go according to plan, that sometimes life gets in the way and that's not the end of the world.

Failure is, perhaps, not quite the right word for what is being described here. Day isn't talking about the cataclysmic, irrevocable mistakes that end up wrecking lives but the kind that generally have a benign ending: tales told from the vantage point of subsequent success, by people who can afford to look back on early rejections as learning experiences (which often translates as people with a financial safety net beneath them).

Just as *Fleabag* shows us a TV version of being damaged, in which our heroine is still always beautifully dressed and can afford to go out for cocktails, Day writes and podcasts about failure from the perspective of a bestselling author with a Sunday newspaper column who is now apparently in a happy relationship. She is upfront about the fact that this is hardly the sort of failure that ends with sleeping in shop doorways and, when one newspaper headlined an extract from her book by talking about the 'agony of childlessness', she urged readers via Instagram to ignore the wording. Trying and not succeeding in getting pregnant was sad, she says, but she has learned to live with it.

And that's perhaps the difference between the American cult of embracing failure – the idea that every successful entrepreneur has a string of bankrupt startups behind them, that success means taking risks and therefore inevitably a few crashes along the way – and this quintessentially English acceptance of disappointment as part and parcel of life.

There is a fine line between celebrating female screw-ups, and undermining female success by making it look prissy and undesirable by comparison. Beware the dangerous inference that men love women best when they're chaotic and needy rather than happy, or the portrayal of professionally successful women as perennially brittle and miserable. But in the right hands, unashamedly reclaiming female failure can feel like a sign of growing confidence. A certain kind of well-connected man has always been able to fail upwards, to bounce miraculously back from disaster, but such second chances are still rare for women – and that makes female setbacks feel somehow especially humiliating. But Fleabag isn't humiliated, she's exultant: a glorious reminder to nervous overthinkers everywhere that, just occasionally, it's fine to break the rules.

The *Guardian* view on Assange and extradition: say no to the US

EDITORIAL

Yesterday, British police bundled Julian Assange out of the Ecuadorian embassy in London, his refuge of almost seven years. With his emergence into daylight, so too came some clarity on the case which the US has been pursuing against him, and on which it seeks his extradition.

The indictment relates to the secret military and diplomatic files provided by Chelsea Manning, the army whistleblower, which unveiled shocking US abuses and shed light on corrupt and repressive governments worldwide. That Ms Manning is once again in jail, for refusing to give evidence to a secret grand jury in a WikiLeaks investigation, is a disgrace. The importance of the material, published by the *Guardian*, the *New York Times* and others, was undeniable. But subsequently we and others strongly disagreed with Mr Assange's decision to bulk-publish unredacted documents.

Two obstacles initially paused the US pursuit. The first was Ecuador's decision to grant him asylum. A change in government has led it to rescind that protection, on the promise he would not be extradited to potentially face the death penalty. The second was the Obama administration's conclusion that pursuing him for publishing the files would set a dangerous precedent, imperilling press freedoms protected by the first amendment.

As a candidate, Donald Trump declared his love for WikiLeaks when the organisation published emails stolen by Russian state hackers from the Democratic National Committee. But six months later, after WikiLeaks released information on the CIA's hacking operations, the service's then director Mike Pompeo declared it a 'hostile intelligence service' and the US described arresting Mr Assange as a priority.

US authorities say they are charging him on the grounds of conspiracy to access a computer, rather than for the publication of the material obtained. This is an important distinction. The high court last year ruled against the extradition of Lauri Love, accused of breaking into US government websites, in a judgment hailed as setting a precedent for trying hacking suspects in the UK, though the circumstances were very different. The US may also add further charges to the sheet. But it would be naive to regard this charge as the cause of the extradition request, rather than the technical grounds for it. And while Mr Assange is accused in this case of assisting in the cracking of a password, many will fear that the conspiracy charge could be more broadly applied, particularly by an administration so hostile to a free, independent press.

Mr Assange now faces up to a year in prison for skipping bail. He was wrong to do so. He entered the Ecuadorian embassy to avoid extradition to Sweden, where he faced allegations of rape and molestation (which he denies), citing fears that Stockholm would hand him to the US. It would be entirely appropriate for Swedish prosecutors to reopen their investigation, as the lawyer representing one of his accusers has requested. None of this alters the dangers of agreeing to his extradition to the US.

16 April

'On our watch we let it burn': Notre Dame fire leaves hole in heart of Paris

ANGELIQUE CHRISAFIS

Hours after the final flames had died down, Notre Dame stood defiant, charred and roofless in the daylight. The huge wooden doors were open as firefighters continued to secure the building, hinting at the dangers and weaknesses that may still lie within.

Inside, beneath a gaping hole above the choir area where the burning spire had crashed down on Monday night, there was rubble, shards of glass, a twist of metal, but the altar and gleaming cross were still standing. 'It felt like I was looking at a bombing,' said Philippe Marsset, the vicar general of Notre Dame, one of the first who had been able to enter to survey the damage.

The cathedral square, usually heaving with tourists brandishing selfie sticks, was cordoned off, eerily silent and deserted, its paving stones peppered with flecks of black ash.

On the edge of the Seine river – where the gothic architectural masterpiece sits proudly on an island – locals were still coming to terms with the fear and panic of the night before when the fire, believed to have begun accidentally, possibly as a result of building work, had raged across the roof.

From the moment the first flames became visible, hundreds had run down to the river shouting, 'Notre Dame is burning!' Then, for hours, stunned crowds looked on as flames soared into the sky and the spire and most of the roof gradually caved in.

Crowds sang church liturgies, many wept, some fell to their knees in grief, and most gasped and wailed at each loud crackle as the spire was engulfed in flames. In a city that has experienced years of terrorist killings – waking to bloodstains on the street – there was relief that no one had been killed.

Some said they felt anger and a sense of shame. 'Think of all the people who built it over centuries, and on our watch we let it burn,' said an older woman with a walking cane, wiping her eyes.

'I came back this morning to check it wasn't just a nightmare I'd wake up from,' said Paul Piron, a 23-year-old literature student. He had stood until midnight singing liturgies and Ave Marias as he watched the cathedral burn.

'We were terrified it would collapse completely,' he said. He had attended vespers there every Sunday for three years. 'It's not just stone, it's a place of life, a parish. I think it will be another 10 years before I can go inside again.'

For Parisians, Notre Dame always seemed immortal. Crusaders prayed here before leaving for holy wars, it had survived through monarchs and the pillaging of the French Revolution. It hosted Napoleon Bonaparte's coronation, survived wars and Nazi occupation, ringing its bells to mark the liberation of Paris. Once again, here it was still standing. But the missing roof and spire left a sorrowful gap.

'There's something empty, missing,' said Eric Zelnick, 69, who lived in nearby Le Marais and had walked past it every day for decades. 'It was the face of Paris, now it's a face missing its teeth.'

Notre Dame was more than a historic house of God; it was a marker, a reference point, even in secular France. The most-visited monument in the capital, with 12 million tourists a year, it is a symbol of literature and history, and the 'zero kilometre' point from which distances are measured.

'There's something very deep that comes up in all of this – we're just a little tiny part of the story of this building,' said Jean Cottin, 55, a film producer who had returned to see the damage after watching the spire fall on Monday night. 'I always came here as a child, it was a place of imagination. Now I'm wondering if I'll ever see it rebuilt in my lifetime. It makes you think about the passing of time: our lives are a blink of an eye in the lifetime of this building.'

The charred structure had become a symbol of endurance. 'It's devastated yet it's still standing – there's a kind of strength from that.'

Firefighters moved along the tops of the bell towers, checking for damage or looking out from viewing platforms once favoured by tourists. The cathedral, which had always reflected the changing colours of the city, had gone from a shocking vision of towering orange flames, to the dark, damaged structure against a white sky of drizzle in the morning.

There was concern in the crowd: would we be up to rebuilding what skilled craftsmen and genius had defied all odds to create centuries ago? Bertrand de Feydeau, from the preservation group Fondation du Patrimoine, said the roof was built with beams from primal forests more than 800 years ago. 'We don't, at the moment, have trees on our territory of the size that were cut in the 13th century.' The roof may never be built exactly the same; it will always carry the mark of this era and will use modern technology.

Catherine, 80, a former nurse from Brittany, who had worshipped at Notre Dame, cycled there to contemplate the damage. 'I'm optimistic that there was talk of rebuilding it before the fire had even gone out,' she said.

She was aware of the long years ahead when it would have to be closed to the public. 'I won't be able to go back into it in my lifetime,' she sighed as she parked her bike to stand and pray.

McKee's letter to her younger self: 'It's going to be OK. You will walk down the street without fear'

LYRA McKEE

Kid, it's going to be OK. I know you're not feeling that way right now. You're sitting in school. The other kids are making fun of you. You told the wrong person you had a crush and soon they all knew your secret. It's horrible. They make your life hell. They laugh at you, whisper about you and call you names. You can't ask an adult for help because if you did that you'd have to tell them the truth, and you can't do that. They can't ever know your secret.

Life is so hard right now. Every day, you wake up wondering who else will find out your secret and hate you. It won't always be like this. It's going to get better.

In a year's time, you're going to join a scheme that trains people your age to be journalists. I know the careers teacher suggested that as an option and you said no, because it sounded boring and all you wanted to do was write, but go with it. For the first time in your life, you will feel like you're good at something useful. You'll have found your calling. You'll meet amazing people. And when the bad times come again it will be journalism that helps you soldier on.

In two years' time, you will leave school and go to a local technical college. Don't worry – you're going to make friends. These will be your first real friends in semi-adulthood, the people who will answer your calls at four in the morning. You'll only keep in touch with Gavyn and Jonny but you'll remember the others fondly. When you're 17, you'll tell them your secret and they won't mind. It will take courage but you will do it. Gavyn will become a Christian and you will fear that he will hate you, but one afternoon you'll receive a text message saying: 'This changes nothing. You'll always be my friend.' Accept him for what he is, as he has accepted you.

You'll go to university, like you planned to, but you'll drop out because it reminds you of school, where people were cold and you had few friends. The campus is just too big and scary. But this experience will be the making of you. You will meet the people who become your best friends. They'll help you replace all the bad memories with good ones. For the first time in your life, you will like yourself.

Three months before your 21st birthday, you will tell Mum the secret. You will be shaking and she will be frightened because she doesn't know what's wrong. Christmas will be just a couple of weeks away. You have to tell her because you've met someone you like and you can't live with the guilt any more. You can't get the words out so she says it: 'Are you gay?' And you will say, 'Yes Mummy, I'm so sorry.' And instead of getting mad, she will reply, 'Thank God you're not pregnant.'

You will crawl into her lap, sobbing, as she holds you and tells you that you are her little girl and how could you ever think that anything would make her love you any less? You will feel like a prisoner who has been given their freedom. You will remember all the times you pleaded with God to help you because you were so afraid and you will feel so foolish because you had nothing to worry about.

You will tell your siblings. No one will mind. Mary will hug you in the food court in Castlecourt as you eat KFC together and tell you she's so proud of you. The others will joke about how they always knew. They will all say some variation of 'I love you', 'I'm so proud of you', 'This doesn't change a thing'.

You will feel so lucky. You watched James get thrown out of his house after coming out to his parents. You were in Michael's house the night his mum said she would 'beat the gay out of him'. You will feel guilty for being the lucky one and getting it easy in the end, even though you went through hell to get there. You will fall in love for the first time. You will have your heart broken for the first time and you will feel like you might die of the pain. You won't. You will get over it.

Right now, you're wondering if you'll ever be 'normal'. You are normal. There is nothing wrong with you. You are not going to hell. You did nothing to deserve their hate.

Life will not only get easier, it will get so much better. You will walk down the street without fear. Your friends will be the best anyone could ask for. You will be invited to parties. You will have a social life. You will be loved. People will use words like 'awesome' and 'cool' and 'witty' to describe you and you'll forget the times the other kids said you were 'weird' and 'odd' and a 'lesbo'.

You will do 'normal' things. You will spend time with your mum. You will work and pay your bills. You will go to the cinema with your best friend every week because that's your ritual – dinner then an action movie where things explode. You will fall in love again. You will smile every day, knowing that someone loves you as much as you love them.

Keep hanging on, kid. It's worth it. I love you.

On 18 April 2019, journalist Lyra McKee was fatally shot during dissident republican rioting in Derry.

22 April

Stephen Smith had to fight for benefits just before he died – when do we start to care?

FRANCES RYAN

You may not remember the name Stephen Smith, but his body is hard to forget: a photo emerged in February that showed a skeletal Smith sitting in a hospital gown, his spine protruding from his six-stone frame. He had just had his disability benefits stopped. It became one of the most notorious images illustrating the cruelty of the disability benefits assessment system: Smith had chronic obstructive pulmonary disease, osteoarthritis and an enlarged prostate that left him barely able to walk and in pain, but he was found 'fit for work' and told to look for a job. It took a year for Smith's benefits to be reinstated. To get them, at the end of last year the 64-year-old was forced to obtain a pass to discharge himself from hospital; ravaged with pneumonia, he had to leave his bed to attend a tribunal and fight his case.

On Sunday night, news broke that Smith had died. The details of his death are not yet known and it's clear he was struggling with numerous health problems. But what we do know is that Smith spent some of the last months of his life fighting to regain the benefits he needed to live on, and that he was put under incredible strain while severely ill.

If it feels like we have been here before, it's because we have. If it feels like campaigners, MPs and charities have repeatedly warned that disabled people are hungry, isolated and even dying as a result of the Conservatives' 'welfare reform', it's because they have.

Since the coalition government rolled out pernicious new testing for both key disability benefits in 2013, these stories have littered the papers, each a parody of grotesque bureaucracy: the woman in a coma told to keep up 'intensive job-focused activity'; the person with Down's syndrome asked when they had 'caught' it; the young woman with mental health problems quizzed over why she hadn't 'killed herself yet'. More than 70 per cent of disability benefits rejections are overturned at tribunal. Academics have linked 'fit for work' tests to increased use of antidepressants and suicides among claimants. The United Nations has even dubbed the UK's treatment of disabled people a 'human catastrophe'.

And yet there has been no mass public outrage. Not one minister has fallen. We are still somehow waiting for a 'Windrush moment', in which the media and politicians – aghast at the incompetence and inhumanity – cross party lines and stand up for basic morality. How many deaths does it take exactly?

It is time the politicians responsible were called to account, and with them the private companies that are profiting from human suffering. The disability benefits system is a national scandal, a disgrace in waiting. All Stephen Smith did was to ask for help. When will we finally say enough is enough?

23 APRIL

Sri Lanka buries its dead with country still in lockdown

MICHAEL SAFI

A father with his arms around the shoulders of his two daughters. Parents and children posing for a family portrait. Dozens of black-and-white photographs of individuals. On posters and leaflets plastered across Negombo, the faces of the dead were everywhere yesterday, as mass funerals were held for those who were killed in Sunday's terrorist attacks.

At St Sebastian's church, the worst hit of the targets with at least 100 fatalities, a makeshift chapel was built under a tent in the courtyard, with more than 20 coffins carried in one by one before a mass funeral service. 'There are so many bodies that we can't accommodate them all at once,' said Anthony Jayakody, Colombo's auxiliary bishop.

Cries filled the air as each coffin was carried past by priests. An older man wept uncontrollably beside a casket carrying his wife; the families of other victims stood aghast and silent.

Mourners, many dressed in white, filled the streets of what had transformed into a city of funerals, with smaller ceremonies held in local houses. Priests and nuns stood on corners comforting the faithful, watched over by machine-gunners and soldiers guarding the lanes that crisscross the majority-Catholic area.

A teacher, Amila Thushranga, said students from his school were among the dead, and he had spent two days visiting the homes of their families. 'Every second house is having a funeral today,' he said.

So as not to overwhelm the city's two cemeteries, an empty lot not far from the church had been turned into a mass burial site, where two dozen bodies had been laid by the end of the day. They were marked out by flower arrangements and numbered wooden crosses. Those who came to pay their respects had to have their clothes and bags checked by police.

A father and his two children were among those buried in the presence of their families and dozens of clerics. At least 45 children died in the bombings, according to Unicef.

Alongside the grief, there was still disbelief at the extreme violence that had struck a quiet community. 'It was so terrible,' said Father Sagara Hettiarachchi, who arrived at the church just after the bomb had exploded. 'Bodies, injured people, lamenting, weeping, crying. As Sri Lankans we never thought such a thing would happen.'

The streets of Negombo and the capital, Colombo, were nearly empty after police called a state of emergency and declared yesterday a national day of mourning. Flags were lowered to half-mast and liquor shops were ordered to close for the day. A three-minute silence was marked nationwide from 8.30am, around the time the first of seven suspected suicide bombers struck. The front page of Sri Lanka's *Daily Mirror* was black but for the words: 'In remembrance of all those who lost their lives.'

Security around hotels and government buildings had been upgraded after warnings that a van carrying explosives was loose in the city and bomb disposal units were called to at least one railway station. A curfew was again in place last night and social media platforms were still blocked.

Questions were raised about whether Sri Lanka's deeply divided government allowed its factional disputes to take precedence over security.

THE BEDSIDE GUARDIAN 2019

The country's prime minister, Ranil Wickremesinghe, said the danger was not yet over. 'There are a few people on the run,' he said, adding he did not know how many. 'We're making progress, that's all I can tell you.'

He said the bombings were likely to dent the tourism industry, which had been hoping for a bumper year after the country was named *Lonely Planet*'s No 1 travel destination. 'At the moment many [tourists] are leaving and that's understandable but we will give the signal when we have the situation fully under control.'

In Colombo, people remained reluctant to openly criticise the police and army, who have been accused of abusing their power in the past.

'We don't want to talk about politics,' said Sunanda Perera, outside St Anthony's church. 'We are sick of it. The politicians don't look after us. These sorts of things should never happen again to the Sri Lankan people.'

24 APRIL

Why you should turn your lawn into a meadow

ALYS FOWLER

My garden sings its own song. It starts after the dawn chorus with the honeybees, followed by the heavier buzz of the bumbles, punctuated by the hoverflies' higher pitch. You can even sometimes hear the rustle and creak of beetles as evening comes. To lie among it, eyes closed, is to hear something exquisite.

My garden sings this song because it is allowed to. I have long been a proponent of neglecting lawns to nurture nature, as Margaret Renkl recently made the case for in the *New York Times* – and there isn't a manicured strip of green that doesn't ache to do the same.

Most lawns have been silenced by the regime of a lawnmower, leaving just a few species of grass. They are biodiversity deserts, barren of beetle and bee, contributing to a vanishing insect population – and, worse still, we pursue this. There are aisles in garden centres promising ever-greener sward, with no moss and weeds. Let there be no misunderstanding: these are chemicals that silence the soil.

There is another way. Your lawn is already a wildflower meadow – every inch of soil is waiting for its moment to burst forth. Those weeds are some of the best insect food, growing despite the weather, endlessly repeat blooming, rich in nectar and pollen. A seed bank is already there – it might even contain orchids. Oh, and perhaps plenty of moss, essential stuff for nests and nature of all sorts.

The simplest route to this is not to abandon your lawn and mower but to learn how to move the mower's blades up, so the cut is higher than 10cm. Hold out for your first cut until the end of June, then leave a month between each cut until autumn. If you need a route to the washing line or shed, mow just a path. The wildflowers will adapt and bloom under your blades, the bees will dance and the birds will sing in praise of it all.

25 APRIL

The Archers' Joe Grundy: farewell from me and the ferrets

NANCY BANKS-SMITH

Poor old Joe. So Farmer's Lung got him in the end. None of us believed he had Farmer's Lung or, even, that it existed. For one thing, he wasn't much of a farmer and for another he was a Grundy.

People like Joe Grundy make the countryside look untidy. People like Joe Grundy are Compo in *The Last of the Summer Wine*, Adam Lambsbreath in *Cold Comfort Farm*, Baldrick in *Blackadder* and, of course, Joe's immediate predecessor in *The Archers*, Walter ('Me ol' pal! Me ol' beauty!') Gabriel. When nice people settle in the smiling countryside they find it is already infested with Grundys. Prospero had this problem.

They toil not, neither do they spin (though the clattering of dishes in the background suggests their wives do both), yet maddeningly they survive and thrive. The consensus of the nice people is that the Grundys are not as green as they are cabbage-looking.

Joe Grundy was in many ways a lucky old man. I cannot personally recommend one's 90s. You tend to fall down in the street, causing unkind comment. Admittedly Joe enjoyed his pint of Shires, a brew so thick you can eat it with a spoon, but Bartleby, his elderly pony, always knew the way home. If nobody offered to pay for his pint, he brewed his own cider. Which actually dissolves spoons.

His saintly daughter-in-law only drew the line at ferrets on the table at mealtimes. And his entire family reacted with that blind rage so characteristic of the younger Grundys at the mere idea of putting him in a home like the Laurels, that black hole which swallows Ambridge residents surplus to requirements. Admittedly, they couldn't afford the Laurels but one appreciated the gesture. He was free of all the fashionable problems that nice people suffer in Ambridge: depression and coercive control and donor insemination. Regular spats with Bert Fry (The Bard of Borchester) kept Joe on his toes.

Bert will miss him dreadfully and is already working on a threnody. 'So! Farewell Joe Grundy! Awkward to the end. If you had died on Sunday it would have made my life easier. Or even Monday. But no! It had to be Wednesday, didn't it?' This week he was teaching his little great-granddaughter to clip a ferret's claws (thus taking her mind off her mother's early death from sepsis and her father's obsessive compulsive disorder). She will remember him fondly.

29 APRIL

Tony Slattery: 'I had a very happy time until I went slightly barmy'

HADLEY FREEMAN

When I moved to London in 1990, I knew that, in order to fit in at school, I had to educate myself about the important British celebrities. While my classmates helped me with regard to the canon – Noel Edmonds, Phillip Schofield, Cilla Black – there was one I found all on my own. Tony Slattery quickly became a source of fascination to me. He was such a ubiquitous presence on television (endless quiz shows and commercials), in theatre (*Me and My Girl*, *Neville's Island*, which got him an Olivier nomination) and film (*The Crying Game*, *Carry on Columbus*, *Peter's Friends*) that *Private Eye* ran a cartoon of him in which his answer machine message was, 'Yes, I'll do it!' But, like most people, I discovered him on *Whose Line Is It Anyway?*, the endearingly low-fi Channel 4 improv show that ran from 1988 to 1999.

Pretty much everyone on that show was great – Josie Lawrence, Mike McShane, Ryan Stiles and, of course, Richard-Vranch-on-the-piano. But Slattery seemed to be in a different orbit: a gifted actor and strikingly handsome, he vibrated with creativity and a barely suppressed inner darkness. You could never be sure how his skits would go, but you knew they would have a jittery brilliance to them, with a left-field lyrical twist or an emotional gut-punch. With his manic energy, he reminded me of Robin Williams, and it was clear that if he learned how to channel his talent there would be no stopping him. And even if he didn't, well, he would still be exciting to watch. But I was wrong. What happened to Slattery was not exciting. It was sad.

Slattery suggests that we meet at the *Guardian* office, which is the first time a celebrity interviewee has offered to come to me. 'Well, I didn't want you coming to horrible Edgware,' he says, which is the corner of north London where he lives. His face suddenly crumples in anxiety: 'But I haven't done wrong by coming here, have I? Did I make a mistake?'

Slattery pretty much vanished from public life in the late 90s, and while 20 years will change anyone, he looks at least a decade older than his 59 years, and close to unrecognisable from his *Whose Line* days. Where once he was energetic and prickly, occasionally accused of grating self-satisfaction and gratuitous cruelty (he once said Jeremy Beadle should be 'clubbed to death'), the man I meet today is like a lost, anxious teddy bear. Heavy-set and visibly nervous, he is still hyper-eloquent, with that familiar melodious voice, but the syllables sometimes stumble on his tongue. It is noon and there is a faint smell of alcohol about him, although he promises he hasn't drunk anything today. 'I made a special effort for you,' he says with a sweet smile. As we walk through the office, I notice that he is limping.

'I've got to get my leg sorted,' he says, rolling up his trousers. His leg is purpled with vivid rashes and lesions. 'It's some kind of cirrhosis,' he says, unconcernedly. Whatever Slattery took out of life when he tore through the 90s British entertainment scene, life has since reclaimed its debt tenfold.

The ostensible reason for us meeting today is that Slattery is reuniting with some of his old *Whose Line* colleagues for a show in Edinburgh this summer. 'So people can come to that and say: "Fuck me, I thought he was dead,"' he says. One of those colleagues will be Richard-Vranch-on-the piano, who, pleasingly, remains one of Slattery's dearest friends, and one of the very few who has stuck by him. Almost all his other celebrity chums and hangers-on vanished 'when the money dried up, which was saddening. Yes, very saddening,' he says, quietly.

I suspect the real reason he has agreed to talk is that he wants people to know he's very much not dead and, hopefully, to attract the attention of an agent. 'I haven't had an agent for a while and I want to get back into the swing of things. I had a very happy time until I went slightly barmy,' he says.

What, in fact, happened was that in 1996, at the age of 36, he had a massive breakdown. After 13 years of nonstop work, fuelled towards the end by a daily diet of two bottles of vodka and 10g of cocaine, he collapsed, physically and mentally. He alternated between what he describes as 'terrible isolationism and an almost comatose state, and then terrible agitation, constant pacing, sitting inside with thoughts whirling round and round'.

Multiple hospitalisations followed – 'all voluntary', he emphasises. At one point, he locked himself in his riverside flat for six months and threw all his furniture into the Thames.

'The river police came by and said: "Tony Slattery, we like you on television, but please stop polluting the river,"' he says, doing a jolly imitation of a policeman. He often breaks into impressions during our time together – of Ken Dodd, Terry Wogan, his mother – and while they are all excellent, it feels as if he is doing them out of an exhausted sense of obligation to keep me entertained.

Media coverage of this part of Slattery's life has tended to focus on the substance abuse, but there was another, then-yet-to-be-diagnosed problem. 'The manic part of me was not because of the drugs and alcohol. I think it was there already. But the drugs and alcohol certainly ignited it,' he says. From the beginning of his career, when he would go on stage he felt like 'a match carelessly tossed into a bunch of fireworks'.

He was eventually diagnosed as bipolar. Finally, he could make sense of the duality in which he still lives – 'the mania, finding things too exciting, then the withdrawal, apathy and bleakness'.

I ask if he thinks the way he binged on drugs and alcohol in the 90s had less to do with substance addiction than with the mania of his mental illness. 'There's no question. Bipolarity often presents itself as something else, like a rash can present as lupus or Lyme disease,' he says.

And was his tendency to say yes to all jobs also part of his bipolar nature? 'Yes, and also I was worried, because I wasn't born into money, so I didn't want to lose it. But I lost the plot and the money.'

Slattery survived this period, just, thanks to the steadfast loyalty of his long-term partner, the actor Mark Michael Hutchinson, whom he met while performing in *Me and My Girl* in the mid-80s. The two are still very much together, living in

Edgware with their cat, and talking about Hutchinson prompts a juddering sob from Slattery.

'He's kept with me when my behaviour has been so unreasonable and I can only think it's unconditional love. He's certainly not with me for my money – we don't have any money. It's the mystery of love. I'm sorry – it makes me very emotional,' he says, trying to pull himself together.

Until very recently, Slattery always refused to discuss his personal life or even confirm his sexuality. I ask if he was shielding his parents, both of whom are now dead.

'Exactly – it was honestly never anything to do with embarrassment. I just knew Mum and Dad would worry themselves to death that I might have Aids. I think Mum knew – she always referred to me as "my bachelor son". But it was just not talked about.'

Slattery grew up on a council estate in north-west London, the youngest of five children and the son of working-class Irish immigrants. He was a quiet child and very close to his parents. He was also a gifted athlete, at one point representing England in under-15 judo, and an even more talented student, aceing his A-levels to get into Cambridge and study modern and medieval languages. He insists he never felt out of place there: 'I knew I was from a different background, but there was a spectrum of people there, from neo-Trotskyites making pipe bombs in a bedsit to people with 14 hyphens in their name who go out shooting rare animals. So you find your friends, and I went there to enjoy everything Cambridge could throw at me.'

Which he certainly did, joining the Footlights in one of its classic heydays, alongside Emma Thompson, Hugh Laurie and Stephen Fry. Previously, Slattery had dreamed of a career in academia, but this got him hooked on laughter and applause – 'two of the most addictive substances known to mankind'. Nonetheless, when these same Footlights reunited to make the

1992 luvvie-tastic *Peter's Friends*, also co-starring Imelda Staunton and Kenneth Branagh (who directed the film), Slattery was cast as the oikish outsider. 'I wasn't part of their class, you see. That's the thing. And as Kenneth Branagh said at the time, this is a film about friendship among people of the same background,' Slattery says.

But Branagh comes from a working-class Northern Irish background, I say. 'That's right, but he ... you know,' says Slattery, and he holds his collar over his face as though donning a mask. I laugh, but he looks down, guilty about teasing Branagh. 'I still feel like I should tread carefully.'

Back in the 90s, articles about Slattery always described him as talented, but this was often undercut with a reference to him being 'hard to warm to'. 'Dark' and 'angry' also came up a lot. 'There was a lot of rage at that time,' he agrees. And yet he says he had a happy childhood, a happy teenage life, a happy university experience, was doing the thing he loved as an adult. Obviously, none of those things is a bulwark against mental illness, but where did the rage come from? Slattery makes a deep, shuddery sigh.

'I have a feeling that what might have been a contributing factor is something that happened when I was very young,' he says haltingly.

When he was a child?

'Um, yeah. Not to do with family. A priest. When I was about eight.'

We sit in silence for a few seconds. I ask if he ever told his parents and he is so overcome at the thought he can only shake his head.

'A psychiatrist once said to me: "Bear in mind that some things are so deeply buried there is nothing to be gained by an archeological dig. Keep it buried,"' he says.

I look at this broken man in front of me, now bent over as if crippled by the weight of a secret he has carried nearly all his life, and ask if he thinks that advice worked for him.

'I think so, because it would have been another bloody thing to deal with, along with the booze, the bipolarity, the overwork, the feeling of being let down by friends, my own bad behaviour. I think that's enough of a cocktail to be getting on with. Some things are so horrible they serve no purpose to be relived,' he says.

I can feel both of us starting to recoil from the subject, him because he doesn't want to think about it any more and me because I am terrified of pulling on the thread that will cause him to unravel entirely. So, to move on, I suggest that maybe he has partly worked through his feelings about what happened to him, if he feels able to mention it now.

'Yes indeed,' he says, but it is the one time in our conversation when it sounds as if he is speaking on autopilot instead of being emotionally truthful.

Not all celebrities who disappear retire into gated-community comfort in Surrey and, contrary to the lie we are sold, fame is no cushion against falling between the cracks. Slattery is charming company – sweet, solicitous, his brain somehow still sharp despite his best efforts to blunt the thoughts that tormented him. He gave up the coke around the millennium when his beloved mother found some in his flat and he was mortified into abstinence. He couldn't afford it now anyway. When I ask what his plans are this week, he says: 'Buy some food, because we've run out. But we're waiting for money to come in from jobs and that often takes a while. So just make it to the weekend.' It is very hard not to measure the distance between what is, what was and what should have been. He does still drink and, yes, he knows it would be better if he stopped completely, but he doesn't think he has the strength to do that. I tell him I am worried that performing will make him drink more. 'I've been quite strict with myself so far,' he says. 'But there have been times when I've thought: "I can't go on stage, I need that half bottle of vodka right now." I'm getting better, but there's still some way to go.'

He is no longer under psychiatric supervision, and he stopped taking his last lot of medication two months ago. 'There was a numbing effect and I thought: "I can't live in this state where you can't feel or see anything." I'd rather be exposed to the fire.'

I walk him back through the office to the front door, where he hugs me goodbye and apologises for 'garbling a load of melodramatic nonsense'. I tell him he did no such thing. I hope an agent gives him a chance, because he deserves more than this, and I tell him so. He smiles and says he just hopes he makes it to his 60th. But that's only in November, I say. 'A lot can happen between now and then,' he replies, cheerfully. And then he walks away, back on to the streets, exposed to the fire.

29 April – 3 May

Sloppy subtitles

LETTERS

There's nothing new about sloppy subtitling. A 1950s western adapted for the French market once had John Wayne's laconic barroom request for 'a shot of red-eye' translated as '*un Dubonnet, s'il vous plaît*'.

Stephen Pardy
London

Here in Wales, it isn't only subtitles that risk being mistranslated. As it is a legal requirement that all road signs be bilingual, the capacity for disaster is increased. My favourite dates to 2008, when Swansea council's injudicious use of their in-house translation service produced a road sign which read, in English: 'No entry for heavy goods vehicles. Residential site only.' The Welsh version read: 'I am not in the office at present. Send any work to be translated.'

Fiona Collins
Carrog, Denbighshire

Re: odd subtitles, I am reminded of the story of the French version of Sam Peckinpah's *Cross of Iron*. After a lengthy battle sequence with no dialogue, someone sticks their head over the parapet and sees a column of armoured vehicles. 'Tanks!' he cries. The subtitles rendered this as '*Merci!*'

Paul Dormer
Guildford, Surrey

2 MAY

I'm a police officer in London. Here's why we've lost control of the streets

ANONYMOUS

There's a saying in the police. It's not sophisticated or clever, really, and it's been passed down from generation to generation of coppers; it's not new. 'The job is fucked,' they say. Only now, it doesn't feel as flippant as it used to.

I'm a police officer in the Metropolitan police, and have been since 2014. I have anxiety and PTSD. I am – and I cannot say this strongly enough – exhausted. I do not feel safe policing London's streets and, moreover, increasingly I do not feel that people in London are safe. Just last night, there was another double stabbing in east London, resulting in the death of a 15-year-old boy.

It's all well and good vaguely debating 'cuts', but on the frontline of service, those things have real meaning. In the borough I am stationed in – much like other boroughs – where there is a population of about 250,000 people, there are on average 10 police officers for the entire area to respond to emergency calls per shift. Only two or three of them can drive on blue lights. Crucially, very few staff carry Tasers. With a big incident, such as a stabbing, it's not unusual to have all of those 10 officers at one crime scene, meaning there is no one else to attend further 999 calls.

I can expect, at the very least, to respond to at least two to three crimes involving knives a month, and that is being generous. Attackers have pulled knives on me. My colleagues – friends – have been stabbed in front of me. I've found myself many times kneeling on the pavement holding parts of bodies together. We are simply not equipped: most of the time when a violent crime comes in, it's only hope that we can depend on. That somehow we can verbally talk a person down from further attacks, or that we can physically overpower them. Or that, miraculously, an officer with a Taser turns up.

There has been, as evidenced by the recent and continuing knife crime debate, a steep upturn in the amount of calls we attend that involve a blade or even a gun. I don't mind admitting I'm scared going out on these jobs. I realise it's part of my duty as a police officer, but the trouble is, I no longer feel we're in control.

The 20,000 frontline cuts don't even begin to cover the reality. Theresa May also sanctioned cuts to civilian staff, ambulance services, crisis teams, call handlers and the people we rely on for intelligence – such as knowing if someone has committed previous crimes, whether they involved a weapon and therefore how prepared we should be. Our duties are being stretched beyond our capabilities to include non-criminal matters regarding mental health and social services, because cuts have debilitated those sectors too.

While on-foot patrols are dangerously diminished, police officers are sent to help the mentally ill, often sitting for hours with people who are a harm to themselves. Should we try to section them, it can take even longer to locate a single bed, so we often end up on the other side of London, away from our borough. Frequently the person is then released an hour later, deemed to be fit, and we get another call from them the following night, at the same address, to deal with the same issue all over again.

As for our own mental health, there isn't really time to recover. You're expected to go straight out on to the next job, sometimes on the same night, even if a situation is debilitating. If you're lucky, you'll get an inspector or a sergeant who's half decent, and asks how you are. Often you think you're all right for a while. But it takes its toll eventually. I have PTSD from particular jobs – I get panicky, and I've had periods of intense flashbacks – but when I asked my GP about being referred for help, he said I had to go through occupational health. I've been waiting for more than six months.

People who have been in the force for 20 years – just 10 years before they qualify for a pension – are leaving. We feel ignored and maltreated by the government, pushed to the brink of exhaustion and our mental capacities.

When I joined the force, stop and search was something that we were told to avoid unless we were absolutely certain there was a solid reason to conduct it. Now, unofficial targets mean that if an officer hasn't performed a stop and search for, say, two weeks, they are being hauled in front of chief inspectors and bollocked. This change – pressure being put on us to meet certain numbers – is not about safety: it's about politics. And policing should never be politicised like that.

It feels like the organisation just doesn't care about the officers, the pressure they are being put under or, as a result, the public. Our normal shift pattern is six days on, four days off. Often that would be seven days, so that we can do training or follow up on crimes. We don't get that day now to follow up – instead we're making up teams in other boroughs. So the service that we're actually able to provide to the public, in terms of reporting your crime, is shocking. We have no faith in the government. Not many people have had the balls to stand up for the police and say that this is wrong; this is unacceptable; this is dangerous. That's what needs to happen now. But it won't, because of Brexit. Our annual leave is in lockdown because of the anticipation of a rise in violence after we leave the EU. For years, people inside and outside the force have been saying that policing is on the brink of collapse. The mood now is that we are no longer on the brink. We have gone over the edge. The job is fucked.

2 MAY

Small Island review – Levy's Windrush epic makes momentous theatre

MICHAEL BILLINGTON

This feels like a landmark in the National Theatre's history: a tumultuous epic about first-generation Jamaican immigrants playing to a genuinely diverse audience. It is based on the novel by the late Andrea Levy which Helen Edmundson has skilfully adapted into a three-hour-plus play directed by Rufus Norris with hurtling energy. If I was moved, it was by the occasion as much as the play, in that it showed theatre exercising a truly national function.

Levy's book allows big themes to emerge through the interwoven lives of four people. Edmundson focuses on just three. One is Hortense, a light-skinned Jamaican who, farmed out by her mother, becomes a prim schoolteacher who arrives in Britain in 1948 with great expectations. She is joining her husband, Gilbert, who, having served in the RAF, is part of the Windrush generation and equally buoyed by the false hope that postwar Britain will be a land of opportunity. The third figure is Queenie, the daughter of a Lincolnshire pig farmer, who becomes landlady to Gilbert and Hortense.

We hear less about Queenie's husband, Bernard, whose reflex racism is partly explained in the book by his experience as a serviceman in partitioned India. Edmundson also takes a more linear approach than Levy and the play's first half, shuttling between Jamaica and Britain, is a helter-skelter affair charting the three main characters' urge to escape.

The second half, set in 1948, paints an unforgettable picture of postwar reality. We see Gilbert, working as a postal driver, routinely asked: 'When are you going back to the jungle?' Queenie is ostracised by her neighbours for her hospitality to what they call 'darkies'. Yet we also see Hortense's shock at realising she and Gilbert have to coexist in a grimly spartan single room.

In the end, it is a play about lies; and the biggest lie of all is that Britain would both welcome and utilise the talents of its fellow citizens from Jamaica. But individual stories take precedence over messages and one of the virtues of Norris's superb production is its ability to focus on people while giving the action a panoramic sweep. Jon Driscoll's projections encompass everything from Caribbean hurricanes and burnished sunsets to the bustle of prewar Piccadilly and the echoing emptiness of Lincolnshire landscapes. Katrina Lindsay's sets also evoke multiple locales with minimal fuss.

In a vast cast there are outstanding performances. Leah Harvey precisely captures Hortense's stiff-backed pride in the face of prejudice. Gershwyn Eustache Jr expertly shows how Gilbert's anger at being denied self-fulfilment is being masked by a surface cheerfulness. Aisling Loftus touchingly pins down Queenie's working-class resilience and, even if Bernard is more shadowy than in the book, Andrew Rothney shows his initial shyness giving way to downright aggression. CJ Beckford also lends a carefree glamour to Jamaican airman Michael, whose story intersects with that of Hortense and Queenie.

From an aesthetic standpoint, there may be better plays this year. But, in showing how aspiring Jamaicans left one small island to land in another of diminished hopes, it will surely rank as one of the most important.

Two Alexas have moved in, and they're terrifying

TIM DOWLING

In the course of my work, I am sometimes sent free stuff that I don't know what to do with. When given the opportunity to review things, I usually turn down such offers, because I find it hard to write nice things about a product I never wanted in the first place. But sometimes the stuff just comes.

In the case of the free Alexa, though, I have already accepted the assignment without quite knowing what it will entail. I'm still awaiting clarification when the box arrives late on Friday afternoon.

In fact, there are two Alexas inside – a pair of black cylinders trailing wires. I'm not sure where they have come from, but they appear to be secondhand – one has googly eyes pasted on it – meaning that someone, somewhere wanted them even less than I do. My wife is away, so I call upstairs to the youngest one. He comes down a minute later.

'You need to set these up,' I say.

'Alexas?' he says. 'I'm not living with those things!'

'It's only for a week,' I say.

'They listen to everything!' he says.

'I think that's the point,' I say. 'I'll find out more on Monday, but in the meantime we need to make them work.'

'Give me your phone,' he says. 'I'm not doing it on mine.'

He downloads the app and plugs in both machines. It takes him just a few minutes to complete the set-up process. When he is done, I turn off the kitchen radio, and we sit across the table from one another.

'What now?' I whisper.

'Alexa!' he shouts. They light up.

'Alexa!' I shout. 'What's the capital of Chile?' There is a short pause.

'Santiago,' Alexa says.

'Whoa,' I say.

'Alexa!' says the youngest. 'How many people are spying on us right now?'

'I don't know the answer,' says Alexa.

'Yeah right,' the youngest says.

'Alexa!' I shout. The dog begins to whimper because of the raised voices.

'You know this thing knows our address?' the boy says.

'It will do,' I say. 'It's logged into my account.'

'You could probably be like, "Alexa! Buy me that laptop!"' he says.

Alexa begins reading out the specifications of the last laptop I bought.

'Uh-oh,' I say. 'What have you done?'

'The price is £530,' says Alexa. 'Would you like to buy it now?'

'No!' we both scream. The dog barks.

'I'm not staying here,' says the youngest, standing up. The dog follows him out. I sit in silence, wondering what to do next.

'Alexa,' I say. 'Play Radio 4.'

'Playing Radio 4,' says Alexa.

At six the next morning I wake to the sound of urgent footsteps on the stairs. The youngest one bursts into my room, eyes wild.

'I just had a nightmare,' he says. 'About Alexa.' From the look in his eyes, he is still having it.

'What kind of nightmare?' I say.

'It was fucking terrifying,' he says. He crawls into bed beside me, and promptly falls asleep. He is 19.

The next day the oldest one drops by for a late lunch. I show him the Alexas.

'I don't really know what to do with them,' I say. 'I now avoid saying "Alexa", because ...'

'I'm sorry,' says one of the Alexas. 'I didn't quite understand that.'

'Because of that,' I say. 'Your brother just avoids the kitchen.'

'Alexa!' he shouts. 'What's the Chelsea score?' Alexa tells him.

'Creepy, isn't it?' I say.

'Quite handy for that sort of thing,' he says. 'Alexa! Who scored the goal?'

On Monday, I have to leave the youngest one alone with the Alexas. He is not happy about this. I am reminded that, of all my children, he is the primary inheritor of my knack for groundless paranoia.

'Walk the dog, feed the cat, don't say "Alexa", and you'll be fine,' I say.

'Great,' he says.

Some hours later, I receive an email informing me that I will not be required to write about Alexa after all. A few minutes after that, I receive an apology from the youngest one, telling me he had to unplug both Alexas: they had started talking to each other.

19 MAY

Rage, rapture and pure populism: on the road with Nigel Farage

PAUL LEWIS

Nigel Farage is barely visible in the middle of a scrum of body-guards, protesters, TV cameras and boom mics barrelling up Merthyr Tydfil High Street. 'There's definitely more cameras than shoppers,' jokes the leader of the new Brexit party.

His entourage ushers him into a vape shop then a nail parlour, but is unable to shield him from the barrage of questions.

Why doesn't he have a manifesto? Or any policies? Does he know this town centre was regenerated with EU money? Is he being bankrolled by the former Ukip donor Arron Banks, who rented him a Land Rover, personal driver and a £4.4 million house in Chelsea?

Farage is unruffled. 'I'm fighting a European election campaign,' he says. 'You can bore on with whatever you want to bore on with.'

The *Guardian* asks if his party has a single non-Brexit policy. 'Massive political reform,' he replies. 'Wholesale. A feeling that politics is broken. A feeling, not just here in Wales but every-where, that there is a detachment between Westminster and ordinary folk.'

What kind of a policy is that? 'It will be very specific.' When? 'We'll have to wait and see.'

In the lead-up to Thursday's election, Farage has the breezy confidence of a politician who believes in his own infallibility. Having abandoned Ukip after its lurch to the far right, Farage is using his nascent outfit – modelled on the Five Star Movement in Italy – to rebrand himself as a new kind of politician who transcends the left–right spectrum.

In less than two months, more than 100,000 people have paid £25 to register as supporters of the party, which appears on course for a thumping electoral victory. The latest YouGov poll predicts the Brexit party will get 34 per cent of the vote – twice the Lib Dems' 17 per cent share. The Lib Dems are two points ahead of Labour in the poll, while the Conservative party is behind the Greens and in fifth place, with 9 per cent.

The question no longer seems to be whether Farage will win the European elections. It is whether he can convert this political moment into a more enduring political force in Westminster.

Farage has been relentlessly touring leave-voting Labour constituencies in recent weeks, in places such as Huddersfield, Newport, Nottingham, Lincoln and Durham. The conventional wisdom is that Labour does not need to fear a Farage assault. While the party is haemorrhaging votes, they are largely fleeing from its pro-remain wing to the Greens and Lib Dems. But the rapturous applause Farage and the former Tory MP (and now Brexit party candidate) Ann Widdecombe received last week in a working men's club near Pontefract in West Yorkshire tells a different story. So too does his reception in Merthyr Tydfil, south Wales, which first elected a Labour MP in 1900.

In the car park of a shopping centre on the edge of town last Wednesday, there were many lifelong Labour voters mingling amiably with Tories and Ukippers. The crowd was mostly white and overwhelmingly male. The one thing many had in common was a belief that mainstream politics had failed and a vague feeling that Farage would shake things up.

'Nigel, he's talking our language, so he's got our vote,' said John Paine, a 64-year-old former labourer, whose daughter, wife and 84-year-old mother-in-law were all poised to abandon Labour for the first time.

Nadia, a middle-aged former Ukip supporter, said the country was divided but 'it has got nothing to do with leave and remain. It is social class. The elitists. The us and the them.' Her husband, Chris, added that his wife was talking about 'Eton and Harrow types'. 'They're not the same as us,' he said.

Farage was educated at Dulwich College, a private school, but that does not seem to bother people such as Steve Bayliss, a 47-year-old support staff worker at South Wales Fire Service. 'They always used to say Labour was for the working class,' he said. 'Now ... Labour is just getting in bed with the Conservatives, and they are the upper middle class. I honestly think Brexit is the new working-class party for poverty-stricken towns.'

When Farage arrives on stage, he gives a tour de force of populist rhetoric. 'I've come to realise that with our existing political system we are never going to get the Brexit that we voted for,' he tells the crowd. 'These two parties, filled with career politicians, influenced by big money, simply won't ever deliver it to us. They are trying to build a coalition of the politicians against the people.'

Shorn of any ideological hue, this is populism distilled into its purest form: rage over a corrupt political establishment's perceived failure to abide by the democratic will of the people. And Farage delivers the message with the engrossing rhythm of pantomime.

Standing by his campaign bus, Farage seems unsure about the populist label. 'You call it what you want to call it,' he says. 'I see the whole of western-world politics utterly dominated by a handful of giant multinationals and a career political class. I've felt that for a very long time. I was miles ahead of the game with some of this stuff.'

Either way, Farage concedes he has 'never had a more straight-forward message. And never have the other side made it easier.'

Why had he not once used the word immigration in his speech?

'Five years ago the burning issue in this country was open-doors immigration. And right now, it is not the burning issue. The burning issue is Brexit. Purely Brexit.'

The following morning Farage makes a brief stop in the Tory stronghold of Brentwood. He had promised this would be a 'celeb event' in the Sugar Hut, a nightclub featured in *The Only Way Is Essex*.

The only VIP who turns up is a boxer, Dereck Chisora, who lingers largely unnoticed beside the bar. A more pressing concern is the set-up. Much to their annoyance, the people have been relegated to the back of the room, behind a VIP rope, their view of the stage blocked by a wall of TV cameras and photographers.

There are shouts of: 'This is a disgrace!' and 'Why are we even here?' Leading the mutiny is Scott Dawkins, a 48-year-old who runs a window-cleaning company. 'It's as if they don't give a toss. You come and show your support, and they ignore you. What's the point in that?'

Ten minutes later, after Farage comes off the stage and submerges himself in the adoring crowd, Dawkins holds up a selfie on his phone and declares himself thoroughly satisfied. 'I think he's brilliant,' he says. 'I think he's a breath of fresh air. It's what we need. The thing is, we're all like the little people. And all these elites think they can do what they want. But they can't now because now we've got a voice.'

Dawkins says he thinks Britain is at a turning point. 'There's going to be a massive uprising. Politics has changed. Brexit has opened so much and more people are getting involved.'

Richard Tice, the real-estate magnate who is chair of Farage's Brexit party, tells me he believes the whole of government – not least the NHS – could be made more efficient if businessmen such as himself were parachuted into the civil service. 'I ran a multinational with a portfolio of over a billion pounds – I think I know how to spend money.'

He shows a photo on his phone of an advertising hoarding highlighting Farage's claim that the NHS could be improved with 'an insurance-based system of healthcare'.

'This is what we are up against,' he says. 'The establishment and the mainstream media keep dredging up things Nigel once said. The people don't give a stuff.'

A few hours later, it is standing room only in the corporate venue Farage's party has rented in Willenhall, West Midlands. 'I have never, ever, ever been into politics,' says Chris Malsbury, 47, who worked in a furniture factory before his job was outsourced to Turkey. 'I never voted, apart from the referendum. The fact the government ignored us really annoys me. They're completely divided from the working man.'

Martin Daubney, a former editor of the lads' magazine *Loaded* and a Brexit party candidate, comes on stage and skewers Alastair Campbell, saying he assumes public opinion over Brexit has shifted because of discussions he's had at 'dinner parties'.

'I'm from Nottingham and I talk to people in car boot sales and chip shops and pubs,' Daubney says. 'I don't go to dinner parties. I hang out with real people.'

Moments later, Farage delivers an especially passionate rendition of his stump speech. Sweat dripping down his neck, he builds to a crescendo using his favoured line about 'a coalition of the politicians against the people'. 'Well let me tell you,' he yells, amid a frenzy of applause, '*we're* the people. The Brexit party are the people. And they are in for the shock of their lives.'

When he comes off the stage, I ask Farage who he's referring to when he talks about 'the people'. 'Everyone defines the people as they choose to do so,' he said. How does he define it? 'The majority. And we have a good majority who want us to leave and get on with it.'

22 MAY

Hadrian's Wall's early visitors would have taken a selfie if they could – and we should too

CHARLOTTE HIGGINS

Ever in search of moral panic, the *Daily Mail* has reported that an excess of tourists taking selfies on Hadrian's Wall has caused a portion of it to collapse. Sadly for this theory, the National Trust, which cares for the stretch of wall in question, says there is no evidence the damage has been caused by selfie-takers.

Erosion, weather and invasive plant species are the most likely culprits, and restoration work will shortly be under way to renovate this section of early-20th-century wall-building. Nevertheless, says the National Trust, please don't walk on the wall, but alongside it.

Ah yes: 20th century. Hadrian's Wall was, it is true, built in AD122. (Its precise purpose is still debated – border control, symbolic marker and propaganda tool are more likely explanations than an order to keep the barbarian hordes at bay.) The wall, as it arcs up and down the Cumbria and Northumberland hills, is impressive – and one of the most beautiful and satisfying walks to be done in England is along its 74-mile (119km) length. But its appearance – and status as a tourist destination and hikers' trail – is the complicated endpoint of a story of depletion, antiquarian rediscovery and the invention of the heritage industry.

William Camden was the first serious scholar to try to catalogue the antiquities along Hadrian's Wall in 1599. It was dangerous territory then, 'full of ranke robbers'. He managed, though, to record that he had seen local women using an altar to the Syrian goddess Atargatis as a washboard. My favourite early visitor to the wall (a man I wrote about in my book *Under Another Sky: Journeys in Roman Britain*) was a 78-year-old called William Hutton. In 1801, he travelled on foot from Birmingham and back, walking along the wall twice – 35 days, 17 miles a day. He railed against its destruction, remonstrating with local landowners who were using the wall for building materials.

It was the lawyer John Clayton (1792–1890), a Newcastle-based antiquary, who bought about 20 miles' worth of the wall (and surrounding lands) to protect it. He had his workmen 'consolidate' the tumbled stones. Those that have collapsed are an Edwardian consolidation of his Victorian consolidation.

For Hutton, the wall was imbued with moral meaning. It should act, he thought, as a monument to human cruelty and wickedness. It 'pronounces the human being as much savage as the brute', he wrote. I don't necessarily disagree. Hutton was, however, wrong on one count – that walking the wall would not take off. 'I am,' he wrote, 'probably the last that will ever attempt it.' If he'd had the chance, I'm fairly sure he would have taken a selfie.

24 MAY

As she says goodbye, Maybot finally shows her humanity

JOHN CRACE

Practice makes perfect. After four previous attempts that allowed her rather more wriggle room than the Conservative party had been expecting, Theresa May finally delivered her fifth and definitive resignation speech. Arguably it was her best speech as prime minister, one that ended with her choking on her words as she tried to contain tears. Unlike David Cameron, who called time on his career with a jaunty hum – 'Di-dum, Di-dee, I didn't do it, it wasn't me, Di-dum, Di-dee' – May really had given a toss all along. It's just a pity it took her so long to show it.

Shortly after 10am, May walked into the Downing Street sunshine to inflict the *coup de grâce* on her time in office. She quickly got to the point. She would be resigning as of 7 June – no one was going to deprive her of a last photo opportunity with Donald Trump – and would step down as prime minister once the Tories had selected a new leader. No ifs, no buts. No more trying to hide inside the fridge at No 10, hoping that her party wouldn't notice she hadn't retreated to Maidenhead as promised. No more blanking out her colleagues in pursuit of the undeliverable deal. This was the end. Beautiful friend, the end.

Then came the sting. A hint of defiance. Yes, she might have been one of the worst British prime ministers of the past 200 years but worse was just round the corner. In six months the whole country might be begging her to come back. The next prime minister would still have to face the challenge of how to deliver Brexit without bankrupting the UK and that person could be Boris Johnson, Michael Gove or Andrea Leadsom: three MPs the Tory party had already rejected as totally unsuitable to lead the country three years ago.

Just imagine Boris as prime minister. A diagnosed narcissist whose entire political career has been constructed through the prism of personal opportunism. A man who as mayor of London wasted millions on pointless vanity projects. Who as foreign secretary insulted the Germans, contributed to a British national being banged up in Iran and couldn't even take responsibility for a Chequers deal he signed off. Who wrote racist columns in the *Telegraph* and never even aspired to being a man of principle. The populist's populist. Both the thinking man's idiot and the idiot's thinking man.

Good luck with that. She would be well out of it.

Old habits die hard, though. Either that, or she couldn't resist making time to be her own Maybot tribute act. The defining hallmark of May's time in office has been her binary view of the world. She has always been right and anyone who has tried to contradict her has been shouted down in a meaningless series of monotone ones and noughts. Brexit means Brexit. Strong and stable. Nothing has changed. A drone in more ways than one. A woman who could make inanimate objects dissolve into tears of frustration.

'Compromise isn't a dirty word,' she observed. Self-knowledge has never been her strongest suit. This from a woman to whom the very idea of compromise is anathema. It was insistence on her red lines that shaped the withdrawal agreement. It was her playing to the gallery of hardline Eurosceptics and her refusal to seek consensus with remainers that sent her spiralling out of control. Even when she reluctantly engaged in cross-party talks, her idea of compromise was to state her position and to expect Labour to fall into line.

Her final plea to be remembered for something other than failing to deliver Brexit fell flat. The best legacy she can realistically expect is to be quickly forgotten, though the country is unlikely to be that forgiving. Her image as Britain's therapist and saviour was never wholly convincing, ever since she commissioned the 'Go home' vans as home secretary.

She tried to run through some of her government's achievements. Successes, she'd had a few. But there again, too few to mention. Her subconscious even compelled her to remember Grenfell, presumably as an act of atonement. On the day after the fire, she hid from the survivors.

After little more than seven minutes at the lectern, May croaked out the last couple of sentences. Here it all became too much and her voice caught in her throat. As the words died on her lips, she turned on her heels and rushed for the front door. Fearful she had revealed too much, when her tragedy has been that she revealed too little.

Was this the real May or was this just fantasy? No one could be certain.

Brexit has broken May, just as surely as it will break her successor. A three-year term in office that started from a seemingly impregnable position of strength ended in masochistic humiliation. But in losing her job, the Maybot finally displayed her humanity.

29 MAY

Redcar: how the end of steel left a tragic legacy in a proud town

HELEN PIDD AND JESSICA MURRAY

It was déjà vu for Brian Dennis last week when British Steel went into administration, putting 5,000 jobs at risk and endangering 20,000 in the supply chain after failing to secure emergency government funding.

In September 2015, Dennis had taken a day off from Redcar's steel plant to attend the Labour party conference when his phone started buzzing. It was the news he had been dreading: after 26 years among the coke ovens and conveyor belts he was out of a job. SSI, the plant's Thai owner, was pulling the plug.

He asked for the microphone. 'I left school at 16 to work in the shipyards and when the government shut them down I moved into the steel industry,' he told delegates. 'The government must step in and act to protect us, our families and our community. All of us steelworkers on Teesside are facing the end of our industry and a very bleak future. Only the government can save us now.'

His plea roused the conference hall to its feet but fell on deaf ears in Westminster. The government blamed EU rules on state aid for preventing it from bailing out SSI and two weeks later the receiver announced there was no realistic prospect of finding a buyer. The blast furnace was turned off and the coke ovens were extinguished, left to cool down from 1,100°C in the salty North Sea breeze. Two thousand direct jobs went and, with them, 170 years of steelmaking on Teesside.

Three and a half years on, Dennis, 53, is no longer a steel-worker. He received money to retrain from the £50 million fund set up by the government to help Redcar's steelworkers start new lives, but packed in his health and safety course after six months. 'My wife kept sending me job adverts and eventually I got the hint,' he said this week, walking his dog on Redcar beach, the hulking steelworks rusting on the skyline.

'There seemed to be a desperate rush to find work, any work,' he remembers. He saw job adverts online for £25,000 positions that would disappear and then come back three days later with a salary of £20,000. 'Just because you've got a thousand people sending you a CV who are hardworking men, should you really be doing that? I think morally it's wrong. It was like a race for the work and I think the employers were trying to make it a race to the bottom, to get what they could as cheap as they could.'

He applied for 50 jobs to no avail. Eventually he begged the jobcentre for feedback on his CV. It told him to take off the fact he was a union rep and a Labour councillor – both proud achieve-ments – and he got the next job he applied for.

Now he works as a supervisor for Calor Gas, overseeing refills of propane gas canisters. He earns £31,000 – when he left the steelworks he was on £46,000.

It is not a subsistence wage, he acknowledges: 'But it's a big drop and the £15,000 comes out of what I call your leisure money – it's your holiday money, your nice things. You've still got to pay your bills, your gas, your electricity, the car ... We've cut back on holidays, eating out. I can't remember the last time we went to the cinema. It's all stopped.'

The Regent Cinema is closed, ostensibly because of structural defects. However, the loss of high-paying SSI jobs and reduced spending in the local economy had an impact on many businesses. Empty shops abound, with pound shops, pawn shops and charity shops dominating the high street.

Employment figures for Redcar and Cleveland look positive on paper. Of the 2,185 SSI and supply chain workers who applied for benefits, 2,167 have ended that claim and nearly 2,000 new jobs have been created through the SSI fund overall, according to the latest figures.

However, most former steelworkers have taken big wage cuts. More than 300 ex-SSI and supply chain workers started their own businesses, helped by a startup support fund. Much of the work was not lucrative, with the steelworkers struggling to transfer their often very niche skills into life outside steel. Five became chimney sweeps; three turned dog walkers, according to the SSI Task Force Legacy Report. Twenty-six went into gardening.

One was Steven Lince, 32, who was profiled as a success story in the report. But a year on, he has thrown in the towel, one of the 10 per cent of SSI startups to fail. With a family to look after and slow business in the winter months, it became unsustainable. He now works as a production operator at a pipe mill just over the river in Hartlepool, earning £22,000 – the same as he earned at 18, and £8,000 less than he was on at SSI.

Insecurity is a huge problem. 'I'm on temporary contracts at the minute, so I'm still in a situation where two months down the line I could get laid off again,' Lince says.

This precariousness, coupled with low wages, has caused some former steelworkers to lose their homes. House prices in Redcar have still not recovered from their 2007 peak and workers have found themselves in negative equity. In February, one three-bed semi with a garden sold for £80,000 – £7,000 less than it changed hands for in 2004.

It wasn't until about two years after SSI closed that houses began to be repossessed, says Carla Keegans, who runs Redcar's

Ethical Lettings Agency. She lets to people 'the council won't help', buying up properties to rent at affordable rates. Those who have lost their homes tend to have terrible credit ratings and often county court judgments against them, making it impossible to rent privately, Keegans says. When they ask her for help they are 'absolutely mortified', she says.

Divorce has often followed, leaving estranged couples searching for two properties on vastly reduced means: 'The stress of it leads to relationship breakdown. What comes with that is domestic violence, mental health problems and alcohol abuse,' Keegans says.

At least two former SSI workers have killed themselves since the plant shut, says Anna Turley, Redcar's Labour MP. Andrew Hodgson, a father of two, was found dead on 8 November 2015, less than a month after the last steel was forged on Teesside. Stress and marriage difficulties were cited at the inquest, and 'the closure of SSI was on his mind also'.

Sue Jeffrey, who had been the Labour leader of Redcar and Cleveland council for only five months when SSI collapsed, says social isolation has been a huge problem: 'The steelworks is a community. It's not just one generation who worked there, it's two or three, sometimes four generations. Therefore, when you go to work you are not just going to meet colleagues ... you are going to work with people who are your family, live in the same community, have the same interests as you, go to the football match with you ... You lose not only your sense of identity in terms of your work experience but also your social identity.'

Initially, mental health charity Mind helped people with sleep problems: they could not adjust to normal bedtimes after a lifetime of shiftwork.

'We're quite a high area for suicides and men are one of our highest-risk groups, so that's something we need to be really vigilant about again,' Veronica Harnett, the chief executive of Redcar

& Cleveland Mind, says. 'It's devastating to lose your job once, never mind twice.'

Though Scunthorpe – where 4,000 people work on British Steel's 2,000-acre site – has hogged the national headlines this week, there are two British Steel sites in Redcar and Cleveland, which took on a number of ex-SSI workers.

The Lackenby beam mill, on the old SSI site, is the UK's only producer of huge steel sections suitable for high-rise buildings. London's skyline, from the Shard to the Olympic Stadium, started life there.

Ten miles down the coast from Redcar in the village of Carlin How is the Skinningrove 'special profiles' plant, which makes sections, such as track shoes, used in earthmovers.

The village was built for steelworkers. On Friday night there was a public meeting at which people begged local politicians to push for the renationalisation of the steel industry. Linda White, whose husband was laid off at SSI after 36 years, organised it. 'I don't want other families to go through what we went through,' she says.

Once the steel industry was privatised in 1988, the stability of Carlin How disappeared, she says. 'We live in a deprived part of the country that has suffered so much from the austerity measures ... The steelworks is right at the centre of our village. I have grown up listening to the clattering and the banging – people who visit ask how we cope with it but to us it's a really good, positive noise.'

Ben Houchen, the Tory mayor of Tees Valley, has broken party ranks to criticise the government. A blistering quote he gave to the local *Gazette* newspaper took up the entire front page on Thursday: 'Yet again the people of Teesside have been shafted by heartless private investors and a government unwilling to pull their finger out.'

Though it is a private investment firm, Greybull, that has left British Steel on the brink of collapse, most anger in Redcar is directed at Westminster. People can't believe the government has refused Greybull a £50 million loan, which the company says it needs to keep the steelworks going. 'If ministers can find £50 million for a ferry contract with no ships, they can find the money to support this strategic British industry and thousands of jobs. They must act,' Turley says.

'As we know in Redcar, once it is lost it is gone for good, leaving behind huge costs for families and the local community.'

Big plans are afoot to turn the Redcar site into a 'special economic area', which the council estimates will bring in £340 million of rates in the next 25 years. But first the site must be painstakingly decontaminated and dismantled at a cost of more than £1 billion. Who will pay is still unclear. Last Thursday Jeffrey was on her way to the plant to interview for a new chief executive of the South Tees Development Corporation, which oversees the site, and wants to ensure Redcar is not as vulnerable to foreign investors in the future.

She stood down earlier this month after Labour took a beating in the local elections, losing 12 seats to the Lib Dems and a string of independents. Dennis decided not to stand again – it was too hard to juggle with his new job and, anyway, he has lost patience with Labour.

Last Thursday he voted for the Brexit party in the European elections: 'I blame Europe; I blame our government for hiding behind EU state-aid rules ... I said to the MEPs, why aren't you screaming from the rooftops saying there are 5,000 jobs on Teesside going to the wall because the government won't help? So I absolutely voted for Brexit ... we can forge our own way.'

16 June

'They're kids, not rioters': new generation of protesters bring Hong Kong to standstill

EMMA GRAHAM-HARRISON
AND VERNA YU

A vast sea of protesters, most dressed in black and carrying white flowers of mourning, have swept through central Hong Kong to denounce a controversial extradition law and demand the city's leader, Carrie Lam, steps down. Organisers claimed that nearly two million people turned out, which would make the demonstration the largest in Hong Kong's history.

They poured in from all over the territory, in numbers so large that the march route had to be extended, and then widened, with crowds spilling from the main road to fill neighbouring streets, and halting all traffic outside government headquarters.

It was an extraordinary show of grassroots political power in a city where residents cannot choose their leaders but are free to take to the streets to denounce them.

'Before this week I had never been on a protest,' said one 28-year-old. 'But I am a teacher, and I realised if I didn't come I wouldn't be able to face my students. This is their future.' Like many others, she had been unnerved by the arrests of activists and did not want her full name printed.

Lam, the chief executive of Hong Kong, had agreed to suspend the extradition bill after a week of protests, perhaps the most serious government climbdown in the face of public pressure since a security law was dropped in 2003. But if she hoped to defuse public anger before yesterday's march, she badly misjudged the city's mood.

'Suspending the law but not cancelling it is like holding a knife over someone's head and saying, "I'm not going to kill you now." But you could do it any time,' said Betty, an 18-year-old protester who had just finished school. 'We're fighting for our freedom.'

Demonstrators turned out in force, calling on authorities to withdraw the bill, free activists rounded up after previous demonstrations, and hold police accountable for violent crowd-control tactics.

Hong Kong's largest historic demonstration was a 1989 protest against Beijing's bloody crackdown on students. 'If today's turnout was at a record high, as organisers claim, Lam would appear to have succeeded in making Hong Kongers just as anxious and angry as they were about Tiananmen Square,' said Antony Dapiran, author of a history of protest in Hong Kong.

Organisers hoping to keep up pressure on Lam have called for students and workers to strike today and for shops to stay shut. They may expect a further boost from the prominent activist Joshua Wong, who became the face of the 'umbrella' movement in 2014 and is due to be released from prison today.

Many have also demanded Lam's resignation. After hours of protests, she issued a fresh apology 'acknowledging that deficiencies in the government's work' have caused controversy and disputes.

'Our demands are clear. She has not addressed any of them,' said William Cheung, a 31-year-old protester. 'And why can't she apologise in front of a camera, rather than in a dry official statement?'

Hong Kong's most dramatic political crisis in years was set in motion a week earlier, when a million people turned out – dressed mostly in white – to protest against the planned extradition law.

The legislation would allow residents and visitors to be sent for trial in China's opaque communist-controlled courts, which critics say would undermine Hong Kong's economy and society. Lam had shrugged off the first demonstration and vowed to ram the bill through Hong Kong's legislature.

On Wednesday, fresh demonstrations spiralled into the worst political violence since the handover from British rule in 1997, with police attacking protesters, and firing teargas and rubber bullets. There were arrests of activists, including in hospital.

With yesterday's march already scheduled, and public anger heightened by police brutality and the detentions, Lam was eventually forced into her dramatic reversal, reportedly after meeting top Chinese officials across the border.

Protesters said they were infuriated by Lam's air of confident determination as she insisted the law was fundamentally sound, defended police violence and insisted her only mistakes were in communication.

There was a sea of protest signs. 'They are kids, not rioters,' read one. 'HK has become China, we're all stuffed,' said another. Others simply held up sombre images of police violence earlier in the week.

Many protesters also carried white flowers in tribute to a man who fell to his death on Saturday after hanging up a large protest banner on a building in the city centre. Several called the 35-year-old man their 'first martyr'.

Older marchers said that although they feared Hong Kong faced the most serious crisis of their lifetime, they had found hope in the numbers of youth protesters.

'I'm very encouraged by the younger people. If it was just us, the city would be finished,' said one 75-year-old. 'I escaped China when there was a famine, and I saw people being shot there. The Communist party isn't to be trusted.'

Outside the central Wan Chai metro station, a prominent dissident and activist, the Rev Chu Yiu-ming, was greeting protesters arriving at the march. His decades of experience as an activist include helping Tiananmen Square protest leaders escape mainland China in 1989, and he said he could not have imagined as he supported them three decades ago that he would one day face such a bitter fight for his rights at home in Hong Kong.

'We know what the law means in China,' he said, referring to a recent case of a jailed activist. 'We must try to prevent Hong Kong from becoming a totalitarian place.'

Protesters, already concerned by police brutality, fear a further crackdown on activists could be on the way.

24 JUNE

I was Boris Johnson's boss: he is utterly unfit to be prime minister

MAX HASTINGS

Six years ago, the Cambridge historian Christopher Clark published a study of the outbreak of the first world war, titled *The Sleepwalkers*. Though Clark is a fine scholar, I was unconvinced by his title, which suggested that the great powers stumbled mindlessly to disaster. On the contrary, the maddest aspect of 1914 was that each belligerent government convinced itself that it was acting rationally.

It would be fanciful to liken the ascent of Boris Johnson to the outbreak of global war, but similar forces are in play. There is room for debate about whether he is a scoundrel or mere rogue, but not much about his moral bankruptcy, rooted in a contempt for truth. Nonetheless, even before the Conservative national membership cheers him in as our prime minister – denied the option of Nigel Farage, whom some polls suggest they would prefer – Tory MPs have thronged to do just that.

I have known Johnson since the 1980s, when I edited the *Daily Telegraph* and he was our flamboyant Brussels correspondent. I have argued for a decade that, while he is a brilliant entertainer who made a popular maître d' for London as its mayor, he is unfit for national office, because it seems he cares for no interest save his own fame and gratification.

Tory MPs have launched this country upon an experiment in celebrity government, matching that taking place in Ukraine and the US, and it is unlikely to be derailed by the latest headlines. The Washington columnist George Will observes that Donald Trump does what his base wants 'by breaking all the china'. We can't predict what a Johnson government will do, because its prospective leader has not got around to thinking about this. But his premiership will almost certainly reveal a contempt for rules, precedent, order and stability.

A few admirers assert that, in office, Johnson will reveal an accession of wisdom and responsibility that have hitherto eluded him, not least as foreign secretary. This seems unlikely, as the weekend's stories emphasised. Dignity still matters in public office, and Johnson will never have it. Yet his graver vice is cowardice, reflected in a willingness to tell any audience what- ever he thinks most likely to please, heedless of the inevitability of its contradiction an hour later.

Like many showy personalities, he is of weak character. I recently suggested to a radio audience that he supposes himself to be Winston Churchill, while in reality being closer to Alan Partridge. Churchill, for all his wit, was a profoundly serious human being. Far from perceiving anything glorious about standing alone in 1940, he knew that all difficult issues must be addressed with allies and partners.

Churchill's self-obsession was tempered by a huge compassion for humanity, or at least white humanity, which Johnson confines to himself. He has long been considered a bully, prone to making cheap threats. My old friend Christopher Bland, when chairman of the BBC, once described to me how he received an angry phone call from Johnson, denouncing the corporation's 'gross intrusion upon my personal life' for its coverage of one of his love affairs.

'We know plenty about your personal life that you would not like to read in the *Spectator*,' the then editor of the magazine told the BBC's chairman, while demanding he order the broadcaster to lay off his own dalliances. Bland told me he replied: 'Boris, think about what you have just said. There is a word for it, and it is not a pretty one.'

He said Johnson blustered into retreat, but in my own files I have handwritten notes from our possible next prime minister, threatening dire consequences in print if I continued to criticise him.

Johnson would not recognise truth, whether about his private or political life, if confronted by it in an identity parade. The other day I came across an observation made in 1750 by Bishop Berkeley: 'It is impossible that a man who is false to his friends and neighbours should be true to the public.' Almost the only people who think Johnson a nice guy are those who do not know him.

There is, of course, a symmetry between himself and Jeremy Corbyn. Corbyn is far more honest, but harbours his own delusions. He may yet prove to be the only possible Labour leader whom Johnson can defeat in a general election. If the opposition was led by anybody else, the Tories would be deservedly doomed. As it is, the Johnson premiership could survive for three or four years, shambling from one embarrassment and debacle to another, of which Brexit may prove the least.

For many of us, his elevation will signal Britain's abandonment of any claim to be a serious country. It can be claimed that few people realised what a poor prime minister Theresa May would prove until they saw her in Downing Street. With Boris, however, what you see now is almost assuredly what we shall get from him as ruler.

We can scarcely strip the emperor's clothes from a man who has built a career, or at least a lurid love life, out of strutting around without them. The weekend stories of his domestic affairs are only an aperitif for his future as Britain's leader. I have a hunch that Johnson will come to regret securing the prize for which he has struggled so long, because the experience of the premiership will lay bare his absolute unfitness for it.

If the Johnson family had stuck to showbusiness like the Osmonds, Marx Brothers or von Trapp family, the world would be a better place. Yet the Tories have elevated a cavorting charlatan to the steps of Downing Street, and they should expect to pay a full forfeit when voters get the message. If the price of Johnson proves to be Corbyn, blame will rest with the Conservative party, which is about to foist a tasteless joke upon the British people – who will not find it funny for long.

26 JUNE

'The river is treacherous': the migrant tragedy one photo can't capture

PATRICK TIMMONS

Under a hot sun beating down on the US border, a family of five can be seen mid-river, struggling against a cruel current of greenish-grey water threatening to sweep them off their feet. It appears to be a couple and their three children, risking their lives in the treacherous Rio Grande that divides Mexico from Texas.

The father clutches a black backpack in his hand, the family's only luggage. On his back he's carrying a small boy wearing a rainbow-striped T-shirt. A little girl is on the woman's back, small arms clasped tightly around her mother's neck.

A third child, older and taller, in a red shirt, between the two adults, is up to his chest in the water and clutching their wrists. He's battling to stay upright but the current surges and swirls and the parents are propping him up, trying to make sure he's not whipped under.

The family were crossing on Sunday, trying to get to Eagle Pass, a small border town in Texas, east of San Antonio. The riverbank on the American side is about 120ft across from the tiny town of Piedras Negras on the Mexican side.

Some miles downstream to the east, a picture was taken this week of a father and his tiny daughter from El Salvador who didn't make it and drowned together, as the mother was waiting her turn to cross, too, from the Mexican side in Matamoros.

They were two of dozens who have drowned in the border river this year. Others, including toddlers, have been dragged from under the water by border agents and resuscitated.

The family wading from Piedras Negras are in mortal danger and don't seem to be moving forward, as the current strengthens the closer they get to the US riverbank.

If they turn back, Mexico's immigration authorities will almost certainly deport them to whichever Central American country they have probably fled. The only way is forward, to try to seek asylum in the United States.

But as the Trump administration has flown in the face of human rights law, taking harsh measures to block people from crossing the border to seek asylum, many stranded in Mexico have taken to desperate measures.

It's clear, even from the Mexican riverbank yards away, that the boy up to his chest in the river is scared. His father is now tugging on his arm, trying to drag the family on.

Three uniformed US border patrol agents on the Texas side are watching, and chatting, though not acting.

Minutes pass. The family has been in the water for over an hour. Then the agents fire up the loud engine on their boat, drive downstream, then head against the current towards the five. They instruct the family to move to a tiny island in the river, then grab the children and let the adults hoist themselves into the boat.

A government van is waiting and the agents offload the family and usher them into the van, disappearing in the direction of the Eagle Pass border patrol station, where they can expect to be detained as they become part of a clogged legal immigration system.

On the riverbank back on the Mexican side in Piedras Negras, a small group of passersby has watched the crossing unfold. One man, Elodio Vergara Martínez, said he had just come back from church. He clutched the Book of Mormon with white knuckles, from the tension of watching the family dice with death.

'I always walk along the riverbank to and from church. Usually I look for crocodiles in the river. But I haven't seen any. I guess that's kind of lucky for this family,' Vergara Martínez told the *Guardian*.

He added: 'The US agents really should have rescued them sooner. They were just trying to make that family suffer.'

The mayor of Piedras Negras, Claudio Bres Garza, a lifelong resident of the area, said in an interview with the *Guardian* on Tuesday that the level of migration through Mexico is unprecedented, especially involving stricken families from Central America.

'I saw the photos of the drowned father and his baby this morning. I've never seen anything like it. More than eight children have drowned in the river this year. It's insane,' he said.

He added: 'Nothing is going to change until Trump is no longer president. He's just doing everything he can to win next year's elections and thinking of his base. Trump knows that our economy depends on the United States. We know who has the upper hand here.'

Numbers of Mexican law enforcement officers have been increasing in recent days as Donald Trump demands that Mexico crack down on migrants before they attempt to cross the border. More than 200 Mexican federal police officers arrived in Piedras Negras on Saturday, reinforcing Mexican national guard soldiers and immigration agents already there. They guard the river and check people's papers day and night.

On Sunday morning, a family of eight migrants from El Salvador arrived at the migrant shelter run by Catholic nuns in Piedras Negras. The Sánchez Reyes family of three adults and five children said they ran a bakery in San Salvador. But gangs began to extort them, eventually taking their house and business, forcing them to flee after killing a teenage niece.

'We aren't against staying in Mexico. We want to find work here,' the matriarch, Flor Sánchez Reyes, said.

But those words may have been a decoy. Later that day, the Sánchez Reyes family slipped away from the shelter to 'go for a walk and bathe in the river' after their six-hour bus ride from the Mexican interior, they told the *Guardian* by text message. It later emerged that apparently, as they approached the river, Mexico's immigration agents stopped them and asked them for their documents, then detained them.

'If immigration agents caught them by the river then they will almost certainly be deported,' said Isabel Turcios, the nun in charge of the Casa del Migrante shelter in Piedras Negras.

Federal police officers stand out in the hot sun by the turbid waters for 12-hour shifts, with no shade, little water or food.

'We've been told to ask for identification from everybody, and especially from people who look like foreigners. This is exactly how it is where you come from,' one officer, who asked not to be named, said. 'Yesterday we came across a drunk American without a valid visa. We took him to immigration detention and he's going to be deported.'

Another said: 'I know we are doing the work of the US border patrol. It makes me feel really sad. We have become Trump's wall. But what can we do? We have our orders.'

Claudia Hernández, a municipal police officer, said the 'really kind of sneaky' migrants try to reach the river as the guards' shifts change, around 8pm, when the officers are really tired.

'That's when they make a break for the river. You would be surprised at how fast they can run. We can't follow them into the river because it's too dangerous,' she said.

She added: 'The river is treacherous and people who aren't from here don't know that. I grew up here along the Río Bravo river [Río Grande]. I wouldn't even go into that water to bathe or swim. There are springs and whirlpools and when the current takes you it can pull you under and you don't resurface. I've been standing guard at the river for the last two months and it's very sad to watch so many parents risking their lives with their children. It happens all the time.'

Meanwhile, Ángel Díaz, a migrant from Nicaragua, crossed the river with six family members, including his newborn daughter, around dusk on Sunday. The family had said they were going to stay for two days at the migrant shelter in Piedras Negras but instead disappeared late on Sunday afternoon. After several hours of not responding to messages, they got in touch, saying they had made it safely across the river to Eagle Pass.

'Nobody even stopped us as we got into the river. We changed out of our wet clothes and waited for ages on the riverbank. We wanted to turn ourselves in to border patrol,' Díaz said. 'But the van never showed up so we decided to walk into Eagle Pass.'

They found a motel and threw themselves on the mercy of its owner, who said they could pay for a night's stay in Mexican pesos.

'We are trying to figure out what to do,' Díaz said. 'Do we turn ourselves in or try to keep going? We don't have any money and so it's going to be difficult to get out of Eagle Pass. Soon we'll have to make a decision. I think we should turn ourselves in to border patrol.' It was hard to discern from WhatsApp messages whether the family was hopeful or frightened.

Back in Piedras Negras, there are simple wooden crosses in the municipal cemetery, marking paupers' graves where unidentified migrants who drowned on the Mexican side of the river this year were taken to be buried.

Like the father and daughter photographed face down in the Rio Grande a few miles east, it is not possible to know exactly what terrors and prayers crossed their minds in their last seconds, but it is all too easy to imagine.

Summer

Alex Mann: the teenage rap fan who lit up Glastonbury

SARAH MARSH

On Sunday afternoon, Alex Mann was an ordinary teenage rap fan from England's smallest city, enjoying himself at his first Glastonbury festival. By Monday morning, he had been plucked from the crowd at the Other Stage to perform flawlessly in front of thousands – and turned into a social media star.

The 15-year-old in a bucket hat from Wells, Somerset, set social media alight with his barnstorming appearance alongside Dave as the pair performed the rapper's track with AJ Tracey, 'Thiago Silva' – named in honour of the Brazil and Paris Saint-Germain football player. It was, he told the *Guardian*, 'the best time of his life'.

In a BBC video of the moment, which has since been shared widely, Dave – full name David Orobosa Omoregie – asked the crowd: 'Who is sober enough to sing these lyrics with me?'

Alex, who was sitting on the shoulders of a friend, was wearing a PSG shirt with Silva's name on the back, and pulled at the club's emblem as his companions pointed at him, trying to get Dave's attention.

Spotting Alex gesticulating wildly, Dave said: 'I see a PSG shirt over there, but do you know the lyrics?' After Alex responded with a few confident lines, Dave concluded: 'He looks like he knows the lyrics ... Yeah, let's take a chance.'

As Alex took to the stage, Dave briefly reassured him that he would only need to cover AJ Tracey's part – but instead, Alex rattled through every single word of the complex, quickfire tune without hesitation, drawing an admiring pat on the back from the slightly upstaged Dave, and the wild adulation of the crowd.

Yesterday, the *Guardian* contacted Alex via his mother, who said that he would be able to speak after he had had a sleep. When fully rested, the 15-year-old said he had no hesitation about heading to the stage after Dave called on him. 'I thought he might be joking so I thought I'd better get up as quickly as possible,' he said.

He added: 'I'm not sure what was going through my head. I was so nervous. I thought: "What if I mess up?" But then I went on stage and performed and it felt so good.'

The flood of messages he was fielding yesterday were not just from the general public. He had clearly caught the attention of Thiago Silva himself. Currently preparing for Brazil's Copa America semi-final against Argentina tomorrow, Silva congratulated him on his performance and asked for his number to speak over the phone.

'I haven't spoken to him yet, but we're in different time zones,' Alex said. 'I'm not really sure what I will say to him. I really like him as a player, so I'll probably just say that.'

Dave, a rapper, singer, musician and songwriter from south London, whose rich, personal lyrics have won him a string of hits and an Ivor Novello, has also been in touch. 'He was supportive and said that I would get a lot of messages today and if I needed anything to let him know. He said if it got overwhelming he would be there,' Alex said. He added: 'When I was on stage, he [Dave] looked at me and said that if I got stuck and didn't know the lyrics I could look him in the eyes and he would help.

'I've listened to the song plenty of times, to be fair, but I was worried when I went on stage. I didn't think I would know all the lyrics but I did ... I pick up lyrics quite fast,' he said.

After the performance, Alex was stunned by the reaction. 'I walked off stage and the security guards took me back down and it was just amazing,' he said. 'People were screaming my name. I had the best time of my life.'

Although the attention had been a lot to take in – he was taking it in his stride. 'Lots of people have started following me on Twitter and Instagram and liking all my posts ... I am not going to let it get to my head too much.'

Some sceptics online have dismissed the video as a stunt. But Alex insisted that there was no such set-up. 'It was 100 per cent real,' he said. 'Completely just happened ... I have only ever seen him once before, in Bristol.'

As for the future, Alex said he had never considered a career in music. The reaction from the crowd made him realise he had some talent, though. 'I'd be up for performing with him again,' he said. 'And being in a video.'

1 JULY

In praise of the mighty Megan Rapinoe

CHARLIE BRINKHURST-CUFF

It was after she scored the second of two goals against France that the image of the US footballer Megan Rapinoe was captured, her arms thrown out to the world, chest as proud as a sculpted bust. She had made herself as big as she could, settling in the ultimate power stance. As someone who has become an avid watcher of football this Women's World Cup, who once felt I couldn't play the game because of my gender, I felt her defiance, and I revelled in it.

Rapinoe has commandeered the global stage with pink-haired aplomb. Last week she said, in no uncertain terms, that she would not be going to the White House if the US won the tournament. In response, Trump tweeted: 'Megan should never disrespect our Country.'

Rapinoe bit back with two excellent goals last week against home nation France on Friday. She might have said she regrets using a profanity when discussing the Trump visit, but the photo of her triumph was an instant 'screw you' to an establishment that continues to violate LGBT rights.

Rapinoe, who is in a relationship with the basketball player Sue Bird, has been politically outspoken for some time. She took the knee in support of the NFL's Colin Kaepernick in 2016, and has consistently spoken up for LGBT rights. She came out during the 2011 Women's World Cup.

'I feel like sports in general are still homophobic, in the sense that not a lot of people are out,' she told *Out* magazine in 2012, speaking about her sexuality for the first time. 'I feel everyone is really craving [for] people to come out. People want – they need – to see that there are people like me playing soccer for the good ol' US of A.'

England are playing the US in the semi-finals today. While I want to believe football's finally coming home, there will be one other person I'll be rooting for on the balmy pitch – someone who can fight back against big, bad presidents, and blast a twirling, crafty shot into the back of the net.

The big scoop: what a day with an ice-cream man taught me about modern Britain

SIRIN KALE

You are only allowed to play the ice-cream jingle for a maximum of 12 seconds, when the van is approaching its destination. But Tony Roach flicks off the *Popeye* tune after only a moment's airtime. 'That wasn't 12 seconds!' I wail. Roach blinks and looks at me oddly, then promises to play it for longer next time. There's something about ice-cream vans that brings out the child in all of us.

I'm riding shotgun in a pink-and-cream 2009 Whitby Morrison Millennium, accompanying Roach on the same round of Eastbourne, his home town, that he has been doing for 40 years. The weather is warm, the sky is cloudless. Humming the *Popeye* tune under my breath, I help myself to another flake from the box above the fridge. It's going to be a good day.

Known to all as Ice-Cream Tony, 57-year-old Roach learned to scoop practically before he could walk. His father, Paul, was in the trade. 'All I can remember is ice-cream vans,' says Roach. 'From the age of six, I was going with my dad in the ice-cream van and helping. It's all I wanted to do.' Paul taught him how to repair the refrigeration units and the engine. Most mechanics won't touch ice-cream vans because they are complex vehicles, so, like an astronaut going into space, you have to be prepared to fix everything yourself. After his father died, Roach restored his

1972 Bedford CF Morrison van. It was an emotional task. 'He was a great geezer. An ice-cream man through and through.'

Roach bought his first van, a 1965 Bedford CA, for £500 in 1979. He follows Paul's route from the 60s. The streets might be the same, but the days in which ice-cream vans were a staple of local communities are gone. According to the trade body, the Ice Cream Alliance, there are between 2,500 and 5,000 vans operational in the UK, but only 10 per cent of them do street trading. In the 50s, there were 20,000. 'We had a lot of competition in those days,' says Roach. 'Now, street trading is dying.'

The past five years have been the worst, even as ice-cream parlours are one of a handful of growing sectors on the high street. Roach blames the downturn on supermarkets selling ice-cream so cheaply, but competition is not the only reason. Children don't play outdoors as much as they used to; you can't hear the chimes of an approaching ice-cream van over an iPad. And don't get Roach started on Jamie Oliver's war on unhealthy eating: 'That didn't help at all,' he says grimly.

We pull up at our first stop, Roselands infant school, where parents are loitering outside. Roach switches off the engine and we sit there with the hum of the Carpigiani soft-serve machine for company. I feel like a lion watching my prey. The bell rings. Children flood out.

Watching Roach spring into action is marvellous. If, as Malcolm Gladwell claimed, it takes 10,000 hours to achieve mastery in any given field, then Roach – who works seven days a week from the February half-term until October, 6am to 11pm – is a master 10 times over. He is the grandmaster of soft-serve; Don Whippy; King Cone.

But fewer people are buying ice-cream than I thought. It's murder at the infant school, and the primary school further down the road, and the third stop, a local park. In two hours, we sell maybe 20 ice-creams in total. At the park, Roach is anxious to tell me that, the day before, the queue was 20 minutes long.

It's not that the product is bad – it's delicious. Roach uses a fresh milk mix from Mediterranean Ices, and is snobbish about providers who make their ice-cream from UHT. 'I can always taste a UHT mix. You notice it when they're walking away from the van. You see how it runs down the edges? It's melting. That doesn't happen with fresh mix.' I look down at the cone I've been holding absent-mindedly, and he's right – no drip.

But people don't have as much money to spend as before. Outside Stafford school, a child whines that his cone isn't big enough. 'That's all the money we have,' says his mother, exasperated. 'I'm not having anything for myself!' Later, at the Kingsmere estate, 40-year-old Christina Ward looks at the menu and says: 'It's well expensive, isn't it?' Roach's kindly mien slips for a moment behind his wraparound shades. 'It's only £2,' he retorts. Ward relents and buys three cones.

Although Roach's products are keenly priced – £2 for a small cone with flake, up to £3 for a large – if you have a few kids, that's not much change from a tenner. Almost everyone buys small cones now, whereas before they would buy big ones, says Roach. 'Since Brexit, people have less money, and less confidence in spending money. They haven't got the money in their pockets they had a few years ago.' (Eastbourne voted leave.) As sales falter, Roach has diversified away from street trading, towards events, which are more lucrative.

Turning ice-cream vans into a novelty for corporate dos and wedding receptions is a social loss; after so many years spent chugging around suburban streets, Roach is part of the fabric of his community. He knows Eastbourne's circadian rhythms: what time the schools get out, when families eat their tea and where children play outside (if they play outside at all – the period after teatime used to be his busiest, but now kids stay in).

Often, as punters approach the van, he tells me their orders. 'He's going to ask for three medium cones with a flake,' Roach says of one older gentleman in a check shirt. (He does.) We serve 17-year-old Brendan Brooks, whose mother bought from Roach as a young girl. In Langley, retired train driver John Carney, 66, has been a customer for 20 years. 'He brings the kids out, and they can see each other, because nowadays we don't let children outside, they're inside being cocooned ... And the mums and dads come out, so it's a chance for us to have a chat, too.'

From his vantage point on Eastbourne's quiet cul-de-sacs, Roach sees social change up close – such as how people don't carry cash any more. 'Two or three years ago, if someone said I'd be taking cards, I wouldn't believe it! But now you have to.' He's an expert on Britain's changing palates. Recently, people have started asking for vegan ice-cream. Roach doesn't have any, but he does have dog ice-cream – not because dogs are more deserving than vegans, but because he did a dog show last week. Roach has observed more worrying trends, too, such as the climate emergency. 'We're having different weather than we had 20 years ago,' he says darkly. 'The weather's changing ... we get very hot spells and then very wet spells.' The Goldilocks weather for selling ice-cream, incidentally, is 21°C, says Roach: 'That's just nice. I don't like it too hot ... people can get a bit grumpy when it's too hot.'

But as our summers buzz longer and hotter, there is one constant: we Brits absolutely love soft-serve ice-cream. 'People's tastes change. But they can't resist a 99.' Mr Whippy is British culture. 'Other countries just don't get it. It's a British thing. It'll be raining on a bank holiday, but we'll still have an ice-cream. It's one of those things only British people understand.'

Soft-serve ice-cream is actually an American import. Mister Softee came to the UK in the 50s, but it wasn't long before we concocted a homegrown rival, Mr Whippy, which was founded in Birmingham in 1958. Mr Whippy is the ultimate leveller, beloved by celebrities – Roach has served Piers Morgan and Davina McCall – and ordinary folk alike. Tony Blair wrote in his 2010 memoir, *A Journey*, about being forced by spin doctors to buy cones for himself and Gordon Brown during the 2005 election trail. (Blair is not a fan.)

Mr Whippy is elemental nostalgia. 'Bing-bong, bingety bongety bong,' wrote Simon Schama in a 2007 *Vogue* essay. 'Mr Whippy is calling, and we, short-trousered, snake-belted, grimy-kneed, snot-nosed, want what he's got. We want a 99, God, how we want it.' You only need to hear the opening bars of 'Green-sleeves' and you're nine years old again, scrambling for change then bolting barefoot out of the door. 'Every time you heard that song played, even when you were little, you knew he was there,' says 44-year-old restaurant worker Stephen Humphreys, handing his daughter Aaliyah a cone. He bought from Roach as a child. 'Quick, get the money together, leg it there before he goes.'

Being an ice-cream man has kept Roach young. He credits his sprightliness to eating ice-cream every day for 40 years. He rarely goes on holiday, but when he does, the first thing he does is have a local ice-cream. ('It's always rubbish. Not as good as mine.') In winter, Roach restores vintage vans – he has a fleet of 12. At the beachfront, we bump into his wife, Yvonne – they have been married for 25 years. She confirms that ice-cream is not just a live-lihood for Roach – he picked her up for their first date in the van. A self-styled 'ice-cream widow', Yvonne says Roach was meant to retire at 50, but keeps putting it off. 'It's never going to happen, and I've accepted it.' Yvonne asks her husband for a cone. 'I hope you've got some money on you!' he says.

During a lull, Roach shows me the trick to making the perfect Mr Whippy: you rotate the cone in a circle, then pull it away from the machine to create the point. (I am lousy.) At the Kingsmere estate, we sell three ice-creams and a slush puppy to 51-year-old reiki master Russell Dobson. 'When they hear the noise,' Dobson says, gesturing to his son, 'you tell them: "There's none left."' 'You can't do that!' Roach exclaims. 'That's what everyone tells them,' Dobson says. 'Did you not know that?' (Later, at a playground, a girl of about five or six runs up to the van and asks if we've sold out. When Roach shakes his head, she looks confused, then enraged.)

The day draws on and Roach and I drive through quietening residential streets, past pebbledash houses and trampolines and garden gnomes. There are mums with prams, dads in tracksuits and flip-flops, children in school uniforms on scooters. Women come out of houses in bathrobes with wet hair and buy ice-cream to take indoors.

Tony Roach holds Eastbourne together with engine grease and dairy cream. Like his father before him, he is an ice-cream man through and through – but he may well be among the last. Roach is at the heart of a dying trade, and a rapidly melting community. It occurs to me that this may be the fictitious Arcadia that Brexiters want: communities where the ice-cream man knows your name and your order, and your mother's order before yours, and her grandmother's order before that, probably. They have been searching for it, but it's already here. This summer, at least.

12 July

Syriza's defeat shows the left needs a plan to hold on to power, not just win it

GARY YOUNGE

The day after Jeremy Corbyn scraped together the parliamentarians' names he needed to get on the Labour leadership ballot in 2015, he headed off in search of voters. 'We didn't have a campaign. We didn't have an organisation. We didn't have any money,' he told me. 'All we had was my credit card and that lasted for about a week.'

He stood so that at least one candidate would make the argument that Labour should oppose austerity and shift to the left. No one ever expected him to win that argument, least of all him. But as the rallies grew, unions came on board and his polling numbers soared, the implausible started to look inevitable.

Just a few weeks before he won the biggest mandate of any candidate in Labour history, his advisers told him to make plans for his victory. Corbyn thought they were tempting fate. 'I'm not even going there,' he told them. 'Please don't talk about it.' Not yet fully accustomed to the notion that his candidacy was viable, he could not contemplate how he would handle victory. It was almost as though he was the last person to take his candidacy seriously – a factor that arguably contributed to the early chaos of his leadership.

That trajectory of oppositionism, exhilaration, shock and denial culminating in the sobriety of actually winning illustrates the story of the western left, from the US to much of Europe, over the past five years. After decades of being on the outside they have surprised themselves, and enthused millions, with an electoral message that provided a way in, now they have to figure out what to do with the trust and credibility invested in them. They used to stand to make a point. Now they stand for power. Having developed a strategy to win, they now have to demonstrate a strategy to lead and govern.

That is why the defeat of Syriza in Greece on Sunday was so significant. After four and a half years in power, the once radical-left party led by Alexis Tsipras lost to the centre-right New Democracy party, led by the scion of a Greek political dynasty. Presiding over anaemic growth, abandoned by the young at the polls where there was a marked slump in turnout, Syriza appeared to become the very thing it sought to replace.

The party's victory in January 2015 was an inflection point in the emergence of a vital and vibrant leftward shift in western politics, providing a response to the financial crisis and the austerity that emerged from it. 'Greece has turned a page,' said Tsipras on election night, 'leaving behind destructive austerity, fear and authoritarianism. It is leaving behind five years of humiliation and pain.'

In July 2015 came the referendum in which the nation emphatically rejected the terms of the punitive bailout conditions imposed on it by the European Union and International Monetary Fund. Before the end of the year, Corbyn was leading Labour; the Left Bloc had doubled its vote in Portugal and was propping up a social democratic government; Syriza won another election and Podemos, a new radical party in Spain that emerged from youth protests, had won 21 per cent at the polls and was threatening to supplant the mainstream left socialist party. The next year started with the democratic socialist candidate, Bernie Sanders, achieving a virtual tie with Hillary Clinton in the first contest for the Democratic presidential nomination.

One election cycle on from Syriza's initial victory, this trend of left insurgency has proved itself to be both viable and vulnerable. It has continued at a diminished pace in different countries with various levels of impact, from eclipsing centre-left parties (France, the Netherlands) to propping up minority governments (Denmark and Sweden). In Britain Labour gained vote share and seats but not power. There have been occasional setbacks (support for Podemos has collapsed) and omissions (electorally, there is little sign of left life in Italy or much change in Germany). The far right, it should be noted, has made even greater strides.

Greece, however, is the one country where the left has actually governed. Some of the lessons of Syriza's defeat are particular to Greece – a relatively small economy, tied into the eurozone. But there are three broader lessons that a left serious about the prospect of government might learn.

First, only propose an agenda to take on powerful interests if you have a strategy to fight them and fully intend to pursue it. After it became clear that the EU and IMF would take no notice of the popular rejection of the bailout proposal, Syriza effectively folded. Unable to beat its creditors, it joined them, implementing all the cuts, privatisations, and VAT increases it had been elected to oppose.

According to the account of Yanis Varoufakis, the finance minister at the time, the Greeks had options, though it soon became clear to him that Tsipras never seriously intended to employ them. There were no guarantees they would have been successful but once they abandoned their own agenda it was certain to fail. Either way, Syriza's defeat was less a failure of left policies than of a left electoral strategy that had no plan B for the predictable obstacles it would face.

Second, there is a limit to how much any election can achieve under neoliberal globalisation – because no matter who you vote for, capital and its proxies always get in. The nation state may be where democratic legitimacy primarily resides but it is just one player among many, from currency traders to international organisations. You cannot simply vote yourself out of it.

That was made clear to Greece. 'Elections cannot be allowed to change an economic programme of a member state,' the former German finance minister Wolfgang Schäuble told Varoufakis. 'There can be no democratic choice against the European treaties,' said the European commission president, Jean-Claude Juncker.

That's not necessarily a reason for the left to eschew electoral politics. But it should frame expectations about what can be achieved and where power lies.

Finally, and consequently, the left cannot limit itself to an electoral strategy alone. Many major social and political advances, from civil rights, workers' rights, feminism and even democracy itself, started as social movements to distribute and democratise power. Professional politicians signed them into law. But it took a coalition between the electoral and the social to make them happen. In power, more than ever, it needs social movements to sustain these advances.

In four years, the left has created electoral and political space it had not imagined possible. Whether it can hold that space depends on what it builds on it.

14 JULY

Lord's, the perfect venue for the greatest one-day game ever played

ANDY BULL

The sun was out when England won the World Cup. It had emerged, at last, from behind the freckles of white cloud and was shining low through the bright blue sky over the Grand Stand.

The shadows stretched all the way to the wicket, the flags licked in the evening breeze, the pavilion glowed soft terracotta. The old place looked pretty as a picture, exactly how we see it in winter when thinking back on the games we saw, and the games we played, in the long, warm days of summer. For the 11 men in this England team, for the thousands in the ground, for the millions watching on TV, that is how they will always see it in their minds, years from now, when they think back on this match: the greatest World Cup final, heck maybe even the greatest game of one-day cricket, ever played.

The dizzying, sickening, drama of those final minutes made for a stretch of sport as compelling as anything else that will happen this year, as gripping as anything, in fact, that has happened in the 14 years since the England cricket team last played live on free-to-air TV in 2005. Accurate viewing figures are notoriously hard to come by but, if Channel 4 could ever get hold of theirs for this broadcast, they will be disappointed with them because, even though all those sets were on around the country, surely most of the people in front of them were too scared to watch what was going on, were hiding behind their sofas or sneaking glimpses from between their fingers.

At Lord's there were old England players, heroes some of them – men who failed to do exactly what this England team were trying to – who were hiding in the toilets, too paralysed with old superstitions to move. 'I thought you weren't supposed to care when you stopped playing,' one of the 2011 team confided as he stared into the mirror over the sink. He was following it all by the gasps and roars coming through the walls. Outside they were living every last second, as though they were the ones who had to make the runs, take the wickets and catches. And even in the pavilion, the stately, sedate members seemed to be screaming and shouting the yeses and noes of those final few runs.

The tension had been growing all day, winding tighter and tighter from way back in the morning, from the moment, in fact, that Kane Williamson won the toss and said he would bat first. After that the prospect of the run chase loomed over the morning and early afternoon like those high tower blocks behind the Mound and Tavern Stands, where the roof terraces and balconies were packed with people taking the long view from over the road. Williamson's decision set it all up to be a stress test. England were shouldering all the pressure that has built up over four years of preparing for this match, and, before that, from 40 more of failure, laced with all that disappointment, humiliation and horror. He was banking on the fact that they would crack.

That approach seemed to inform his batting strategy, too. New Zealand got just enough. And when England were 86 for four, Jason Roy, Jonny Bairstow, Joe Root and Eoin Morgan all gone, and their luck seemingly used up on inside edges that flew past the stumps and an lbw call that was an umpire's whim away from being given out, it looked as if just enough was going to be more than they needed.

England's fans were suffering now. They had hope, if not faith, their stores of that diminished by the transgenerational trauma of following the team's futile efforts to win this tournament before, the memories of Mike Gatting trying to hit that reverse sweep off Allan Border, of Wasim Akram's inswingers, of being battered by South African all-rounders, bashed up by Lance Klusener and bowled out by Andrew Hall, of Freddie Flintoff's 4am jaunt in a pedalo, of being belaboured by Kevin O'Brien, steamrollered by Tillakaratne Dilshan.

So optimism was rationed like wartime jam. For most of the day Lord's was alive with anxious chatter, a jittery, skittery babbling, 'what do you think, can they, could they, will they, maybe?' It rose to a new pitch in the penultimate over, when England needed 22 runs to win with nine balls to go. There was that catch at long-on by Trent Boult, who stepped on to the boundary rope and slipped over backwards even as he tried to toss the ball up to his team-mate Martin Guptill to complete a relay catch that would have won the match. Then there was the six Stokes hit in the next over, clean, this time, over mid-wicket, to make it nine needed from the last three. And that ricochet away when Guptill's throw from deep mid-wicket hit Stokes's bat as he dived in for his second run.

New Zealand hardly seemed to believe it but it meant there were three needed off two balls. England got two of them. But everyone knows that, of course. Everyone in earshot of a TV or a computer, in hearing distance of a radio or within sight of a newspaper surely knows already how the game went to a super over and how, when it was all over and the two sides had made 15 runs each without losing a wicket, the only way they could be separated was by counting back the boundaries they had scored.

Well, it will stand the retelling, here and countless times ever after, in pubs and clubs and bars, magazine articles, TV documentaries and books. Maybe, when they tell it then, some will say they always knew how it was going to play out. Do not believe them – because until Jos Buttler swept off the bails that last time to make the final run-out, everyone was still thinking of the team England were, not the team they are. Now, after that and everything else that happened this Sunday in the high summer of 2019, no one will make the mistake again.

16 JULY

Trump's 'go back' racism is crude, but may be dangerously effective

AFUA HIRSCH

Pity Donald Trump. Even his racism is the most unsophisticated kind. Every black and brown person knows a 'go back to where you came from' racist. For many of us who have never been migrants, to have this muttered at us was the first signal that to be a visible minority means to be forever perceived as an immigrant. And that being perceived as an immigrant is bad.

'Go back' racists are rarely intellectually capable of engaging with the question of whether the destination they deem so suitable for us actually exists. Trump's latest outburst – in which he said four congresswomen should 'go back and help fix the totally broken and crime-infested places from which they came', is a case in point. For the US president to say of Ayanna Pressley, Ilhan Omar, Alexandria Ocasio-Cortez and Rashida Tlaib, 'if they're not happy here, they can leave', makes no sense because the women in question are Americans. Yet it makes perfect sense because they are not white.

The idea that Pressley, who is African American – a community which this year marks the 400th anniversary of having been forcibly brought to the US – should be driven out because she has a view that Trump finds inconvenient is exactly the racism that bigots have always expressed.

It seems obvious to me that Trump knew his remarks were racist; they were intended to be so. Not only did he claim these congresswomen had other countries to go back to – when three of the four were, in fact, born in the US – he then characterised those places not only as 'crime-infested' but with governments that are 'a complete and total catastrophe, the worst, most corrupt and inept anywhere in the world'. After a short break from Twitter, a round of golf and a chance to see the reaction, Trump then reiterated his remarks in person, at a press conference on the White House lawn.

The president denies the racism, of course. His latest tweet claims, laughably, that he doesn't 'have a racist bone in his body', while his Twitter feed alternates between evidence of his racism and denials of it: a Fox story celebrating 'cool' new Republicans of colour, and a video of a black man wearing a 'Keep America Great' cap denouncing the idea there is anything racist about Trump. It was cringe-inducing to see vice-president Mike Pence's chief of staff, asked about the row, playing the 'I have black friends' card. Trump isn't racist, Marc Short insisted, 'he has an Asian woman of colour in his cabinet'. The congressional Republican party's response was deafening in its silence.

On the whole, however, Americans have been fairly unambiguous about calling a spade a spade. Those who recognised that a line had been crossed included George Conway, the husband of Trump's adviser Kellyanne Conway – who wrote powerfully about his experience of similarly racist remarks in his own childhood – and Will Hurd, the sole black Republican House member, who described Trump's tweets as 'racist', 'xenophobic' and 'inaccurate'.

'Go back' racism is all of those things. But that doesn't mean it isn't incisive. As with most prejudice, it says so much more about the person making the remark than it does the intended recipient. It reveals a person who subscribes to the myth of 'indigeneity' (that a person cannot fully belong to a nation if they're not of a certain race); that they fantasise about their multicultural nation reverting to an imagined past steeped in the fantasy of white, racial purity. It shows an interpretation of the relationship between citizens and the state that is rooted in whiteness – believing, like Trump, that people of colour have no right to criticise power, even though democracy depends on it.

It's ugly and yet, as a black British person, I find a certain relief in witnessing the US version of this problem. As our leaders are fond of saying, we have more in common than divides us. Both our nations are in the grip of populist movements. Both have governments that attack the identities of people of colour in a race to the bottom for nationalist support. Both have depicted immigration as an existential threat, and both have policies that are merging questions of immigration status into questions of race.

In the UK, the 'hostile environment' saw British people of Caribbean and African heritage with a right to stay in the country – in the case of the Windrush scandal, specifically invited into it decades earlier – treated like criminal stowaways. In the US, Trump's immigration and customs enforcement raids have seen black and brown US citizens feeling compelled to carry their documents around with them to avoid being wrongly identified as illegal immigrants. In both countries, we know that to be a visible minority means to face a presumption of guilt when it comes to our immigration status. The difference between Britain and the US, however, is that while Americans are having an argument about their known problem of racism, in Britain we are still having an argument about whether an argument even needs to be had.

Theresa May, who brought in the 'Go home' immigration vans, felt able to condemn Trump's remarks about the four congresswomen as if from a position of moral authority. Media personalities such as Piers Morgan – who has questioned my right to criticise British 'heroes' – or columnists who say that black British figures such as Stormzy should be 'grateful' to be in their own country, vigorously deny racism is intended.

Americans are more likely to acknowledge the existence of the kind of racism about which British people remain in denial. The problem in the US is that racism still has its uses. The question for the next presidential election will increasingly be, how many are willing to be complicit in the cost of that racism in exchange for the benefit – in this case, the support of an electoral base fired up by the president's reviling of migrants and people of colour.

In a press conference responding to Trump's remarks, the congresswomen affected expressed a desire not to let Trump's tweets achieve what is, in reality, always racism's true intent: distraction. 'We should not take the bait,' Pressley said. She is right. Trump is turning on these congresswomen quite deliberately, having calculated that, regardless of their policies – which are centred substantially on addressing class inequality – US voters aren't ready for a Democratic party which looks like them.

Yet it would be wrong to be dismissive of rhetoric as racist as this. Its intended purpose is certainly to play on the fears our racialised pasts have deposited in the present. But that can be a very reliable political strategy.

18 JULY

What I've learned as a nurse watching people die in remote rural Scotland

COLLETTE COWIE

There are very few experiences as unique, sobering and intimate for a nurse as entering a stranger's house in the middle of the night and watching them die.

THE BEDSIDE GUARDIAN 2019

There's no hospice provision where I'm based in rural north Scotland. For those diagnosed with progressive, incurable illnesses such as cancer or heart failure, a health professional will offer them a preferred place of death. It's a stark choice: a bed in the local community hospital (if available) or die at home.

For most of the farming families I visit, it's an easy decision. 'They'll have to carry me out of here in a box' is a familiar refrain. The farms have been passed down from generation to generation and with it a way of life that is all-encompassing – right up to the point where it ends.

I was once called to visit an elderly woman in the terminal stages of her illness. Lying barely conscious in the bed, she no longer had the strength to lift herself up, though the agitation in her face and limbs indicated she had not stopped trying. 'Can you believe she was out in the yard counting the cows this morning?' her daughter asked me in astonishment. 'And complaining because I was ushering her back inside.'

Earlier that afternoon the district nurse had inserted a tube into her bladder to allow the urine to drain. It had fallen out and a new one was required. 'Did she pull it out?' I asked, wincing at the sight of the intact balloon that should have been sitting at the neck of the bladder, and contemplating the potential journey it had made from there to freedom. 'Ah, no. It just dropped out,' said the daughter over her shoulder as she continued with the washing-up. 'She's had so many children I'd be surprised if anything stays up there for long now.'

The farms are often sprawling stone buildings surrounded by fields and potholed tracks, impossible to find by satnav, unlit and barely noticeable in the middle of the night. They're positioned high on hills so steep that when the weather is heavy the professional composure you assumed when disembarking from the car is lost and you find yourself sliding back down the slope, feet unable to grip, flailing like a cartoon.

People who live out there are tough, melded by the work and the weather, with a rare stoicism.

I work night shifts. In the small hours, driving around the countryside can be spectacular. Mine is the only vehicle on the road, swerving round deer startled by the headlights or slowing down for lolloping badgers and panicking pheasants. At the height of summer, the light barely fades at night and, once or twice, I've been caught awestruck beneath a meteor shower, the vast open night sky totally filled with light for an instant.

Pain is a big potential issue during the dying process – for both the patient and their family. Sometimes I feel totally inadequate as I open the so-called 'just in case' box and look at the handful of vials I can administer for pain, agitation or nausea.

My colleague likes to tell of a patient whose unresolved abdominal pain was a huge problem as she neared death, and the eventual solution that became like the holy grail among practitioners. It finally came when the nurse had a conversation with the elderly patient who confided that, as a proud woman, she did not want anyone to see her without her dentures.

The thing she feared most about death was someone removing her teeth after the event and being powerless to stop them. The moment the nurse reassured her she would ensure the teeth would be left intact, the woman's pain, untreatable by morphine and any amount of adjunct therapy, simply dissolved. She experienced a peaceful death.

The deaths I see are rarely just about one person dying. The family and loved ones are part of the experience, as, I guess, are us nurses. The journey towards death can be hard to navigate. Sometimes it is not peaceful and we cannot resolve the pain or agitation. 'They'll have to take me out of here in a box' seems glib when you're watching a patient or loved one unable to articulate their experience and tossing and turning restlessly for hours, turning us all into onlookers who can only guess what they might need. But it's also a truly human experience, the point that all our lives lead to – and, for me as a nurse, as humbling as that meteor shower.

23 JULY

Boris Johnson's election as Tory leader

STEVE BELL

245245245245

A cabinet purged: 'I hope Boris has thought this through properly'

JESSICA ELGOT

Boris Johnson promised time and again to Tory MPs who came for cosy chats before his leadership bid that he would not call an election. Yet his first hours in office, when he sacked 18 of his cabinet ministers and promised a top team that looked like 'modern Britain', set teeth on edge among Tory MPs in parliament.

Arriving back at Downing Street after an hour of defenestrations in his new House of Commons office, Johnson installed leading faces of Vote Leave in the top jobs: Priti Patel, Dominic Raab, Michael Gove and Andrea Leadsom.

Inside, his staff look like the referendum backroom team reassembled, including Dominic Cummings and Lee Cain, his new director of communications. 'He has effectively got Vote Leave back together,' one Johnson-backing MP said. 'And if I was the Spartans [the hardcore Brexiters who have resisted voting for a deal], or the Labour party, I would be scared of them because they are very, very good.

'There's nobody else in politics better than them at campaigning. It's a wink saying, "I might just have an election, you know." And that's all deliberate. The Labour and Conservative mutual interest is in not having an election before Brexit is done. So that is the way you get the deal through. It's "vote for the deal or hold an election".'

Another frontbencher said that an election looked like an implicit threat. 'Doing this helps you get a deal through – you look ready,' the MP said. 'It is such an obvious play, as is filling your cabinet with all these potential rebels and sacking the people who will vote for you anyway.'

The appointments have not only unnerved the soft wing of the party. Cummings' appointment has also alienated a number of Eurosceptics. One source said veteran Brexiters including Johnson's campaign chair Iain Duncan Smith, Bill Cash and Owen Paterson were furious. Cummings, a former director of Vote Leave, where he clashed repeatedly with old-time Eurosceptics, had previously worked for Duncan Smith, but then publicly branded him 'incompetent'.

For a politician given to rambling speeches, Johnson's first afternoon as prime minister was ruthlessly efficient. He was greeted at the door of No 10 with a firm handshake from the cabinet secretary Mark Sedwill, but the new prime minister spent barely half an hour behind the black door with his new civil servants before he jumped in his motorcade to parliament to set the wrecking ball on May's cabinet.

'There is a sense of urgency,' one source close to Johnson said. 'He has always made clear he wanted this done straight away.'

Johnson spent just over an hour sacking ministers inside his Commons office, to spare them the humiliation of walking up Downing Street. The first dismissal came as the biggest shock. Penny Mordaunt, the first female defence secretary, was out of her job after just two months. Allies of Mordaunt said she had been desperately keen to stay, but the overnight briefing that the role had been offered to Jeremy Hunt had been hurtful.

'She was sacked, she did not resign or turn down anything else,' one source close to her said.

Hunt was offered the job of defence secretary on Tuesday night and made it clear that he could not accept what he considered to be a demotion. One close ally said he was horrified that Mordaunt was then sacked and he was called in to be offered the job of defence again – and made that clear to Johnson.

'How could Jeremy have done that to Penny, when she'd been such an asset to the campaign?' the source said. 'It was unthinkable.'

As Johnson raced through the rest of his appointments, his leadership rival headed out for a long boozy dinner with his friend and fellow sacked departee, Liam Fox.

'Sacking Jeremy was massively unnecessary,' one of his team fumed. 'That's 40 per cent of the party who backed him – where on earth does this get Boris?'

Another high-profile Hunt backer called the promotions of Raab and Patel in particular, as Hunt and Mordaunt went the other way, 'quite difficult for a lot of us'.

A shake-up had been expected, but only the previous night Johnson had promised 'the love-bombing starts here' to MPs at the backbench 1922 Committee. 'This is more like an actual bomb,' one MP said.

A passing minister, watching some of the cars depart, said: 'I hope Boris has thought about this properly.'

Another MP, a close friend and former colleague of Johnson, said he had not expected such mass firings. 'I know these guys really well,' he said. 'But this surprises even me.'

Yet some gave a more cutting verdict on the departing ministers and several observed they were all people who could be relied on not to rebel. 'The political strategy is he knows he must get a deal through – and these people will vote for anything,' one frontbencher said.

'It is very bold – but how many of those who were sacked would you really want in your cabinet? Who is going to honestly

THE BEDSIDE GUARDIAN 2019

get outraged about Karen Bradley or Chris Grayling or James Brokenshire?'

Several of those who had waited to be sacked rather than walk already knew their time was up. The outgoing business secretary, Greg Clark – who did not pre-emptively resign – did hold pre-emptive leaving drinks, carrying trays of wine for his team late into the evening on the Commons terrace on Tuesday night.

Four resignations came even before Johnson entered No 10, though none were surprising. The chancellor, Philip Hammond, and the justice secretary, David Gauke, made pointed comments in speeches behind closed doors before handing over their resignations.

Hammond gave his closest aides red wine and crisps in his office on Tuesday evening, before chatting to Treasury civil servants on his way out yesterday.

'He said people should keep an eye on his Twitter and he expects to be a lot more active,' one Treasury source said. 'He underlined how important it would be for the incoming chancellor to have a smooth relationship with No 10.'

Hammond's resignation letter devoted precious little space to praising his outgoing boss.

Gauke, the departing justice secretary, gave a farewell speech to staff inside the Ministry of Justice, where sources said he used his own parting blow to loudly champion the need for an independent and bold civil service.

The new machine still had a few loose cogs. Despite an overnight press release which briefed that Tracey Crouch would be handed a big cabinet job, it appeared no one from Johnson's team had bothered to check whether that would be OK with her. She said she would prefer to spend the summer with her young son.

Some MPs were still expecting a further clear-out of the junior ranks. Even so, MPs said they expected many of Johnson's beaming acolytes to be disappointed.

Some have already taken roles below what they had hoped for – both Liz Truss and Matt Hancock had publicly lobbied for the roles of chancellor or business secretary.

'I don't know how unhappy Matt will be, to be honest,' one MP said of Hancock, who will stay as health secretary. 'He looked this morning like someone who was extremely worried he was about to have his head chopped off.'

One minister likened the number of supporters expecting jobs to an overbooked easyJet flight: 'Everyone thinks they've got a seat, but some aren't even on the waiting list. Some are just looking hopefully at their compensation vouchers in the lounge.'

27 JULY

Holidaying alone is glorious – what took me so long to admit it?

GRACE DENT

At 6am in Portugal, at the pristine breakfast buffet, unbesmirched by human hand as I'm its first customer, I fill a plate with sugary pastries. Yes, they'll bloat me in my bikini, but who cares? I'm holidaying alone. Flying solo. A 'single Pringle', one holidaymaker joked, as I chuckled along at our shared bit of fun, inwardly imagining hammering him to death with a flip-flop.

But the fact is, 'single occupancy' has turned out to be so much fun, I wonder if its life-enhancing loveliness has been hushed up for decades? By travel agents and multidenominational faith leaders, and other forces dedicated to preserving the status quo.

I've long suspected that the term 'family holiday' is an oxymoron, and now I feel more sure.

I pen this missive from the sun-battered Algarve, where I've spent seven days in glorious isolation and, for long stretches, in complete silence. I've tottered about from dawn to dusk like a slighty less pickled Princess Margaret, quite literally pleasing myself. This was not meant to happen when I booked a last-minute break, sensing that yet again, as a child-free woman, I was about to let summer ride past without downtime, covering the gaps of other people's summer breaks, letting July quickly become September. I wasn't meant to prefer it. I wasn't meant to think: 'Next time: two weeks.' This break has made me realise just how much a normal #squad holiday is about compromise – exactly like everyday life. We bite our lips and bury our needs. We're on holiday, so let's not bicker. No, I don't mind washing up. No, I won't upgrade my flight if you can't. Oh, you like bullfighting, how charming! On holiday alone, I have not been available for this bullshit.

As a naturally very early riser, I've been first in the hotel gym, before grabbing the best-positioned pool lounger. No dead wood has held me back. Apologies to all friends and family who have vacationed with me in the past, but we all know that getting five grownups plus kids to a beach within 120 minutes is like a terrible *Crystal Maze* puzzle. During the day, I've cut a solo figure on the tourist trail, examining eerie skull-encrusted crypts in Faro – which I know would have been too brutal for some eyes. I've cracked into a goldfish bowl-sized G&T on the cusp of midday and taken a long, indulgent nap by mid-afternoon. At night I dine earlier than a pensioner, then pass out asleep as the resort goes out partying.

Repeat seven times, blissfully, swapping out 'visit to the bone crypt' for 'round trip of the resort on the silly Noddy Train with the parpy horn'. It was the sort of train that I always want to go on when I'm on holiday with my partner or in a group, but everyone always says is ridiculous. The thing is, I am ridiculous. I love a stupid parpy tourist train. It reminds me of the train at Pontins when I was a little girl, trundling along, holding hands with my dad. I like waving back at strangers when they wave at me. 'Hello! Look at me! I'm on a train!' I say, flapping my hand. It's pure joy.

This is my very first holiday alone and it pains me that I've waited so long. And although I wasn't stopped by fear, because I've flown all over the world for work purposes for decades, I was certainly held back by shame. 'Are you meeting friends there?' asked the British Airways hostess, as she served me champagne (I upgraded: bite me), which felt a little like pity but could also have been surveillance on whether I was trafficking narcotics into the east Algarve in my ridiculous boil-washed Helena Bonham Carter crow's nest hair. I've watched at least 100 episodes of *UK Border Force* on channel Pick, I know what goes on.

'Yes, they're all out there already,' I lied, wondering if I should embellish further. Add in some children? No, no more lying, I told myself. If anyone else bothers to inquire, I shall answer their nosiness with unflinching honesty. It happened a few days later at dinner, when I found myself chatting to a group in a restaurant. My situation had intrigued them. Was I a widow? A divorcee? An air hostess? Just chronically antisocial? No, I said, I am none of these things, I am just a normal human being and very tired. My partner is working right through the summer and my friends presently need to holiday in places with ball pits and nightly Macarena Kids' Club performances.

And, well, my father is dying. Slowly, very slowly, of Alzheimer's, which has left me in a perpetual decade-long state of what I realise now is ambiguous grief, a grief which never truly has closure, because although he is no longer here, he is here. Vivid and breathing. This makes it easy (and I think it's like this for a lot of people, in different hard situations) to believe that the trick is to keep going. To keep working. To keep being useful. To never, ever take a holiday. Because who could holiday when all this is happening? And when I get there on this holiday, a woman alone, what will strangers think?

The answer to this, after a long pause, was a stunned but empathetic nod, and then more silence. But seeing as I love silence, and I was having the greatest holiday of my entire life, this worked out incredibly well.

1 AUGUST

Word of the week: 'Boosterism'

STEVEN POOLE

Asked this week what his new economic policy was, Alexander Boris de Pfeffel Johnson replied: 'Boosterism!' He wanted to put 'rocket boosters' on the British economy, as a way of 'turbocharging' it. Turbocharging (in aviation, originally 'turbo-supercharging') sounds perfectly thrilling, as long as the vehicle one turbocharges is not heading straight for a concrete wall. But is it quite the same as 'boosterism'?

A rocket 'booster' is the massive first stage of a multipart rocket, such as the Saturn V that delivered the Apollo 11 astronauts to the moon. But the verb 'to boost', as well as meaning 'to steal' in thieves' cant, has also long meant to support or encourage. And so 'boosterism', since 1926, is the act of talking something up, whether it be a dodgy stock or one's own reputation, a new invention or a country. (Some left-wing intellectuals during the Cold War were accused of 'Soviet boosterism'.)

Quite appropriately for the new prime minister, in particular, the *Oxford English Dictionary* notes that boosterism is 'the expression of chauvinism'. Whether a Trump-like boosterism is all a post-Brexit economy needs to function remains to be seen.

7 AUGUST

Toni Morrison: farewell to America's greatest writer – we all owe her so much

CHIGOZIE OBIOMA

It was with a heavy heart that I woke up, like many, to the news of the passing of the great African American writer Toni Morrison. As I have mourned and digested the news, my reaction has slowly gone from shock to dismay, then to a sense of inchoate peace.

If we judge being old as a more feeble state, or characterised by a gradual withdrawal from work, then Morrison, like most great writers, had not become old. At the age of 88, she had continued to give us her stories and thoughts. *The Source of Self-Regard* – a further exploration on some of the broader themes of race and dignity that she explored throughout her life in novels such as *Beloved* and *The Bluest Eye* – was released only a few months ago, published outside of the US under the title *Mouth Full of Blood*. And until recently, we have seen a steady stream of novels from her, including *God Help the Child*, which was published on the same day as my debut novel *The Fishermen*, in 2015. There was no sign that the end of our constant supply from her reserve of wonderful stories and ideas was anywhere near.

With the death of Morrison, many writers today feel like we have lost our literary mother. Although I grew up in a town in Nigeria, the two first American writers I ever read were black: Richard Wright and Morrison. I read *Black Boy* around the age of 11 or 12, then Morrison's *The Bluest Eye* a year or two later. It is a devastating story of a black girl who is destroyed by the low self-esteem imposed on her by a society in which her race and culture are diminished as ugly and unworthy. As a young boy in Nigeria, then slowly coming to the understanding that Africans were perceived by the rest of the world as being just like the black people in *The Bluest Eye*, I saw the light in this grim story. I realised that if we begin to look deeper into ourselves and take pride in our heritage, we will see the true beauty of who we are; what the rest of the world says about us, or how they see us, will be unable to kill our spirit. Morrison herself credited the great Nigerian author Chinua Achebe for helping her discover this, what she called 'the freedom to write'. But it was more a freedom to see that we can tell our own stories – and, by so doing, lift our people.

Reflecting on her life, I feel a sense of peace because I know I have learned a lot from Morrison. On the craft level, I believed until this morning that she was the greatest living American writer (an honour Cormac McCarthy now holds), and one of the best prose stylists in the world, on the same plane as Martin Amis, Wole Soyinka, Salman Rushdie and others. She set out to do 'unimaginable' things with the English language, a language she considered 'at once rich and deeply racist'. Counting myself as one of many writers from former colonial states who now write in the English language, which has become our national tongue, we have had to find ways to subdue and conquer it, and bring it into submission to our cultural sensibilities. Part of that conquering is not only writing in the English language the way we desire, but also *what* we desire. This was exactly what Morrison did throughout her life. In a time when African stories are not seen as important unless they are set outside Africa or created to align with western sensibilities, Morrison encouraged me to write about African traditional religion, culture and philosophies without reserve, even if the rest of the world – and even Africans themselves – see it as backward and unpleasant. I find peace because a new generation of black and African writers will continue to do just that, encouraged by the great work she has left us – and for this, I thank her.

8 AUGUST

Country diary: the few swallows we see are already preparing to leave

PAUL EVANS

At dusk, the campsite owner popped his head into the washing-up hut and the clatter of tin mugs to ask me to come outside. He wanted me to see swooping dots in the sky, a flight of swallows, maybe a hundred strong, preparing to roost. There had been more than 2,000 swallows here a couple of years ago; he attributed their decline to Chinese mist nets around the Mediterranean, particularly in north Africa, where millions of migrant birds have been trapped to be eaten.

I thought of Sir Philip Sidney's 1590 poem *The Countess of Pembroke's Arcadia* when he talks about man's cruelty to animals: 'Worst fell to smallest birds [...] At length for glutton taste he did kill them; /At last for sport their silly lives did spill.' Hundreds of years later, the situation is even more desperate for migrating birds.

Chaucer (in *The Parliament of Fowls*) called the swallow a murderer of 'the fowles small that maken hony of flowres fresshe of hewe', i.e. bees, and there were both swallows and bees flying over the coastal footpath the following day – but not as many as there should be.

Rounding on to the headland revealed a patch of flowers: lilac thistle, pink bramble and purple knapweed, supporting a circus of flying butterflies: an embarkation of painted ladies, a creaking of gatekeepers, a mowing of meadow-browns. I haven't seen a gathering of so many butterflies in one place for decades and, although it couldn't counteract the horror story of migrating birds caught in nets, it was a joyous flutter of the heart.

That evening as darkness fell into Traeth Lligwy (Lligwy Bay), so the swallows dropped in family groups or clans into the reeds of the Afon Lligwy estuary. Before sleep – if that's what they do, do they dream? – the swallows filled the quietly spoken reedbeds with a hushed twittering that, far from expressing 'silly lives', held a language of community wisdom, the swallow story in which each voice spoke as one, and each one was known to the other.

Now Lammas has passed the birds were talking themselves out of here, making plans for navigation in convoys, the lode-stones in their heads swinging south, towards Africa, towards the mist nets.

16 AUGUST

Peterloo: the massacre that led to a new democratic era

RICHARD J EVANS

Two hundred years ago, on 16 August 1819, the event we've come to know as the Peterloo massacre took place, as a public meeting on St Peter's Fields in Manchester was violently broken up by troops acting on the orders of the local magistrates. The meeting had been called as part of a wider movement to demand parliamentary representation for the rapidly growing industrial city of Manchester, which had no MP at the time.

The economic depression that followed the end of the Napoleonic wars, made worse by a series of poor harvests, had led to widespread unemployment, wage cuts and desperate poverty in the area, and people had no means of making their wishes known to parliament except by extra-parliamentary means.

The meeting was convened legally, and an estimated 60,000 people, many of them in their Sunday best, and including many women, some of them advocates of female suffrage, turned up to hear an open-air speech by the radical reformer Henry 'Orator' Hunt. The crowd was peaceful and orderly, but the magistrates, all of them strong opponents of parliamentary reform, issued a warrant for the arrest of Hunt and his entourage, and sent in the local yeomanry (described as 'younger members of the Tory party in arms'), who went into the crowd, 'cutting most indiscriminately to the right and to the left to get at them', as *The Times* reported.

Hunt and some others around him (including the *Times* reporter John Tyas) were duly arrested, but thinking the yeomanry were being assaulted by the crowd, the magistrates now sent in regular cavalry, who charged from one end of the field while mounted yeomanry charged from the other. Escape routes were blocked by troops, and one officer was heard to shout: 'For shame! For shame! Gentlemen: forbear, forbear! The people cannot get away!' Altogether an estimated 18 people were killed, and around 650 injured, some of them seriously.

The massacre of peaceful protesters sent shock waves across the country. It was soon dubbed the Peterloo massacre, an ironic reference to the allied victory at the Battle of Waterloo some four years previously. Commemorative mugs, handkerchiefs and other souvenirs were made by supporters of the radical cause, while the event was followed by the foundation of this newspaper in 1821 (as the *Manchester Guardian*) and immortalised in Shelley's bitter poem 'The Mask of Anarchy'.

The bicentenary of Peterloo is being marked in many ways, including a major film by Mike Leigh, and radio and television programmes. However, not everyone has considered the event worth commemorating in such style. Paradoxically, given its own reporter's work (a 10,000-word dispatch) was followed by a thunderous denunciation of the behaviour of the troops in a leading article, *The Times* has chosen to cast doubt on Peterloo's significance. In a recent editorial it attacked the BBC's decision to broadcast 'no fewer than 10 radio programmes on the massacre', and disputed the framing of a Radio 4 documentary (presented by Katharine Viner, editor-in-chief of the *Guardian*) entitled *Peterloo: The Massacre That Changed Britain.*

The editorial declared that, 'contrary to the BBC's demonology', Peterloo had 'no wider historical significance, and did not "change Britain" beyond feeding a tendentious account by left-wing historians of Britain's traditions of radical protest'. It blamed this 'Marxist version of Britain's past' on EP Thompson, who in his 1963 book *The*

Making of the English Working Class, threw together 'wholly disconnected movements' – including the one that led to Peterloo – to form a misleading narrative that took an 'isolated outrage' out of context.

What *The Times* seems to object to is what it takes as a sympathetic account of revolutionary activity. Surely, it suggests, such protests were unnecessary, given the fact that parliamentary reform acts eventually brought universal suffrage 'without recourse to the revolution that governments had feared since 1789'. Daniel Finkelstein, a Tory peer and former executive editor of *The Times*, has echoed these sentiments, declaring in a column that 'a romantic desire to suggest that Britain's path was decided by street protest and a contemporary hint that it might work again can't be allowed to make Peterloo bear more weight than it can carry'.

The Times' leader concludes with the claim that using the past 'as a prism through which to interpret current politics is bad history'. Ironic, then, that these articles themselves use Peterloo to condemn the exercise of 'street protest' in the present day.

It's not hard to see why Conservatives in this country are worried about the effect the bicentenary of Peterloo might have on contemporary politics. We're only a few weeks away from what's looking increasingly like a no-deal Brexit, with warnings multiplying about social unrest, street violence and public disorder, and troops apparently being put on alert to deal with food riots and political marches. The establishment's anxiety is palpable.

There are echoes here of the fears of 'the mob' felt by the magistrates in 1819 and their masters in the Tory government. It was repeated a century later in a similar massacre whose anniversary we are also marking this year, at Jallianwala Bagh in the Indian city of Amritsar – where at a peaceful protest, more than 400 unarmed protesters were shot down by British troops commanded by an army officer who later said his purpose was 'to punish the Indians' for their effrontery.

Just as the Amritsar massacre proved a turning point in the struggle for Indian independence, so Peterloo proved a turning point in the fight for the right to demonstrate. This had nothing to do with violent revolution and everything to do with peaceful reform. Thompson was not creating any 'Marxist' political narrative when he concluded that 'since the moral consensus of the nation outlawed the riding down and sabreing of an unarmed crowd, the corollary followed – that the right of public meeting had been gained'. Beyond this, national horror at the massacre provided a real impulse for the campaign to extend the right to vote, gained just over a decade later, in 1832.

The crowds at Peterloo were ultimately placing their faith in the power of parliament to represent the people once its archaic constitution had been amended. That power needs defending more than ever now, at a time when it is threatened by an unelected prime minister who shows every sign of wanting to push through an immensely damaging policy without its consent.

19 AUGUST

'It's a sign of panic': EU nationals on the UK's threat to end free movement (extract)

MATTHA BUSBY AND AMELIA GENTLEMAN

EU citizens living, working and studying in the UK have spoken of their fears for the future after the Home Office announced plans to end freedom of movement immediately after a no-deal Brexit.

Silvia González moved to Wales from Spain in 2015 after falling in love with British culture during a year studying when she was young. Brexit has turned her 'dream into a nightmare'.

'I have a stable, permanent job and a good support network, and I can speak English quite fluently,' said González, 40. 'But I still have sleepless nights about what will happen. I can't even think what those hundreds of thousands of people who are in far worse positions than mine are going through. Now this reckless, senseless, stupid move to stop freedom of movement on 31 October means turning the craziness up another notch.'

González was critical of the Home Office's use of a constitutive application system for settled or pre-settled status instead of a 'simple, declaratory registration system'. She said ending freedom of movement straight after a no-deal Brexit would mean the government was going against its promises not to change the rights of EU citizens living in the UK. 'If freedom of movement ends on 31 October, where does that leave us?' she asked. 'I haven't applied for settled status yet as I haven't been here for five years yet.'

Applying now would mean having to go through checks, ID verification and potentially having to send additional information, only to go through the process again in a couple of months, she said.

Her husband applied and had to send in his passport by post in December because the app did not work properly for him.

'We spent 10 days in agony right before Christmas until he got it back,' she said. 'I don't want to put myself through that if I can help it but not doing so with this latest development would mean putting myself at risk. How is anyone going to tell me apart from someone coming from Spain in three months' time? What checks is any employer going to need to do?'

González said she feared for all the people in more vulnerable positions than herself, such as those who spoke poor English, had health issues or could not keep abreast of the latest developments.

'It is mind-blowing, really,' she said. 'I've never felt so powerless and less protected by my government, because even though I'm not allowed to vote they are supposed to be working to safeguard my rights too, as a person living in the UK and paying their taxes.'

Micael Jose Ribeiro is a student from Portugal and wants reassurances that the government would respect the status of those who applied for settled and pre-settled status. 'The Home Office has a bad record when it comes to migrants,' said the Greenwich University software engineering student. 'I don't trust them.'

He said he has also not registered for pre-settled status because of that lack of trust, despite living in the UK for three years. 'I'm hoping parliament will extend this further,' he said. 'I don't want to give them sensitive details which could compromise my stay in the UK. There's no one to hold the Home Office to account.'

The status of European and UK nationals had not been agreed between the EU and the British government, he said, warning that safeguards were not in place in case the negotiations collapsed.

Describing the announcements around the settled and pre-settled status schemes, he said the way they were handled – as well as the earlier failure to guarantee the rights of European nationals in law – made it seem like EU citizens 'didn't matter'.

'EU citizens are still being used as bargaining chips in negotiations,' he said. 'They have been doing that by saying they're ending freedom of movement on 31 October. But that's just a lie. What tells them they have pre-settled status and the next person doesn't? They're just doing politics to impress the tabloids, show they're tough and prepare for an election.'

He said the UK needs migrants to run public services, and that calls to impose salary requirements of more than £30,000 for potential EU migrants were 'ridiculous'. 'I don't know many people who earn that,' he said. 'The UK needs migrants for the NHS.'

Although the Home Office said yesterday that EU citizens resident in the UK before 11pm on 31 October will be eligible for settled status and that no such people will be barred from re-entering the UK when free movement ends, Ribeiro reflected on the confusion and distrust experienced by many EU nationals amid a number of differing media reports.

'If I had plans to come home on 1 November, would I be able to come back into the country? I don't know,' he said.

22 AUGUST

Far-right violence is on the rise. Where is the outrage?

OWEN JONES

Mohammed Saleem was murdered by a terrorist, and yet you've probably never even heard of him. It was 29 April 2013, and the 82-year-old was walking home from evening prayers at a mosque in Small Heath, Birmingham.

A Ukrainian neo-Nazi terrorist – who had bombed three mosques – stabbed him three times from behind. 'He was a very beautiful, educated man who empowered all of his five daughters – and his sons as well – to pursue education, and loved and appreciated everything Britain gave him,' says Maz Saleem, his daughter. 'I've spent six years tirelessly campaigning for him to be recognised on a mainstream platform.'

Three weeks later, the murder of Lee Rigby by Islamist funda-
mentalists sparked national outrage and an emergency Cobra
meeting: not so for Saleem. 'It was brushed under the mat,' Maz
tells me. Or what of Mushin Ahmed, an 81-year-old grandfather
who was killed by two British racists in August 2015 as he walked
to pray at a Rotherham mosque? As one of his assailants screamed
that he was a 'groomer', he was kicked with such force that his
dentures shattered and the imprint of a trainer was left in his
face. Or what of a 32-year-old black man in east London who, in
June 2018, had to crawl on his knees to the A12 to escape a racist
attack: he'd been stabbed five times.

I was on the receiving end of an attack in the early hours of last
Saturday: my friends were punched defending me and I suffered
very minor injuries. But as a white man with a media platform,
what happened to me garnered far more interest than the racist
murders or serious hate crimes that have far worse consequences
than bumped heads and bruises. The far right is emboldened,
legitimised and ever more violent, and hate crimes are surging.
When we discuss Islamist fundamentalist terrorists, we ask: who
are the hate preachers radicalising them in mosques or on the
internet? We have yet to engage seriously in a similar debate
about far-right terrorism for a simple reason: the hate preachers
are mainstream politicians, commentators and media outlets.

Consider the scale of the threat. The far right has always had
two principal enemies – minorities and the political left – and
nothing has changed. Eight years ago, the Norwegian far-right
terrorist Anders Breivik slaughtered dozens of predominantly
young socialists on the island of Utøya. His reason? The left's
anti-racism meant they were the driving force behind what
he described as the 'Islamisation' and therefore destruction of
Christian Europe. This was a particularly violent expression
of a persistent far-right conspiracy theory and, while left-wing

teenagers died on that Norwegian island, this narrative did not. Members of the left are, according to this mindset, traitors to their nation, seeking to destroy it through mass immigration of culturally hostile aliens, and are allies of a despised enemy – Islam as a demonised religion, Muslims as a people.

Far-right terrorists feed off the hatred that is often fanned by elites when it suits them. The recent El Paso terrorist attack, in which Latin American people were slaughtered, cannot be divorced from the systematic demonisation of Mexican immigrants by right-wing media outlets and Republican politicians, and now in an undiluted form by a US president who labels them rapists and criminals. Jews – who have been targeted for 2,000 years – were butchered and maimed in Pittsburgh less than a year ago. The alleged terrorist reportedly accused Jews of trying to bring 'evil' Muslims to the United States – here was an ancient hatred married to a more modern manifestation: Jews as disloyal and rootless, seeking to destroy western civilisation by importing dangerous Muslims. Chillingly, in overtly antisemitic remarks, Donald Trump this week accused Jewish Americans who vote for Democrats of 'great disloyalty'. The 2015 far-right terrorist attack on a black church in Charleston cannot be understood in isolation from the fact that slavery, which has bequeathed an extensive racist legacy, was abolished just two lifetimes ago. In New Zealand's Christchurch massacre, more than 50 Muslims – people with a faith that has been targeted not just by the far right but several mainstream media outlets and politicians – were murdered.

In Britain, the Labour MP Jo Cox was murdered by a white far-right terrorist who gave his name in court as 'death to traitors, freedom for Britain'. What lesson was learned? How was Nigel Farage able to brag that Brexit had been won 'without a single bullet being fired', and later declare he'd 'don khaki, pick up a rifle and head for the frontlines' if Brexit wasn't delivered,

THE BEDSIDE GUARDIAN 2019

without his political or media career suffering? How did the far-right terrorist plot to murder Labour MP Rosie Cooper with a machete not lead to national shock and horror? What of the far-right attack on Muslim worshippers in Finsbury Park, whose perpetrator expressed a desire to murder Jeremy Corbyn and Sadiq Khan as terrorist supporters?

The hate preachers radicalising far-right extremists are not ranting on soap boxes on street corners: they get splashed on front pages. They use rhetoric such as 'Enemies of the people' and 'Crush the saboteurs'; they deploy distortions, myths, half-truths and lies to whip up hatred against Muslims, migrants and refugees, and to scapegoat them for crimes committed by the powerful.

In the clash between fascists and antifascists in Charlottesville, Trump infamously declared there 'were very fine people on both sides', and in doing so founded 'both-sideism': the idea that advocating white supremacy is morally equivalent to opposing racism and wanting rich people to pay higher taxes. Yet this moral equivalence – which includes claiming that the left is equally violent – is beyond dangerous. The far right might be committing murderous terrorist atrocities against minorities, but some guy poured a banana and salted caramel milkshake on Nigel Farage's favourite suit! Sure, there are members of minorities being murdered on the streets by racists with little media coverage, but the US neo-Nazi Richard Spencer was punched once, so who is to say who is worse?

There is a systematic campaign to delegitimise the very few left-wing voices in mainstream media and politics, orchestrated not just by the right, but by some self-described 'moderates' and 'centrists' too. The attempt to construct a false equivalence between a far right that is on a murderous rampage against minorities and their allies, and a left committed to resisting its hatred and violence, is perverse. Mainstream politicians and several media outlets are legitimising ideas that fuel ideologically driven far-right terrorism and violent racist and bigoted attacks. Many more will be injured, and will die, as a consequence, and because they are not white, and because they lack a national platform, you will probably never hear their names.

23 AUGUST

In Bolsonaro's burning Brazilian Amazon, all our futures are being consumed

ELIANE BRUM

The Amazon is the centre of the world. Right now, as our planet experiences climate collapse, there is nowhere more important. If we don't grasp this, there is no way to meet that challenge.

For 500 years, this has been a place of ruins. First with the European invasion, which brought a particularly destructive form of civilisation, the death of hundreds of thousands of indigenous men and women and the extinction of dozens of peoples. More recently, with the clearance of vast swaths of the forest and all life within it. Right now, in 2019, we are witnessing the beginning of a new, disastrous chapter. The area of trees being cleared has surged this year. In July, the deforestation rate was an area the size of Manhattan every day, a Greater London every three weeks. This month, fires are incinerating the Amazon at a record rate, almost certainly part of a scorched-earth strategy to clear territory. Why is this happening now? Because of a change in power.

A predatory form of politics called Bolsonarism has assumed nearly total, and totalitarian, power in Brazil. President Jair Bolsonaro's chief project is to create more ruins in the Amazon forest, methodically and swiftly. This is why, for the first time since Brazil became a democracy again, it effectively has a minister against the environment.

For more than 30 years no environment minister has enjoyed the same autonomy as Ricardo Salles. He is a gofer for agribusiness, which is responsible for the majority of the deaths in the fields and forests, and Brazil's greatest destructive force. The landowners' lobby has always been part of Brazil's government, formally or not. But today, this has reached a new level. They are not just in the government, they are the government.

Bolsonarism's number one power project is to turn public lands that serve everyone – because they guarantee the preservation of natural biomes, the life of native peoples and regulate the climate – into private lands that profit a few. These lands, most of which lie in the Amazon forest, include the public lands to which indigenous peoples have the constitutional right to use, the public lands settled by *ribeirinhos* (people who have for over a century made their living by fishing, tapping rubber, and sustainably gathering Brazil nuts and other forest products), and the collective-use lands of *quilombolas* (descendants of rebel slaves who won their right to territories occupied by their ancestors).

Infighting is constant in the government, in part because the Bolsonaro administration employs the strategy of simulating its own opposition so it can occupy every possible space. Yet there is a consensus about opening up indigenous peoples' protected lands and conservation areas. When it comes to transforming the planet's largest tropical forest into a place for raising cattle, growing soybeans and mining ore, there is no fighting at all. A few somewhat dissonant voices have already been deleted from the government.

Bolsonarism goes well beyond the man after whom it is named. At some point, it might even do without Bolsonaro. Deeply entwined with our global democracy crisis, Bolsonarism has been influencing the entire Amazon region, drawing out figures who have been hiding in sewers for years, sometimes decades, in other Latin American countries, where the fate of the world's largest tropical forest is also being decided. And Bolsonarism, it bears repeating, is not a threat just to Brazil but to our planet, because it destroys the forest that is strategically vital to controlling global heating.

How do we resist this tremendous destructive force, this skilled destructive force?

For us to be capable of resisting, we must become the forest and resist like the forest, the forest that knows it carries ruins within itself, that carries within itself both what it is and what it no longer is. We must lend shape to this political, affective feeling in order to lend meaning to our actions. This means shifting a few tectonic plates in our own thinking. We have to decolonise ourselves.

The fact that the Amazon is still regarded as something far away, on the periphery of our vision, shows just how stupid white western culture is. It is a stupidity that moulds and shapes the political and economic elites of the world, and likewise of Brazil. Believing the Amazon is far away and on the periphery, when the only chance of controlling global heating is to keep the forest alive, reflects ignorance of continental proportions. The forest is at the very core of all we have. This is the real home of humanity. The fact that many of us feel far away from it only shows how much our eyes have been contaminated, formatted and distorted. Colonised.

In the big cities of Brazil and the rest of the world, we are distanced from the deaths in which our small daily acts are accomplices. We have the privilege of not being forced to question the origin of the clothes we wear or the food we eat. But in the Amazon, if you eat beef, you know for sure it is beef from deforestation. If you buy wood, you know there is (almost) no truly legal lumber in Brazil. If you purchase a table or a wardrobe, you look at the furniture and think about how it was most likely made with wood torn off indigenous land or from an extractive reserve. In the Amazon, in the centre of the world, our relationship with the death of the forest and forest peoples, as well as with the death of family farmers, is direct. It is inescapable.

We need to humbly ask if the forest peoples accept us alongside them in the fight. They are the ones who know how to live despite the ruins. They are the ones who have experience resisting the great forces of destruction. If we are to have any chance of producing a resistance movement, we must understand that, in this fight, we are not the protagonists.

We are the ones who need to let ourselves be occupied and allow our bodies to be affected by other experiences of being on this planet. But not as a form of violence, like the colonisation of the Amazon and its peoples; the colonisation still under way today, and going on at an ever faster pace. Rather, this time, as a form of exchange, a blending, a relationship of love.

Bolsonaro is not just a threat to the Amazon. He is a threat to the planet, precisely because he is a threat to the Amazon. Confronted with Bolsonarism's accelerated forces of destruction, all of us, of all nationalities, must emulate the enslaved Africans who rebelled against their oppressors. We must forge communities like those established by Brazil's escaped slaves. And since we don't know how to do this, we will have to be humble enough to learn with those who do.

What is best, and most powerful, about today's Brazil and the Amazon, in all its regions, are the peripheries that demand to be the centre. Our best chance lies in joining forces with the real centre of the world where the battle for the future is being waged.

23 AUGUST

Poor Prince Andrew is 'appalled' by Epstein. Let that be an end to it

MARINA HYDE

It's basically your classic men-of-the-world vignette. Lying in business dress in the New York mansion of his friend Jeffrey Epstein, Prince Andrew is receiving a foot massage from a young, well-dressed Russian woman. Other men are in the room while this is happening, and they include Epstein (also being foot-massaged by a Russian woman) and the literary agent John Brockman, who runs a foundation connecting scientists and intellectuals with billionaires. As the young Russians work on their feet, Andy is complaining about his lot. 'In Monaco,' he says, according to Brockman's account, '[Prince] Albert works 12 hours a day but at 9pm, when he goes out, he does whatever he wants, and nobody cares. But, if I do it, I'm in big trouble.'

Waa waa waa. What could be a more effective heartstring-tugger than 'other European princes have it better than me'? It's right up there with Chandler's line from *Friends*: 'My wallet's too small for my 50s, and my diamond shoes are too tight!'

The scene is recalled in an email revealed by Brockman's soon-to-be former client, the tech author Evgeny Morozov. He is one of many divesting themselves of even tenuous Epstein association in the wake of the billionaire financier's suicide in a Manhattan jail earlier this month, as he awaited trial for sex trafficking, underage and otherwise.

But what of Andy? Under some scrutiny, he and ex-wife Duchess Fergie private-jetted away from Balmoral last week, then on to the luxury bit of Sotogrande, where they are said to be gracing private barbecues. Briefings suggest, distractingly, that they might be getting back together. Their daughter Princess Beatrice might be getting engaged to her boyfriend. 'They're going to get married,' royal expert Ingrid Seward declared this week, divertingly. 'I was told by a member of the family.' So, on go the Yorks. It really is the full fairy tale. By which I mean: fairly Grimm.

Back to the foot massage scene, then, where the chaps seem to have got on to Prince Albert's night-time freedom via the subject of Julian Assange. Brockman reports Andy saying: 'We think they're liberal in Sweden, but it's more like northern England as opposed to southern Europe.' Is the implication that Swedish authorities investigating sexual assault allegations are being illiberal?

Either way, you don't get all that nanny state stuff on Epstein's private Virgin Islands property, reportedly known locally as 'Paedophile Island'. Or as Buckingham Palace finally put it in a statement denying any impropriety on behalf of the prince: 'The Duke of York has been appalled by the recent reports of Jeffrey Epstein's alleged crimes.'

I'm slightly sorry for the royal flunkies who had to issue this line, given that most of us are suffering eyeball strain from all the rolling we're doing. Even so, I do feel we need further clar-ification on what the Duke is appalled by. Is it just the 'recent reports'? Because if we're meant to believe that Prince Andrew is appalled by ALL of the crimes of Jeffrey Epstein – both the ones alleged and the ones he served actual jail time for – then allow me to treat this statement with all the dignity it deserves. To wit: BULL. SHIT. Bullshit Prince Andrew didn't know what sort of guy his friend was when he was snapped walking with the Tier 1 sex offender, after he got out of jail, in a photo the *New York Post* headlined 'PRINCE & PERV'. Bullshit he didn't know why his close friend WENT TO PRISON FOR A YEAR, but kept hanging out with him anyway. Bullshit if, as Brockman recounts, he lay on his back in that guy's house, with a Russian attending to his feet, talking over her head about the nocturnal licence afforded to minor European royals, and he didn't know roughly what he was swimming in. Bullshit. I get we have to pay for Andrew's lifetime of jollies; but we don't have to have our intelligence insulted by him.

I'm not even going to wheel out that old writing device where one says that either Prince Andrew is stupid or deeply compromised, and wonder archly which it is. Guys, he can be both! In fact, the one feeds the other.

The plain fact is that Andrew continued to be friends with Epstein even after he pleaded guilty to procuring an underage girl for prostitution. I guess it was the old she-said, he-said thing. Or as the then Palm Beach police chief put it: 'This was 50-something "shes" and one "he" – and the shes all basically told the same story.' Obviously, Epstein got away lightly with his grotesque plea deal, because 50-something:1 isn't the ratio you need. Even last year, they still needed 60 accusers to stop Bill Cosby. Donald Trump's 17:1 she–he ratio is nowhere near enough to keep him from the highest office on the planet.

As for where we go from here, perhaps a multimillion-pound royal wedding would indeed be helpful. It should be quite the opposite. Where Princess Anne pointedly didn't, Prince Andrew demanded all the titles and trappings for his two daughters and was furious when denied some of them. Yet Beatrice and Eugenie still live like ... well, princesses.

So instead of distracting from the miserable stories of the female attendees of various Epstein mansions, these gilded lives should throw them into even more shameful relief. They suggest the kind of man, and we've all met them, who has a two-tier view of the female sex. There is a world for their daughters, hopefully insulated from men like their friend Jeffrey – and then there is another world for girls who service their friend Jeffrey.

Yet decent people know there aren't two kinds of women and girls – there are just women and girls. I'm reminded of the climactic line in *All My Sons*, where the wartime profiteer Joe Keller has been finally made – by his own son's suicide note – to see how his actions were responsible for the fate of so many other young men. 'I think to him they were all my sons,' Keller reflects. 'And I guess they were. I guess they were.'

And so with the girls in the stories that swirl around Epstein and his circle, which includes the Duke: either broken, or yet-to-be-broken. But, ultimately, breakable. They are all daughters, too, your Royal Highness. The Russian masseuse on your feet, the 17-year-old runaway on whose bare hip you have your hand in that fateful picture in London, the terrified 14-year-old who ran screaming from your great friend's house in her underwear, who you must have read about at the time, because I did, and I didn't even know the guy. They are each someone's daughter. They all once played at princesses and castles and imagined their own fairy-tale weddings. Funny how dreams die, isn't it – and who helps to crush them.

26 AUGUST

Bury's demise is a grim warning that small-town Britain is still being left behind

DAVID CONN

The threatened expulsion of small town Bury from the English Football League – which could happen if the owner, Steve Dale, does not conclude a sale of the club by 5pm on Tuesday – has been a touch more emotional for me than many of the football traumas I have investigated as a journalist over the past 20 years. I grew up in north Manchester, five miles down the road, and went to school in Bury. Twice a day I used to pass the club's Gigg Lane ground and wonder at it from the top of the 35 bus: a proper football home, bedded in with all its history behind a pleasing line of trees.

In these crisis-stricken months for Bury – a club founded in 1885 – many people have rightly pointed with bewilderment to English football's violent inequalities; to Manchester City and United 10 miles away, owned by overseas billionaires, making multimillionaires of their players and managers. Supporters have despaired at the gaping holes in football's governance, its painfully limited 'fit and proper persons test' for owners, so long campaigned for but which still fails to protect beloved clubs from needless ruination.

But the details of Bury's crumbling expose an alarming, knacker's-yard wreckage that is more broadly worrying for the economies of Britain's old industrial places at this time of imminent national shock. Football, the national sport, has always reflected the country and its times. When Bury, Bolton, Black-burn, Preston and other north-west and Midlands towns formed the late-Victorian professional clubs, they were powerhouses of mills and manufacturing. The former public schoolboys who founded the Football Association in London in 1863 remained amateurs and opposed professionalism for years – partly because they did not need the money to compensate them for time off to train and play.

Today, the ruins of Bury FC expose the wider vulnerability of its surrounding town and many places like it around the country on the brink of Brexit: a disruption engineered by politicians who never took the bus to school, apparently incubating extreme ideologies for a country from which they were always kept detached.

Bury's financial instability was evident for five years under the previous owner, Stewart Day, a Blackburn-based property developer specialising in accommodation blocks for students. In 2014 his company borrowed money secured on Gigg Lane at 10 per cent interest a month, which compounded into 138 per cent annual interest. That, sadly, did not clang enough alarm bells and Day continued building his flats, and loading borrowings on to Bury, until it all collapsed.

When he announced in December that he had sold the club to Dale, for £1, Day said he wanted to spend more time with his family, while Dale spoke of it as a philanthropic venture. Day's financial difficulties were laid bare within weeks, as his companies fell into insolvency and administration.

Some people involved in new or expanding universities in northern former mill towns have described their growth as economic regeneration, but it has always seemed shaky to base a recovery on government-backed loans taken out by young people facing uncertain futures. Day's property ventures were not even supported by banks; he had borrowed heavily from Lendy, a model based on attracting money from thousands of individual investors, which has itself collapsed and is now subject to a Financial Conduct Authority investigation. Day also pre-sold individual flats, promising guaranteed returns from students' rent payments, and many investors are now distraught at seeing life savings lost.

At Bury itself, loans now up to £3.7 million, secured on Gigg Lane, were taken from an outfit called Capital Bridging Finance Solutions, based in Crosby, with 40 per cent commissions paid to still-unnamed third parties as introduction fees. The publicly filed documents state that Capital in turn mortgaged Bury's ground to a company registered in Malta, whose own lenders for the deal were eight companies domiciled in the offshore tax haven of the British Virgin Islands. Perhaps you have to know and have been to Gigg Lane, a football haven amid terraced streets just off Manchester Road, to feel in your guts the ludicrous nature of such house-of-cards economics.

A further look at Dale's business record revealed a trader in insolvent companies that had mostly been dissolved or liquidated. Any philanthropic intentions were overtaken by his voluble complaining at the financial hole vacated by Day. On the way to Bury's own insolvency Dale laid off hardworking staff and failed to pay £4 million of creditors including £1.1 million to HMRC, as well as players who are still owed substantial back wages.

Bury's council leader, David Jones, told the *Guardian* last week that losing the club would be a 'nail in the coffin' for the town. Since David Cameron and Nick Clegg formed their coalition government in 2010, the council has suffered cuts of £85 million, 61 per cent of its annual budget, he said. Boris Johnson is now presenting a no-deal Brexit as easy to cope with, when the government's own assessment is that the north-west's already patchy and unequal economy will suffer a -12 per cent hit.

That is the broader context of the Bury collapse and its defining image: the former director Joy Hart, chaining herself to a drain-pipe outside the club's closed offices, pleading for salvation.

On 27 August 2019, Bury FC were expelled from the English Football League.

27 AUGUST

'A storm has hit my life': the Kashmiri families torn apart by mass arrests

AZHAR FAROOQ AND
REBECCA RATCLIFFE

There was only one knock at the door before police officers entered Tanveer Sheikh's home. Armed men climbed through the windows and began searching room to room, asking for Tanveer.

'We have young girls at home and they were woken from sleep,' said Maryam, Tanveer's mother. 'I told the policemen, how could they barge in like this? We could have been naked.'

Tanveer, who is 16 or 17 years old, according to the family, was not at home in Srinagar, in Indian-administered Kashmir, at the time, so officers took his uncle Naseer instead. The police did not explain why they wanted to detain Tanveer. 'They said: "You hand over Tanveer and we will let Naseer go,"' said Maryam.

Naseer's son keeps asking for his father, who has been held for 11 days. 'He is two years old,' Maryam said. 'What will we tell him? He will not even understand what has happened.'

Naseer is among thousands of people reportedly detained by police as part of a major crackdown launched after the Indian government revoked the region's special status three weeks ago.

Prominent politicians, including former chief ministers, are understood to be among the detained, as well as business owners and lawyers. Most of those arrested are young men.

According to local media reports, some prisoners have been flown out of Kashmir to prisons in Lucknow, Bareilly and Agra. It is possible that people are being held under the Public Safety Act, a controversial law that allows authorities to imprison someone for up to two years without charge or trial.

UN human rights experts said last week they were 'deeply concerned' by the developments. Groups including Amnesty International and Human Rights Watch have also expressed alarm.

A communications blackout, which has lasted more than three weeks, has severely hampered work by activists to document potential human rights abuses. The suspension of phone and internet services has also left relatives unable to call one another. The revocation of special status from the state of Jammu and Kashmir has stripped it of any autonomy, removing its constitution and rules that have prevented outsiders from buying land. Many Kashmiris fear the change will alter the demographic and traditions of the territory, India's only Muslim-majority state.

Despite heavy security, sporadic protests have continued over the past two weeks. A sympathiser of a banned political group, who asked not to be named, told the *Guardian* last week the region was a 'burning volcano' that would 'erupt any time'.

Delhi's actions have also escalated tensions with Pakistan, which claims Kashmir and has suggested India could carry out ethnic cleansing.

Outside Srinagar's central jail, families from across Kashmir queued to visit their loved ones. Aamina said her 22-year-old son, Junaid Nabi Wani, was arrested after Friday prayers two weeks ago.

'He was sitting on the roadside with neighbours and relatives when police came and asked for his identity card,' Aamina said. A police officer then placed his arm around Wani's shoulder and asked him to take a walk. An armoured vehicle was waiting, she said, and he was bundled into it and taken away. It is not known why he was detained. 'His cousin was with him and he came running to us. We rushed outside and tried to resist but the policemen cocked their guns and pointed them at us,' said Aamina. She was assigned the number 56 by prison staff and asked to wait for her chance to enter the jail. She carried a small lunch box with food for her son.

Sarwar left her home in north Kashmir's Hathlong village at dawn in the hope of visiting her son, Aqib. She said he was detained in a midnight raid eight days ago. She said no reason was provided for his arrest.

'May God's wrath fall on them! My son was innocent, trust me, he has done nothing,' she said. Her neighbour, Fareeda, had also travelled to meet her son, Bilal, who was detained along with Aqib.

Families waited for hours to see their relatives. 'He said nothing. He only cried,' Fareeda said afterwards, breaking into tears. On her arm, a stamp read 'ostrich' and 'crocodile' – a code that is changed daily which allows entry into the jail.

According to estimates collected separately by Associated Press and Agence France-Presse, between 2,300 and 4,000 people have been detained. Officials said recently there had been 'a few' detentions, to prevent disorder.

Amnesty International accused the Indian government of 'deliberate silencing of voices in the region'.

Naseer's family say he is being held to ransom until his nephew is handed over. Such arrests are common, according to several families in Srinagar's old city, traditionally a flashpoint for anti-India protests.

A family in the Gojwara locality said police raided their home at midnight on 8 August and asked for their 25-year-old son. 'He was not at home, so they detained his father. He is 70 years old,' the family said. They asked to remain anonymous because their daughters had not been informed. 'When they [daughters] come, we tell them their father has gone out for a walk. When some time passes, we tell them to leave and go home early,' a family member said. 'The police ask us to bring our son and take the father back,' they added. Amnesty International India has previously documented cases where fathers were asked to bring another son for detention if they wanted their first son to be released. 'These detentions are not just unlawful but also lead to harassment and intimidation of the families,' said Mrinal Sharma, a policy adviser for the rights group. Meenakshi Ganguly, the south Asia director at Human Rights Watch, said detainees must be allowed access to proper legal counsel and families should be told where relatives were being held. 'International law prohibits indefinite detentions and all those in custody should be swiftly released or charged,' she said.

Aamina said she was scared to be at home and had barely slept since her son was taken. 'I promise if he is released I will leave this place. I will beg but I will go somewhere where no one knows us,' she said.

Her husband died last year and her other son has spent two years in prison. 'I am all alone now,' she said. 'A storm has hit my life.'

3 SEPTEMBER

The Painted Bird review – savage, searing three-hour tour of hell

XAN BROOKS

One day they'll make a film about the first public screening of *The Painted Bird*, inside the Sala Darsena at the 2019 Venice film festival. It will feature the man who fell full-length on the steps in his effort to escape and the well-dressed woman who became so frantic to get out that she hit the stranger in the next seat. The centrepiece will be the moment 12 viewers broke for the doors only to discover that the exit had been locked. I'm seeing this film as a disaster movie along the lines of *The Towering Inferno*, or perhaps a slapstick comic version of *The Painted Bird* itself.

Film festivals need masterpieces to marvel at and turkeys to laugh about. But they also need a film like *The Painted Bird*, a film that makes a mockery of star ratings. I can state without hesitation that this is a monumental piece of work and one I'm deeply glad to have seen. I can also say that I hope never to cross its path again.

Czech director Václav Marhoul spins war-torn history into phantasmagorical horror, rattling around ravaged eastern Europe for just shy of three hours. *The Painted Bird* is adapted from a 1965 novel by Jerzy Kosiński, which was cobbled together from survivors' accounts, and takes its title from a scene in which a starling daubed with white paint is mistaken for an enemy and pecked to death by its flock. The movie shows this incident in complete grisly detail. It's one of its lighter, gentler moments.

Petr Kotlar plays the unnamed Jewish stray, identified in the credits only as Boy. He's part Odysseus, part Job in that the tale has him caught in the eddies of the second world war, washed from one nightmarish episode to the next. Marhoul shot the film over several years, so that we watch Kotlar ageing as the movie progresses. He fills out on screen as the audience thins out.

The first mass walkout is prompted by Udo Kier's jealous miller, who gouges out a man's eyes and then feeds them to his cats. The second, most violent exodus occurs when the local nymphomaniac (Jitka Čvančarová) is set upon by the townsfolk, while the third is so perfectly synchronised to a Cossack attack that the desperate dash of the spectators mirrors that of the villagers on screen. After it's over, the auditorium is hardly half full. Those who remain have decided to ride the rollercoaster right through.

Judged purely on visual terms, *The Painted Bird* is gorgeous: a lush black-and-white tour of birch forests and bulrushes and remote rustic hamlets. Judged as drama, it is brazenly brutal, a pitiless chronicle of a land red in tooth and claw, so steeped in primitive suspicions that it's startling to suddenly see a 20th-century plane or a truck, or spot actors from less threatening pictures. Look, there's Stellan Skarsgård playing a foursquare German; Harvey Keitel as a misguided Catholic priest; Julian Sands as the paedophile parishioner who is eager to take the boy in. Sands is in a death scene that may haunt me for weeks.

Marhoul's film is unremittingly savage and searing. It knows exactly what it's doing and, by that logic, never puts a foot wrong. What this sets out to depict is an eastern Europe in crisis, rocked by war with its core melting down and psychosexual radiation bleeding into the surrounding countryside. The boy is so tormented and traumatised that it's small wonder he eventually becomes a tormentor, too.

The Painted Bird plumbs the depths, but rest assured that those hardy souls who stay the course are rewarded with the smallest glimmer of hope. This takes the form of a few lines drawn in the

condensation of a bus window. After three hours in hell a lone
crumb of comfort can fill us up like a banquet.

4 SEPTEMBER

Boris Johnson's electoral gamble
risks wrecking the Tory party

JONATHAN FREEDLAND

When some of the best-known Conservative figures of the last
half-century are booted out of their party, when a new prime
minister loses his first parliamentary vote and his governing
majority on the same day, when historians are referring to this as
a 'revolutionary moment', you know something of great significance is going on. But what exactly is it?

What we are witnessing is another round in the same historic
struggle that powered the English civil war of the 17th century:
the contest between the executive and the legislature. At its
simplest, the House of Commons has voted – once again – to take
control of the Brexit process, in order to prevent the UK crashing
out of the European Union with no deal on 31 October. That's
the substance of the bill that MPs will vote on, and are likely to
pass, today, having cleared the procedural hurdle in dramatic
fashion last night. The comparisons with the 17th century are
not hyperbolic, because what this move represents is a bid by the
legislature – parliament – to grab powers that have traditionally
been the preserve of the executive.

That contest is not over. If MPs succeed today, they will have
decided – against the wishes of Boris Johnson – to seek an exten-

sion of Britain's EU membership until 31 January 2020, if no exit agreement has been secured before then.

Johnson has said he will refuse to act on MPs' wishes, that he will simply not request such an extension from Brussels. To avoid the MPs' instruction, he would rather empty out the current House of Commons and have a general election to fill a new one, one more sympathetic to his aims. But that can only happen if MPs allow it, by voting for it. Under the current rules, he needs two-thirds of the Commons to agree to an early election and Labour has said it won't do it – fearing a ruse that would allow Johnson to crash out of the EU during an election campaign.

In other words, parliament is asserting itself and its rights, refusing to be pushed around by an overmighty executive (in the form of Johnson this time, rather than Charles I). Indeed, I'm told that MPs are pondering a means to ensure their will is done over the head of the prime minister: one senior opposition figure has a bill ready that would mandate the Speaker, John Bercow, to apply to Brussels himself for that extension on behalf of the British parliament.

There's a deep paradox here. It was the champions of Brexit who back in 2016 posed as the defenders of parliamentary sovereignty, determined to reassert the supremacy and independence of the Commons from the supposed encroachments of Brussels. Yet here they are now, fighting parliament at every turn: first proroguing, or suspending, parliament for five weeks; then expelling MPs from their party, even those with decades of devoted service; now seeking to defy parliament's will. It's quite a reverse, one captured well by that photograph of the leader of the house, Jacob Rees-Mogg, stretching out contemptuously on the Commons frontbench.

This is not the only revolutionary upheaval under way. Something of that order is currently convulsing the Tory party. A purge that expels two former chancellors and a man who a matter of weeks ago was a candidate for the leadership is an epochal event for the Conservative party. It is changing shape, refashioned by Johnson into the Brexit party by another name – a nationalist, populist party of the hard right.

There is some debate over whether all this – the prorogation, the expulsions – is a series of improvised moves born of panic or, on the contrary, a cunning plan. Within that question is a related one: is the PM's chief aide, Dominic Cummings, an evil genius or what Marina Hyde calls a 'crap svengali'? One of the victims of the Tory purge – Tory grandee and Churchill's grandson Nicholas Soames – told BBC's *Newsnight* he believes this is all very deliberate. The assumption is that Cummings is intentionally baiting MPs so that he can trigger an election that Johnson will then cast as a populist battle of 'people v parliament'.

If that's right, it is surely the most high-risk electoral strategy ever attempted in this country. It knowingly alienates moderate Tory voters who have always quite liked, say, Ken Clarke, thereby writing off a string of seats – in the south and the West Country – that are likely to fall to the Liberal Democrats. It similarly dooms the Tories in Scotland. So Johnson will begin the next election campaign with that immediate handicap. The Cummings plan is to make up for those lost seats, and gain many more, by winning pro-leave seats in the Midlands and north of England, many of them Labour-held, chiefly by neutralising the Brexit party. Why vote for Nigel Farage when you can get a no-deal, full-monty Brexit with Johnson?

The trouble with that is, there are plenty of onetime Labour voters who were happy to vote leave in 2016, happy even to vote for Farage in May's European elections, who may nevertheless balk at voting Tory. Still, Cummings and Johnson are gambling on the belief that they can burn down every other plank of historic Tory support, but win power by delighting the hardcore Brexit base. Win the 35 per cent, enrage everyone else.

A few weeks from now we might be watching a triumphant Johnson returned to Downing Street with a healthy majority, forced to applaud the strategic genius of Dominic Cummings. Or we might marvel that a man who inherited a precarious political situation went on a rampage of revolutionary destruction, thereby making that situation much, much worse.

4 SEPTEMBER

Britain is mired in a democratic crisis – but it goes much deeper than Brexit

ADITYA CHAKRABORTTY

Growing up, I learned that leaders who threaten democracy normally came decked out in khaki green, in front of troops toting shiny hardware. They commandeered broadcast studios, captured national buildings and imposed curfews on the streets. What is happening in Britain this week looks nothing like those grainy TV pictures, but it nonetheless marks an assault on our democracy.

The government wants to shut down parliamentary democracy, claiming it is acting for the good of parliamentary democracy. From within No 10 Dominic Cummings threatens to end the career of elected MPs. And David Gauke, the Conservative MP who just six weeks ago was secretary of state for justice, wrote to his former government colleagues on Monday to ask them to obey the rule of law.

Just because the paradoxes are so glaring it makes them no less dangerous. The self-proclaimed party of law and order has this summer dropped the first bit to become merely the party of order. In this battle of Brexit-blocking politicians versus the people, the tribune of us plebs is none other than Jacob Rees-Mogg. His leader is Boris Johnson, perhaps the most slovenly would-be authoritarian in contemporary history.

Yet the public protests across the country against all this are not especially large; away from the keyboard warriors of social media, the mood is not particularly restive. A friend messaged from a bus in central Bristol last Saturday where two fellow passengers, 'ladies in their late 60s or early 70s', looked out at a march against Johnson's coup and loudly advised the driver to run them over. Yesterday, while the world's media camped out on College Green for wall-to-wall chaos coverage, another friend posted on Twitter from a dentist's waiting room in Newcastle. 'Three Tory MPs debating Brexit on BBC News channel. Nobody watching.'

Some of this indifference is both eternal and welcome. Amid the greatest disaster, wrote Auden in his poem 'Musée des Beaux Arts', 'the dogs go on with their doggy life and the torturer's horse / Scratches its innocent behind on a tree'. But there is a more pressing and profound puzzle with which we must wrestle. When renowned historians are comparing this attempted putsch to the Reichstag fire, when denunciations are raining down from constitutional experts, when MPs and BBC broadcasters speak of little else apart from Britain's democratic crisis – why does such heated talk leave most of the public so cold?

I detect no signs that Johnson has become the people's prime minister, capturing the hearts of a grateful nation. Rather, over the past five years he has gone from being the Heineken Tory –

reaching the parts of the electorate other Conservatives just can't reach – to a Marmite politician who sharply polarises public opinion. Nor do I believe that what is happening this week has gone either under-reported or misunderstood – it is blatant subversion of the British way of doing politics.

The approach to the answer lies again through Auden's poem: '[T]he ploughman may / have heard the splash, the forsaken cry, / But for him it was not an important failure ...' If today's residents of Downing Street can so easily gut our democratic institutions, it is largely because many of those institutions long ago lost their importance to the public. In his own pseudo-bumbling fashion, Johnson is taking a leaf out of the book of Donald Trump, Narendra Modi, Jair Bolsonaro: he is deliberately outraging the norms that have governed politics and society, safe in the knowledge that for much of his electorate those conventions have already rotted away to useless totems.

Put bluntly: yes, Britain is mired in a democratic crisis. But it is one that is older, wider and deeper than this week's debacle over Brexit and parliamentary sovereignty, and it features across our everyday lives. It's there in our privately run academy schools, which will get another wodge of cash in Wednesday's expected spending round from chancellor Sajid Javid. Under the auspices of today's arch-Brexiters, Cummings and his then frontman at the Department for Education, Michael Gove, turned our schools system into what an LSE study calls 'highly opaque', marked by 'little transparency, democratic accountability or public or parliamentary scrutiny'.

It's plain as day in the London borough of Barnet, where the Tory council outsourced the vast bulk of local authority functions to giant private businesses and then – when the evidence of service failure and ballooning costs grew too thick – this summer gagged local residents from asking too many questions at council committee meetings. It's there in the sweetheart deals big builders cut with local councils and the one George Osborne cut with Google over their tax bill.

The master-text on the moment we're in was published nearly 20 years ago. 'Coping with Post-Democracy' was an alarm sounded by the British political scientist Colin Crouch towards the end of Tony Blair's first term as prime minister. He coined the term 'post-democracy' to refer to a country that still had its ballot boxes and elected chamber and rowdy journalists – only all were being drained of meaning. Democracy, argued Crouch, 'thrives when there are major opportunities for the mass of ordinary people to participate'.

But the post-democratic order he saw taking shape was 'a tightly controlled spectacle managed by rival teams of professional experts in the techniques of persuasion', in which the interests of multinationals and big businesses would always trump 'the political importance of ordinary working people', especially with the withering-away of unions.

From here it was a short step to today's Westminster of 'retail politics', parties touting their 'offer' and the apparatus of marketing. For a while, the sorcerers of the new post-democratic system could buy our consent, as long as house prices kept rising and cheap credit could be thrust down our throats. But then came the banking crisis, which just showed our debt was the financiers' credit and that they would always collect.

From the wreckage of that system came much of the 2016 vote for Brexit and it today ensures the indifference of the public as a bunch of posh boys try to strip us of our hard-won rights. Years before the advent of Facebook and Twitter, Crouch warned of a public habituated to a 'negative activism of blame and complaint', no longer interested in formulating constructive demands – but merely demanding some MP's head on a pikestaff.

This is a different critique of what ails our democracy than the ones you and I are used to seeing, full of complaints about our arthritic institutions and calls for a written constitution alongside token gestures such as moving parliament to the Midlands. Such prescriptions will do no harm, although what the burghers of Dudley have done to deserve the sudden imposition of Peter Bone, I don't know; but they don't get near what we are seeing in Britain this week. The public will not be moved by finagling in parliament or cases put forward by well-intentioned lawyers – important as both are. To do that, our political parties, chiefly Labour, need to show the public what use they are in the 21st century. That means providing advice to voters, not just members, on welfare, housing and employers. It means acting to collectively procure cheap utility deals. It means laying on classes in how politics and economics work and why they matter. Real democratic renewal will not come through Westminster manoeuvring, or new pieces of legal text, but through building serious and sturdy new institutions.

Index